Fodor's 92
San Diego

Fodor's Travel Publications
New York and London

Fodor's San Diego

Editor: Larry Peterson
Editorial Contributors: Kevin Brass, Bruce David Colen, Pamela Faust, Sharon K. Gillenwater, Tara Hamilton, Dan Janeck, Marael Johnson, Maribeth Mellin, David Nelson, Jane Onstott, Marcy Pritchard
Art Director: Fabrizio La Rocca
Cartographer: David Lindroth
Illustrator: Karl Tanner
Cover Photograph: Tim Holt, Photo Researchers, Inc.

Design: Vignelli Associates

Special Sales

Contents

Maps

Foreword

Visitors come to San Diego for many reasons, but the beautiful weather year-round, the fine beaches, and the many opportunities for outdoor activities must be primary. Accordingly, this new edition of *Fodor's San Diego* has expanded coverage of participant sports (including not only golf and jogging but Frisbee golf and windsurfing) and beaches. Many of the hotels cater particularly to travelers who want to spend active days in the sun, and our Sports and Fitness chapter calls attention to hotels with the best facilities.

While every care has been taken to ensure the accuracy of the information in this guide, the passage of time will always bring change, and, consequently, the publisher cannot accept responsibility for errors that may occur.

All prices and opening times quoted here are based on information supplied to us at press time. Hours and admission fees may change, however, and the prudent traveler will avoid inconvenience by calling ahead.

Fodor's wants to hear about your travel experiences, both pleasant and unpleasant. When a hotel or restaurant fails to live up to its billing, let us know and we will investigate the complaint and revise our entries where the facts warrant it.

Send your letters to the editors of Fodor's Travel Publications, 201 E. 50th Street, New York, NY 10022.

Highlights'92 and Fodor's Choice

Highlights '92

Sailors and crews from all over the world started congregating in San Diego in mid-1991, gearing up for an attempt to win the America's Cup from the San Diego Yacht Club. The **America's Cup XXVIII** races will be held in San Diego in May 1992. Preliminary challenges and skirmishes began in the winter of 1991 and it's a safe bet that many of those Australian, Italian, and Russian sailors will hang on through the summer of '92 as well.

The ever-changing downtown skyline will provide the backdrop for the races, with the nautical theme carried through in the design of the San Diego Convention Center, which looks like a futuristic sea creature capped by gigantic sails. The opening of the center in 1990 served as catalyst and reward for those who have invested heavily in the downtown area through decades of redevelopment.

The waterfront **Embarcadero** area has become an exciting place to stay, thanks to the new hotels, restaurants, and nightclubs that have opened by the harbor. Major cruise lines now dock at the B Street Pier, and a seafaring taxi service sails from one waterfront hotel to another. The San Diego Trolley's Bayfront Line now connects the convention center and waterfront hotels with the center of downtown and with the ever-increasing number of trolley lines running east and north into the surrounding county and south to the Mexican border.

The **San Diego Zoo** celebrated its 75th birthday in 1991 with the opening of **Gorilla Tropics,** the latest in a series of new bioclimatic exhibits that far surpass the cages of old. The zoo's animals climb, cavort, burrow, and leap in habitats that resemble their homeland haunts, and endangered species are especially pampered. **Seaport Village** is undergoing a $40 million expansion that will include the redevelopment of the abandoned Spanish-Colonial police headquarters and a "Night Court" area with clubs, restaurants, and bars.

San Diego has an international airport again. **Alaska, Continental,** and **AeroCalifornia** now fly from San Diego to Mexico, and negotiations are underway for other international flights.

The **Golden Triangle,** east of La Jolla, has become a booming commercial center, with corporate headquarters, exclusive hotels, upscale restaurants, and architectural masterpieces, while North County's canyons and hillsides are being covered with high-priced residential communities. The backcountry mountains and desert, however, remain blessedly uncrowded and tranquil.

The building boom has spread south to Baja California, where the Mexican government and private investors are banking on prosperity. Rosarito Beach now boasts exclusive condos and time-share resorts, and new hotels and restaurants are springing up continually. Ensenada is changing just as quickly, becoming much more than a weekend getaway. U.S. tour buses are allowed across the Mexican border now, and a new crop of tour companies specializing in Baja make the trek south hassle-free.

Fodor's Choice

No two people will agree on what makes a perfect vacation, but it's fun and helpful to know what others think. We hope you'll have a chance to experience some of Fodor's Choices yourself while visiting San Diego. For detailed information about each entry, refer to the appropriate chapters within this guidebook.

Restaurants

The Belgian Lion, Beaches *(Very Expensive)*

Dobson's, Downtown *(Very Expensive)*

George's at the Cove, La Jolla *(Very Expensive)*

Issimo, La Jolla *(Very Expensive)*

Hard Rock Cafe, La Jolla *(Inexpensive)*

Panda Inn, Downtown *(Inexpensive)*

Lodging

Hotel Del Coronado, Coronado *(Very Expensive)*

La Valencia, La Jolla *(Very Expensive)*

San Diego Princess Resort, Mission Bay and Beaches *(Very Expensive)*

U.S. Grant Hotel, Downtown *(Very Expensive)*

Humphrey's Half Moon Inn, Harbor Island/Shelter Island *(Expensive)*

Favorite Zoo Exhibits

Flamingos

Koalas

Gorilla Tropics

Sun Bear Forest

Tiger River

Special Moments

Driving across the San Diego–Coronado Bridge

Evening stroll above La Jolla Cove

Hauling in a marlin from deep-sea waters

Hiking at Cabrillo National Monument on Point Loma, with views of downtown and Coronado

Sunday picnic in Balboa Park

Beaches

La Jolla Cove

Torrey Pines State Beach

Mission Beach

Favorite Outdoor Activities

Scuba diving off La Jolla Cove

Golfing at Torrey Pines

Roller skating on the Mission Beach boardwalk

Jogging along the Embarcadero

Volleyball on Ocean Beach

Windsurfing on Mission Bay

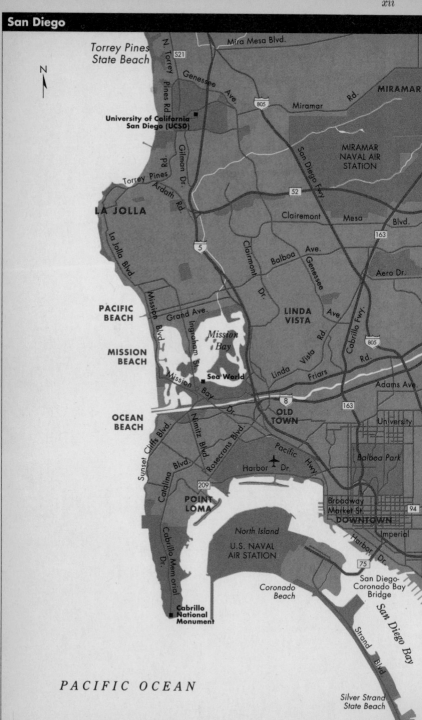

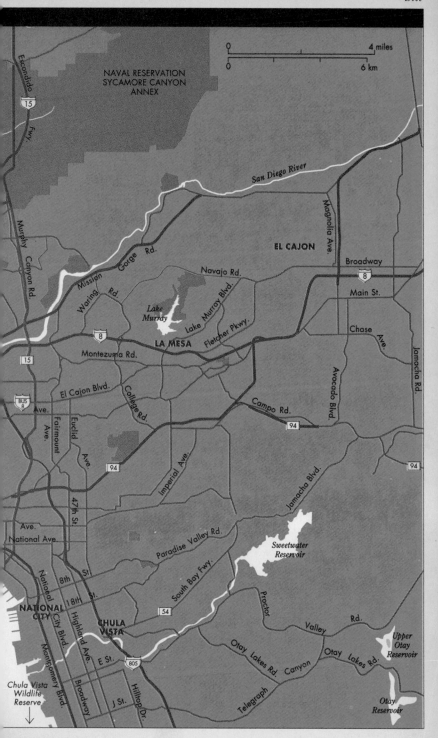

NAVAL RESERVATION
SYCAMORE CANYON
ANNEX

Escondido Fwy.

15

Murphy Canyon Rd.

San Diego River

Magnolia Ave.

EL CAJON

Broadway

8

Main St.

Mission Gorge Rd.

Navajo Rd.

Lake Murray Blvd.

Waring Rd.

Lake Murray

Lake Murray Blvd.

Fletcher Pkwy.

Chase Ave.

8

LA MESA

Montezuma Rd.

15

Avocado Blvd.

Jamacha Rd.

El Cajon Blvd.

College Rd.

Campo Rd.

94

BUS 8

Ave.

Fairmount Ave.

Euclid Ave.

94

94

Imperial Ave.

Jamacha Blvd.

47th St.

Ave.

National Ave.

Paradise Valley Rd.

Sweetwater Reservoir

South Bay Fwy.

8th St.

18th St.

National City Blvd.

Highland Ave.

54

CHULA VISTA

Proctor

Valley Rd.

Upper Otay Reservoir

NATIONAL CITY

E St.

805

Montgomery Blvd.

Otay Lakes Rd.

Canyon

Otay Lakes Rd.

Chula Vista Wildlife Reserve

Broadway

J St.

Hilltop Dr.

Telegraph

Otay Reservoir

0   4 miles
0   6 km

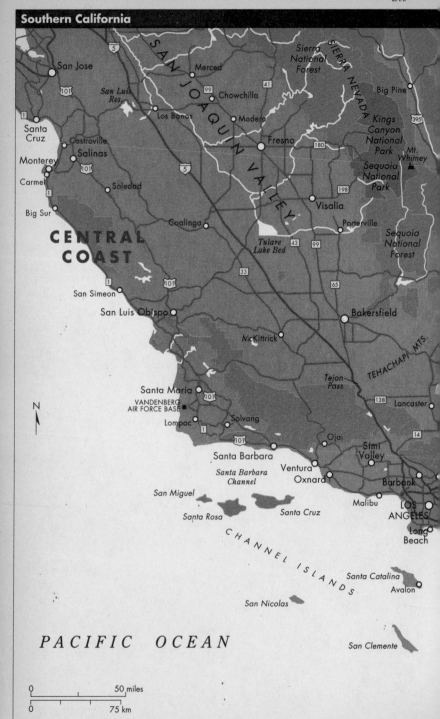

Southern California

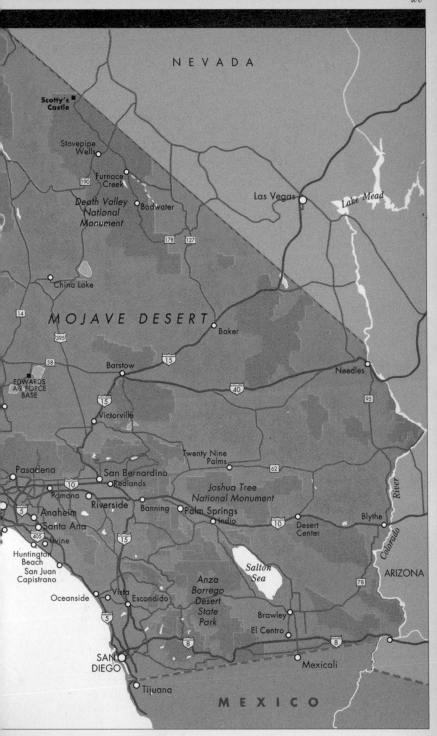

World Time Zones

International Date Line

MONDAY
SUNDAY

+12 +13 -9 -10 -11 -10

+11 +12

Numbers below vertical bands relate each zone to Greenwich Mean Time (0 hrs.).
Local times frequently differ from these general indications,
as indicated by light-face numbers on map.

Algiers, **29**	Berlin, **34**	Delhi, **48**	Istanbul, **40**
Anchorage, **3**	Bogotá, **19**	Denver, **8**	Jerusalem, **42**
Athens, **41**	Budapest, **37**	Djakarta, **53**	Johannesburg, **44**
Auckland, **1**	Buenos Aires, **24**	Dublin, **26**	Lima, **20**
Baghdad, **46**	Caracas, **22**	Edmonton, **7**	Lisbon, **28**
Bangkok, **50**	Chicago, **9**	Hong Kong, **56**	London (Greenwich), **27**
Beijing, **54**	Copenhagen, **33**	Honolulu, **2**	Los Angeles, **6**
	Dallas, **10**		Madrid, **38**
			Manila, **57**

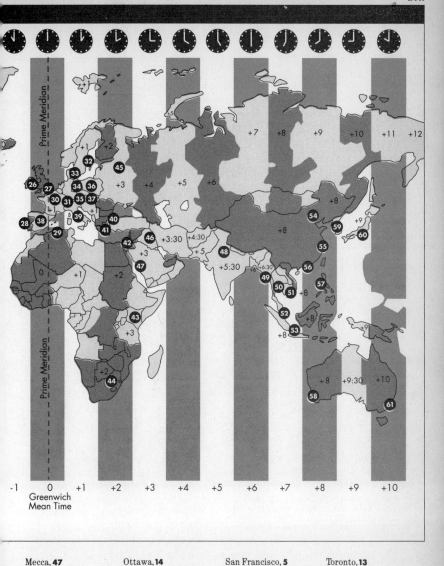

-1   0   +1   +2   +3   +4   +5   +6   +7   +8   +9   +10
Greenwich
Mean Time

Mecca, **47**
Mexico City, **12**
Miami, **18**
Montreal, **15**
Moscow, **45**
Nairobi, **43**
New Orleans, **11**
New York City, **16**

Ottawa, **14**
Paris, **30**
Perth, **58**
Reykjavík, **25**
Rio de Janeiro, **23**
Rome, **39**
Saigon, **51**

San Francisco, **5**
Santiago, **21**
Seoul, **59**
Shanghai, **55**
Singapore, **52**
Stockholm, **32**
Sydney, **61**
Tokyo, **60**

Toronto, **13**
Vancouver, **4**
Vienna, **35**
Warsaw, **36**
Washington, DC, **17**
Yangon, **49**
Zürich, **31**

Introduction

*by Maribeth
Mellin*

*A longtime
resident of San
Diego, travel
writer and
photographer,
Maribeth Mellin
is a former senior
editor at* San
Diego *magazine,
author of* Fodor's
Baja, *and
contributor to
several
magazines and
newspapers.*

Each year, San Diego absorbs thousands of visitors who are drawn by the climate: sunny, dry, and warm nearly year-round. They swim, surf, and sunbathe on long beaches facing the turquoise Pacific, where whales, seals, and dolphins swim offshore. They tour oases of tropical palms, sheltered bays fringed by golden pampas grass, and far-ranging parklands blossoming with brilliant bougainvillaea, jasmine, ice plant, and birds of paradise.

They run and bike and walk for hours down wide streets and paths planned for recreation among the natives, who thrive on San Diego's varied health, fitness, and sports scenes. They drive by Mission Bay, a 4,600-acre aquatic park, where dozens of colorful, intricate kites fly over hundreds of picnickers lounging in the sun. They wander through the streets of downtown, where the fanciful Horton Plaza shopping center serves as a vibrant city center, with theaters, restaurants, and shops drawing crowds from nearby steel-and-glass office towers.

San Diego County is the nation's seventh largest—larger than nearly a dozen U.S. states—with a population of over 2 million. It sprawls east from the Pacific Ocean through dense urban neighborhoods to outlying suburban communities that seem to sprout overnight on canyons and cliffs. Its eastern boundaries are the Cleveland National Forest, where the pines and manzanita are covered with snow in the winter, and the Anza-Borrego Desert, where delicate pink and yellow cactus blooms herald the coming of spring. San Diegans visit these vast wildernesses for their annual doses of seasonal splendors, then return to the city, where flowers bloom year-round and the streets are dry and clean. The busiest international border in the United States marks the country's southern line, where nearly 70 million people a year legally cross between Mexico's Baja California peninsula and San Diego. To the north, the marines at Camp Pendleton practice land, sea, and air maneuvers in Southern California's largest coastal green belt, marking the demarcation zone between the congestion of Orange and Los Angeles counties and the more relaxed expansiveness of San Diego.

The city of San Diego is the state's second largest, behind Los Angeles. It serves as a base for the U.S. Navy's 11th Naval District and a port for ships from many nations. A considerable number of its residents were stationed here in the service and decided to stay put. Others either passed through on vacation or saw the city in movies and TV shows and became enamored with the city and its reputation as a prosperous Sunbelt playground. From its founding San Diego has attracted a steady stream of prospectors, drawn to the nation's farthest southwest frontier. Nearly 10,000 new residents arrive in San Diego each year.

Tourism is San Diego's third largest industry, after manufacturing and the military. In the past few years, the San Diego Convention and Visitors Bureau and other local boosters have courted and won internationally important events that have brought uncalculated benefits of tourism to the city. Sports fans shivering elsewhere in the winter cold saw the sun tanning spectators at the 1988 Super Bowl on TV while sailors from around the globe have been practicing the course for the America's Cup Races, to be held in San Diego in May of 1992. Such worldwide media events keep San Diego a highly visible vacation option.

The waterfront has a whole new look and ambience since the 1990 opening of the 760,000-square-foot San Diego Convention Center. The convention center's completion has spurred development of downtown's waterfront at an unprecedented rate, and the thousands of conventioneers who are expected to visit San Diego in 1992 will boost the downtown business climate and image like never before. Built along the harbor's edge at the foot of Fifth Avenue, the center boasts a sail-like rooftop thrust before downtown's skyline. Hotels are rising all over town, seemingly on every patch of available land. San Diego's politicians, business leaders, and developers have set the city's course toward a steadily increasing influx of visitors—which gives residents some pleasant attractions and not-so-enjoyable distractions. With growth comes congestion, even in San Diego's vast expanse.

Fortunately, there are many reminders of the city's more peaceful times. In Old Town, San Diego's original city center, the courthouse, newspaper offices, and haciendas are historical adobe buildings covered with ancient twisted vines. The village of La Jolla, often compared to Monte Carlo, has retained its gentle charm despite continuous development. And Balboa Park, the city's centerpiece, is a permanent testimonial to the Spanish architecture and natural ecology that give San Diego its unique character and charisma.

If San Diego sounds just a bit too laid-back and serene, consider its proximity to Mexico. Tijuana, a typically colorful and frenetic border town and an intrinsically foreign land, is only 30 minutes away. San Diegans consider Tijuana and all the Baja peninsula to be their backyard playground, a place to escape American sensibilities and immerse themselves in Mexican sensations.

During Prohibition, Americans drove their jalopies and roadsters down dusty, rutted roads to the spectacular gambling halls of Tijuana, Rosarito Beach, and Ensenada, where unbridled hedonism was not only tolerated but encouraged. Hollywood stars settled in for the duration, waiting out the dry days north of the border in lavish grandeur and investing their dollars in Mexican real estate.

Some of Baja's grandest hotels were built during this era, when U.S. financiers recognized the value of the peninsula's rugged coastal wilderness.

Those pleasure palaces of the past have since crumbled, but Baja is undergoing a new surge of development since the Mexican government targeted the area as a premier tourist destination. In Rosarito Beach alone, nearly a dozen hotel and resort complexes are under construction along the waterfront, and the dusty trails leading to run-down cabanas have been replaced with paved roads and slick motels. Weekends bring bumper-to-bumper traffic through the seaside towns and crowds of shoppers to the stalls along Tijuana's Avenida Revolución.

Visiting Baja is easier than ever, thanks to the San Diego/ Tijuana trolley, which runs from the Santa Fe Depot in downtown San Diego to the international border in San Ysidro. The trolley travels south through the suburbs of National City and Chula Vista, where giant shipyards and fish canneries have been replaced by fancy marinas. Near San Ysidro, the trackside billboards display Spanish ads for Tijuana's shopping centers, highlighting bargains in brand-name clothing from Ralph Lauren and Guess?. On the pedestrian overpass leading from the trolley stop into Tijuana, Mexicans and Americans mingle. Still, for all its familiarity, Tijuana could never be mistaken for an American town. Therein lies its appeal.

If you prefer more organized attractions, San Diego has its share of theme parks and specialized museums. Sea World, on the shores of Mission Bay, highlights San Diego's proximity to the sea with spectacular aquariums, whale shows, shark exhibits, and penguin habitats. The San Diego Zoo, often called the country's finest zoological/botanical park, is a must-see attraction. The Wild Animal Park, 30 minutes east of downtown, preserves the natural wonders of San Diego's chaparral country while protecting endangered wildlife from around the world. Balboa Park, site of the 1915 Panama-California Exposition, houses not only the zoo but the city's finest museums in historical Spanish-Moorish palaces set amid lush lawns and rocky canyons.

San Diego has always been recognized as an environmental paradise. As the city grows, its cultural base expands to meet more sophisticated demands. Today San Diego retains its sense of a western frontier as it develops into a major cosmopolitan centerpiece for the nation. No wonder visitors from all over the world come for vacation and decide to stay for life.

1 Essential Information

Before You Go

Visitor Information

The **San Diego Convention and Visitors Bureau** (1200 Third Ave., Suite 824, San Diego 92101, tel. 619/232–3103) will provide you with a wealth of information about the San Diego area. Brochures on accommodations, restaurants and attractions, maps, and quarterly calendars of special events are yours for the asking. A truly internationally minded city, San Diego can give you brochures in English, French, German, Japanese, and Spanish. Once you are in the area, all walk-in visitor services are provided at the International Visitor Information Center (11 Horton Plaza, San Diego 92101, tel. 619/236–1212).

The **San Diego Visitor Information Center** (2688 East Mission Bay Dr., San Diego 92109, tel. 619/276–8200) will send you its newspaper, *Pathfinder*, if you include a self-addressed, stamped envelope with your request. They will also make reservations for your lodging.

In addition, a number of communities within San Diego County maintain visitors' bureaus or chambers of commerce, which will send you information about attractions and facilities in their particular area. Some of these are:

Borrego Springs Chamber of Commerce (Box 66, Borrego Springs 92004, tel. 619/767–5555).
Carlsbad Convention and Visitors Bureau (5411 Avenida Encinas, Carlsbad 92008, tel. 619/434–6093).
Chula Vista Information Center (99 Bonita Rd., Chula Vista 92010, tel. 619/239–0512).
Coronado Convention & Visitors Bureau (1330 Orange Ave., #315, Coronado 92118, tel. 619/457–8788).
Del Mar Chamber of Commerce (1401 Camino Del Mar, Suite 101, Del Mar 92014, tel. 619/755–4844).
Escondido Convention & Visitors Bureau (720 N. Broadway, Escondido 92025, tel. 619/745–4741).
Julian Chamber of Commerce (Box 413, Julian 92036, tel. 619/765–1857).
La Jolla Town Council, Inc. (Box 1101, La Jolla 92038, tel. 619/454–1444).
Oceanside Visitors & Conference Center (928 N. Hill St., Oceanside 92054, tel. 619/721–1101).
San Diego North Coast Visitors Center (550 Via de la Valle, Solana Beach 92075, tel. 619/481–1811).

A handsome and detailed 200-page book, *Discover the Californias*, available free of charge through the California Office of Tourism by calling 800/862–2543, includes maps and a calendar of yearly events.

Tour Groups

Joining a tour group has some advantages: Someone else worries about travel arrangements, accommodations, and baggage transfer; you are likely to save money on airfare, hotels, and ground transportation; and you will probably cover a lot of territory. The major disadvantages, on the other hand, are that you'll have to adjust to someone else's time schedule and you won't be as free for independent explorations.

When considering a tour, be sure to find out (1) exactly what expenses are included, particularly tips, taxes, side trips, meals, and entertainment; (2) the ratings of all hotels on the itinerary and the facilities they offer; (3) the additional cost of single, rather than double, accommodations if you are traveling alone; and (4) the number of travelers in your group. Note whether the tour operator reserves the right to change hotels, routes, or even prices after you've booked, and check out the operator's policy regarding cancellations, complaints, and trip-interruption insurance. Many tour operators request that packages be booked through a travel agent; there is generally no additional charge for doing so.

General-Interest Tours   A sampling of options is listed here; for additional possibilities, check with your travel agent or the San Diego Convention and Visitors Bureau (1200 Third Ave., Suite 824, San Diego 92101, tel. 619/232–3101). Most group tours combine San Diego with a number of other California cities.

Casser Tours (46 W. 43rd St., New York, NY 10036, tel. 212/840–6500 or 800/251–1411).

Domenico Tours (751 Broadway, Bayonne, NJ 07002, tel. 201/823–8687 or 800/554–8687).

Globus-Gateway/Cosmos (150 S. Los Robles Ave., Pasadena, CA 91101, tel. 818/449–0919 or 800/556–5454).

Maupintour (Box 807, Lawrence, KS 66044, tel. 913/843–1211) or 800/255–4266).

Mayflower Tours (1225 Warren Ave., Downers Grove, IL 60515, tel. 708/960–3430).

Talmage Tours (1223 Walnut St., Philadelphia, PA 19107, tel. 215/923–7100).

Special-Interest Tours   **Atlas Travel Service** (4577 Viewridge Ave., San Diego, CA 92123, tel. 800/854–2608 or 800/542–6082 in CA or 800/754–6742 in Canada) will arrange golf tours, a wide range of leisure-time activities, and individual or group tours of Mexico, Disneyland, and San Diego from hotels in the Atlas chain.

Hector Lam y Asociados (Box 803, San Ysidro, CA 92073, tel. 011–52-688–3364). This Tijuana resident leads fascinating tours of Tijuana for groups and individuals, in English or Spanish.

La Palmas Tours (522 E. Chase Ave., El Cajon, CA 92020, tel. 619/444–9929) has groups and individual tours to area attractions in San Diego, Baja, Orange County, and Los Angeles.

Package Deals for Independent Travelers

A wide range of packages is available to the independent traveler. Most airlines have packages that include car rentals and lodging along with your flight. American Airlines (tel. 800/433–7300) has "Sunshine Holiday" packages to San Diego. USAir's (tel. 800/223–2929) "Great Escapes Vacations" package to Southern California gives you a choice of attractions and special fares for children. Alaska Airlines (tel. 800/468–2248) serves the West Coast and Alaska and offers sightseeing packages. Also check with **United Vacations** (tel. 800/328–6877) and **Delta Dream Vacations** (tel. 800/872–7786).

Hotels often have packages for weekends or for off-season, in addition to the packages tied in with major tourist attractions. For example, hotels and motels in San Diego may offer a package for lodging and admission tickets to the San Diego Zoo and the San Diego Wild Animal Park.

Amtrak offers tours to major attractions in California. For a brochure and specific information, call 800/872–7245 (Tours Department), or write to Amtrak Public Affairs (1 California St., Suite 1250, San Francisco, CA 94111).

Packages are increasingly popular as marketing strategies; always ask about package options when you are making reservations. Often visitors bureaus and chambers of commerce will have information for you, and, of course, travel agents are always good sources.

Tips for British Travelers

Passports You will need a valid, 10-year passport (cost: £15). You do not need a U.S. visitor's visa if you are staying less than 90 days, have a return ticket, and are flying with a major airline. There are some exceptions to this, so check with your travel agent or with the **United States Embassy, Visa and Immigration Department** (5 Upper Grosvenor St., London W1A 2JB, tel. 071/499–3443). The embassy no longer accepts visa applications made in person.

No vaccinations are required for entry into the United States.

Customs If you are 21 or over, you can take into the United States: 200 cigarettes, 50 cigars, or 2 kilograms of tobacco; 1 liter of alcohol; and duty-free gifts to a value of $100. Be careful not to take in meat or meat products, seeds, plants, fruits, etc., and avoid narcotics like the plague.

Returning to Britain, you may bring home (1) 200 cigarettes or 100 cigarillos or 50 cigars or 250 grams of tobacco; (2) two liters of table wine and (a) one liter of alcohol over 22% by volume (most spirits), or (b) two liters of alcohol under 22% by volume (fortified or sparkling wine); (3) 60 milliliters of perfume or (c) two more liters of table wine; and 250 milliliters of toilet water; and (4) other goods up to a value of £32, but not more than 50 liters of beer or 25 cigarette lighters.

Insurance We recommend that you insure yourself to cover health and motoring mishaps with **Europ Assistance** (252 High St., Croydon CRO 1NF, tel. 071/680–1234). Its excellent service is all the more valuable when you consider the possible costs of health care in the United States. It is also wise to insure yourself against trip cancellations and loss of luggage. For free general advice on all aspects of holiday insurance, contact the **Association of British Insurers** (Aldermary House, 10–15 Queen St., London EC4N 1TT, tel. 071/248–4477).

Tour Operators The price battle that has raged over transatlantic fares has meant that most tour operators now offer excellent budget packages to the United States. Among those you might consider as you plan your trip are:

American Airplan (Airplan House, Churchfield Road, Walton-on-Thames, Surrey KT12 2TZ, tel. 0932/231322).
Cosmosair plc (Ground Floor, Dale House, Tiviot Dale, Stockport, Cheshire SK1 1TB, tel. 061/480–5799).
Jetsave (Sussex House, London Rd., East Grinstead, W. Sussex RH19 1LD, tel. 0342–32823).

Kuoni Travel Ltd. (Kuoni House, Dorking, Surrey RH5 4AZ, tel. 0306/740888).
Premier Holidays (Premier Travel Center, Westbrook, Milton Rd., Cambridge CB4 1YQ, tel. 0223–611611).
Speedbird (Pacific House, Hazelwick Ave., Three Bridges, Crawley, West Sussex RH10 1NP, tel. 0293/611611).

Airfares We suggest that you explore the current scene for budget-flight possibilities. The small ads in daily and Sunday newspapers or magazines such as *Time Out* are a good source of cut-price tickets. Some of these fares can be extremely difficult to come by, so be sure to book well in advance. Also, check on APEX and other money-saving fares, since, quite frankly, only business travelers who don't have to watch the price of their tickets fly full-price these days—and find themselves sitting right beside APEX passengers!

When to Go

Any time of the year is the right time for a trip to San Diego. The second-largest city in California and the seventh-largest city in the United States, San Diego has a wealth of activities and attractions all year long. The climate is as close to perfection as one can imagine, with an average annual high temperature of 70 degrees Fahrenheit, an average annual low of 55 degrees, and an average annual rainfall of less than 10 inches.

Climate A group of meteorologists once voted San Diego as the "only area in the United States with perfect weather," and the statistics seem to bear them out.

Typical days are sunny and mild, with low humidity, providing ideal conditions for sightseeing and for almost any sport that does not require snow and ice.

The following are average maximum and minimum temperatures for San Diego.

Jan.	62F	17C	May	66F	19C	Sept.	73F	23C
	46	8		55	13		62	17
Feb.	62F	17C	June	69F	21C	Oct.	71F	22C
	48	9		59	15		57	14
Mar.	64F	18C	July	73F	23C	Nov.	69F	21C
	50	10		62	17		51	11
Apr.	66F	19C	Aug.	73F	23C	Dec.	64F	18C
	53	12		64	18		48	9

Current weather information on over 750 cities around the world is only a phone call away. Dialing WeatherTrak at 900/370–8728 will connect you to a computer, with which you can communicate by touch tone—at a cost of 95¢ per minute. The number plays a taped message that tells you to dial the three-digit access code for the destination you're interested in. The code is either the area code (in the United States) or the first three letters of the foreign city. For a list of all access codes, send a stamped, self-addressed envelope to Cities, 9B Terrace Way, Greensboro, NC 27403. For further information, call 800/247–3282.

Festivals and Seasonal Events

January **Whale watching.** From the vantage point of the Cabrillo National Monument on Point Loma, watch the gray whales in their migration along the California coast. Tel. 619/557–5450.

February **Golf.** The Shearson-Lehman-Hutton Open Golf Tournament features a $700,000 purse. Tel. 619/281–4653.

March **Wildflowers** bloom in the desert. Anza-Borrego Desert State Park is one of California's last frontiers, where wildflowers still transform the desert into a rainbow of colors. Tel. 619/767–5311.

Ocean Beach Kite Festival is an annual kite-decorating and flying contest for all ages at Ocean Beach. Tel. 619/223–1175.

April **San Diego Crew Classic** brings together more than 2,000 athletes on college teams from across the United States for a rowing competition at Crown Point in Mission Bay. Tel. 619/594–6555.

Downtown ArtWalk. This annual open house for downtown's art galleries has become a weekend-long festival with live entertainment, performances, and special showings at the ever-increasing collection of galleries in the G Street neighborhood. Tel. 619/232–9915.

May **Cinco de Mayo Festival** is an annual Mexican celebration, with entertainment and booths, in Old Town State Park and the Bazaar del Mundo. Tel. 619/296–3161.

Del Mar National Horse Show. Thousands of show horses compete at the Del Mar Fairgrounds. Tel. 619/259–1355.

Pacific Beach Block Party is an annual street fair with live music, food stands, and games. Tel. 619/483–6666.

June **The Old Globe Festival,** which runs from June until September, features works of Shakespeare in repertory with other classic and contemporary plays at the Old Globe Theatre in Balboa Park. Tel. 619/239–2255.

The Indian Fair attracts American Indians from throughout the Southwest for arts, crafts, ethnic foods, and dances at the Museum of Man in Balboa Park. Tel. 619/239–2001.

San Diego County Fair at Del Mar is a classic county fair, with flower and garden shows, a carnival, displays, and livestock shows. Tel. 619/259–1355.

July **Over-the-Line Tournament** is a rowdy, weekend-long party with more than 1,000 3-person teams competing at a cross between softball and stickball on Fiesta Island. Tel. 619/297–8480.

Sand Castle Days at Imperial Beach Pier is America's largest sand-castle event. Tel. 619/424–6663.

August **America's Finest City Week** is an annual celebration with a half-marathon, parades, and concerts. Tel. 619/236–1212.

September **Cabrillo Festival** commemorates the 1542 landing in San Diego Harbor of Juan Rodriguez Cabrillo and his discovery of the West Coast. Tel. 619/557–5450.

October **Zoo Founders Day** means that everyone is admitted free to the world-famous San Diego Zoo. Tel. 619/234–3153.

November **The Dixieland Jazz Festival** presents a weekend filled with performances by well-known bands at the Town & Country Hotel. Tel. 619/297–5277.

Mother Goose Parade in El Cajon is a two-hour, nationally tele-vised spectacular with 200 floats, bands, horses, and clowns. Tel. 619/444–8712.

December   **Christmas on El Prado** is sponsored by the museums in Balboa Park. Tel. 619/239–2001.
San Diego Harbor Parade of Lights brings colorfully lit boats through the downtown harbor. Tel. 619/222–0561, ext. 307.

What to Pack

Clothing   San Diego's casual lifestyle and year-around mild climate set the parameters for what you'll want to pack. You can leave for-mal clothes and cold-weather gear behind.

Plan on warm weather at any time of the year. Cottons, walking shorts, jeans, and T-shirts are the norm at tourist attractions. Pack bathing suits and shorts regardless of the season. Casual attire is generally acceptable; only a few restaurants require a jacket and tie for men. Women may want to bring something a little dressier than their sightseeing garb.

Evenings are cool, even in summer, so be sure to bring a sweat-er or a light jacket. Rainfall in San Diego is not heavy; you won't need a raincoat except in the winter months and even then, an umbrella may be sufficient protection.

A note about shoes: Be sure you take proven, comfortable walk-ing shoes with you. Even if you don't walk much at home, you'll find yourself covering miles sightseeing on your vacation, and nothing puts an end to pleasure sooner than sore feet.

It's always important to pack light; porters and luggage trol-leys may be hard to find. Don't take more luggage than you can handle comfortably yourself.

Miscellaneous   While it is true that you can buy film, sunburn cream, aspirin, and most other necessities almost anywhere in San Diego, it's a nuisance to be searching for staples, especially when time is limited. Take along a reasonable supply of those things you know you will be using routinely and save your vacation time for sheer enjoyment.

An extra pair of glasses, contact lenses, or prescription sun-glasses is always a good idea; the loss of your only pair can put a real crimp in your vacation. Pack any prescription medicines you use regularly, as well as any that might be important on oc-casion, such as allergy medication. If you are prone to certain medical problems and have good, simple ways of dealing with early manifestations, take along what you might need, even though you may never use it; it's worthwhile insurance.

Sunglasses are a must in San Diego. Also remember that binoc-ulars can be a pleasure on a trip; tuck in a small pair.

Traveling with Film

If your camera is new, shoot and develop a few rolls of film be-fore leaving home. Pack some lens tissue, and don't forget an extra battery for your built-in light meter. Invest about $10 in a skylight filter and screw it onto the front of your lens. It will protect the lens and also reduce haze.

Film doesn't like hot weather. In summer, don't store film in a car glove compartment or on the shelf under the rear window; put it behind the front seat on the floor, on the side opposite the exhaust pipe.

On a plane trip, never pack unprocessed film in check-in luggage; if your bags get X-rayed, you can say good-bye to your pictures. Always carry undeveloped film with you through security checks, and ask to have it inspected by hand. (It helps to isolate your film in a plastic bag, so it's ready for quick inspection.) Inspectors at U.S. airports are required by law to honor requests for hand inspection; abroad, you'll have to depend on the kindness of strangers.

The old airport scanning machines—still in use in some Third World countries—use heavy doses of radiation that can turn a family portrait into an early morning fog. The newer models— used in all U.S. airports—are safe for anything from five to 500 scans, depending on the speed of your film. The effects are cumulative; you can put the same roll of film through several scans without worry. After five scans, though, you're asking for trouble.

If your film gets fogged and you want an explanation, send it to the National Association of Photographic Manufacturers (550 Mamaroneck Ave., Harrison, NY 10528). NAPM representatives will try to determine what went wrong. The service is free.

Cash Machines

Virtually all U.S. banks belong to a network of ATMs (Automatic Teller Machines) that dispense cash 24 hours a day in cities throughout the country. There are some eight major networks in the United States, the largest of which are Cirrus, owned by MasterCard, and Plus, affiliated with Visa. Some banks belong to more than one network. These cards are not automatically issued; you have to apply for them. Cards issued by Visa and MasterCard also may be used in the ATMs, but the fees are usually higher than the fees on bank cards. There is also a daily interest charge on credit card "loans," even if monthly bills are paid on time. Each network has a toll-free number you can call to locate machines in a given city. The Cirrus number is 800/4–CIRRUS; the Plus number is 800/THE–PLUS. Check with your bank for information on fees and on the amount of cash you can withdraw on any given day.

Traveling with Children

The watchwords for traveling with children are plan ahead as much as possible. The trip will be a lot more fun for all of you. Have a good supply of things to keep them busy on the plane, in the car, on the train, or however you are traveling. When you are sightseeing, try to include some things that will be of special interest to your children. They may tolerate a museum, and even show some interest in a historic building or two, but put a zoo into the itinerary when you can.

When you are traveling by car, you'll have an option you can exercise: Stop frequently. Just getting the children out of the confines of the car for a little while is an advantage; an even bigger advantage comes when you can stop at a park and children can run or use a playground.

Lodging At many hotels and motels, children stay free in the same room with their parents, with nominal charges for cribs and $5 to $10 charges for extra beds. Most **Days Inn** hotels (tel. 800/325–2525) charge only a nominal fee for children under 18 and allow children 12 and under to eat free. **Rancho Bernardo Inn** (17065 W. Bernardo Dr., San Diego 92127, tel. 619/485–6530) has a children's camp during Spring Break and the month of August.

Baby-sitting Services For baby-sitting services, first check with the hotel concierge. Agencies in San Diego include the **YMCA Childcare Resource Service** (tel. 619/275–4800) and **Sitter Service** (tel. 619/281–7755).

Publications *San Diego Family Press* is a monthly newspaper for parents, filled with listings of events and resources; it is available free at such places as libraries, supermarkets, and museums. For a small fee, you can have an issue sent to you before your trip; write to Box 23960, San Diego 92123 (tel. 619/541–1162).

Two books that might prove helpful are *Places to Go with Children in Southern California,* by Stephanie Kegan (Chronicle Books, $7.95), and *Great Vacations with Your Kids: The Complete Guide to Family Vacations in the U.S.,* by Dorothy Ann Jordon and Marjorie Adoff Cohen (E. P. Dutton, $11.95).

Family Travel Times is an 8- to 12-page newsletter published 10 times a year by TWYCH (Travel with Your Children, 80 Eighth Ave., New York, NY 10011, tel. 212/206–0688). A subscription includes access to back issues and twice-weekly opportunities to phone for specific advice.

Getting There On domestic flights, children under 2 not occupying a seat travel free. Various discounts apply to children from age 2 to 12. If possible, reserve a seat behind the bulkhead of the plane; these offer more leg room and usually enough space to fit a bassinet (supplied by the airlines). At the same time, inquire about special children's meals or snacks, which are also offered by most airlines. (See "TWYCH's Airline Guide," in the February 1990 and 1992 issues of *Family Travel Times,* for a rundown on children's services offered by 46 airlines.) Ask the airline in advance if you can bring aboard your child's car seat. For the booklet Child/Infant Safety Seats Acceptable for Use in Aircraft, write to the **Federal Aviation Administration** (800 Independence Ave. SW, Washington, DC 20591, tel. 202/267–3479).

Hints for Disabled Travelers

California is a national leader in providing access for disabled people to the attractions and facilities of the state. Since 1982, the state building code has required that all construction for public use must include access for the disabled. State laws more than a decade old provide special privileges, such as license plates allowing special parking spaces, unlimited parking in time-limited spaces, and free parking in metered spaces. Special plates from states other than California are honored.

The **San Diego Trolley** (tel. 619/231–8549), which runs to the Mexican border, has lifts for wheelchairs. About one-third of the bus lines are served by buses with elevator ramps; check with San Diego Transit (tel. 619/233–3004).

The **Community Service Center for the Disabled (CSCD)** (2864 University Ave., San Diego 92104, tel. 619/293–3500, or for the hearing impaired, TDD 619/293–7757) publishes lists of hotels, motels, and restaurants with access for the disabled. Ask for the Housing Department.

At the **San Diego Zoo** (tel. 619/231–1515) some enclosures are accessible; others are dangerous for wheelchairs because of steep hills. The **San Diego Wild Animal Park** in Escondido is almost completely accessible.

The Information Center for Individuals with Disabilities (Fort Point Pl., 1st floor, 27–43, Wormwood St., Boston, MA 02210, tel. 617/727–5540; TDD 617/727–5236) offers useful problem-solving assistance, including lists of travel agents who specialize in tours for the disabled.

Moss Rehabilitation Hospital Travel Information Service (1200 West Tabor Rd., Philadelphia, PA 19141–3009, tel. 215/456–9600; TDD 215/456–9603) provides information on tourist sights, transportation, and accommodations in destinations around the world. The fee is $5 for each destination. Allow one month for delivery.

Mobility International USA (Box 3551, Eugene, OR 97403, tel. 503/343–1284) has information on accommodations, organized study, etc., around the world.

The Society for the Advancement of Travel for the Handicapped (26 Court St., Penthouse, Brooklyn, NY 11242, tel. 718/858–5483) offers access information. The annual membership costs $45, or $25 for senior travelers and students. Send a stamped, self-addressed envelope.

Greyhound-Trailways (tel. 800/752–4841; TDD 800/345–3109) will carry a disabled person and companion for the price of a single fare. **Amtrak** (tel. 800/USA–RAIL) requests 24-hour notice to provide redcap service, special seats, and a 25% discount.

The Itinerary (Box 2012, Bayonne, NJ 07002, tel. 201/858–3400) is a bimonthly travel magazine for the disabled.

Access to the World: A Travel Guide for the Handicapped by Louise Weiss offers tips on travel and accessibility around the world. It is available from Henry Holt & Co. for $12.95 (tel. 800/247–3912; the order number is 0805001417).

Hints for Older Travelers

There are many discounts available to older travelers: for meals, lodging, entry to various attractions, car rentals, tickets for buses and trains, and campsites.

The age that qualifies you for these senior discounts varies considerably. The American Association of Retired Persons will accept you for membership at age 50, and your membership card will qualify you for many discounts. The state of California will reduce the cost of your campsite, but you must be at least 62.

Our advice, if you are 50, is to ask about senior discounts, even if there is no posted notice. Ask at the time you are making reservations, buying tickets, or being seated in a restaurant. Carry proof of your age, such as a driver's license, and, of course, any membership cards in organizations that provide discounts for seniors. Many discounts are given solely on the basis of your age, without any sort of membership requirement. A 10% cut on a bus ticket or a 10% cut on a pizza may not seem like a major saving, but they add up, and you can cut the cost of your trip appreciably if you remember to take advantage of these options.

The American Association of Retired Persons (AARP, 1909 K St., NW, Washington, DC 20049, tel. 202/662–4850) has two programs for independent travelers: (1) *The Purchase Privilege Program,* which offers discounts on hotels, airfare, car rentals, and sightseeing, and (2) the *AARP Motoring Plan, provided by Amoco,* which offers emergency aid and trip routing information for an annual fee of $29.95 per couple. AARP members must be 50 or older. Annual dues are $5 per person or per couple.

When using an AARP or other identification card, ask for a reduced hotel rate when you make your reservation, not when you check out. At participating restaurants, show your card to the maitre d' before you are seated, since discounts may be limited to certain set menus, days, or hours. When renting a car, be sure to ask about special promotional rates which may offer greater savings than the available discount.

Travel Industry and Disabled Exchange (TIDE, 5435 Donna Ave., Tarzana, CA 91356, tel. 818/368–5648) is an industry-based organization with a $15 per person annual membership fee. Members receive a quarterly newsletter and information on travel agencies and tours.

National Council of Senior Citizens (925 15th St., NW, Washington, DC 20005, tel. 202/347–8800) is a nonprofit advocacy group with some 5,000 local clubs across the country. Annual membership is $12 per person or per couple. Members receive a monthly newspaper with travel information and an ID card for reduced rates on hotels and car rentals. The council runs frequent tours to Disney World.

Mature Outlook (6001 N. Clark St., Chicago, IL 60660, tel. 800/336–6330), a subsidiary of Sears Roebuck & Co., is a travel club for people over 50, with hotel and motel discounts and a bimonthly newsletter. Annual membership is $9.95 per couple. Instant membership is available at participating Holiday Inns.

Golden Age Passport is a free lifetime pass to all parks, monuments, and recreation areas run by the federal government. People 62 and over should pick it up in person at any national park that charges admission. A driver's license or other proof of age is required.

The California state park system has more than 200 locations and provides a $2 discount on campsites (ask for this discount when you make advance reservations) and a $1 discount on day-use admission for anyone 62 or over and others in the same private vehicle.

September Days Club is run by the moderately priced Days Inns of America (tel. 800/241–5050). The $12 annual membership fee for individuals or couples over 50 entitles them to reduced car rental rates and reductions of 15–50% at some 95% of the chain's more than 350 motels.

Greyhound-Trailways (tel. 800/752–4841; TDD 800/345–3109) and **Amtrak** (tel. 800/USA–RAIL) offer special fares for senior citizens. Amtrak has a free access guide.

The Senior Citizen's Guide to Budget Travel in the United States and Canada is available for $4.95, including postage, from Pilot Books (103 Cooper St., Babylon, NY 11702, tel. 516/422–2225).

The Discount Guide for Travelers over 55, by Caroline and Walter Weintz (Dutton, $7.95), lists helpful addresses, package tours, reduced-rate car rentals, etc., in the United States and abroad. To order, send $7.95 plus $1.50 shipping and handling to NAL/Cash Sales (Bergenfield Order Dept., 120 Woodbine St., Bergenfield, NJ 07621, tel. 800/526–0275).

Further Reading

There is no better way to establish the mood for your visit to Old Town San Diego than to read Helen Hunt Jackson's 104-year-old novel, *Ramona.* As one reviewer said recently, "Although not set in Old Town, it could have been. The book is the classic romantic depiction of 'Old California.'" The Casa de Estudillo in Old Town has been known for many years as Ramona's Marriage Place because of its close resemblance to the house described in the novel. A best-seller for more than 50 years, *Ramona* is still readily available in paperback and hardcover editions.

Other novels with a San Diego setting include Raymond Chandler's mystery about the waterfront, *Playback;* Wade Miller's mystery, *On Easy Street;* Eric Higgs's gothic thriller, *A Happy Man;* and David Zielinski's modern-day story, *A Genuine Monster.*

Arriving and Departing

By Plane

There are regularly scheduled nonstop flights to San Diego from many U.S. and Mexican cities. Direct flights, with one or two stops en route and no change of plane, or connecting flights, requiring two or more stops on two or more airplanes, make the city accessible by most major and regional carriers.

The Airlines San Diego is served by AeroCalifornia (tel. 800/258–3311), Alaska Airlines (tel. 800/426–0333), America West (tel. 619/560–0727), American (tel. 619/232–4051), Braniff (tel. 619/231–0700), Continental (tel. 800/525–0280), Delta (tel. 619/235–4344), Northwest (tel. 619/239–0488), Skywest (tel. 800/453–9417), Southwest (tel. 619/232–1221), Trans World Airlines (tel. 619/295–7009), United (tel. 619/234–7171), and USAir (tel. 800/428–4322).

Luggage Regulations Each passenger is permitted two pieces of hand luggage that can fit either under the seat or in the overhead bin. In addition, each passenger may check in two or three bags, which cannot weigh more than 70 pounds per piece or be larger than 62 inches (length + width + height). Luggage regulations may vary slightly with each airline.

Lost Luggage Airlines are responsible for lost or damaged luggage up to $1,250 per passenger on domestic flights. Additional lost-luggage insurance may be purchased through travel agents and at airline ticket counters and airport insurance booths. The usual cost is $1 for each additional $100 of insurance, with a maximum coverage of $25,000. Be sure to itemize the contents of each bag in case it becomes necessary to file a claim. Your name and address should be clearly labeled on every piece of luggage.

Smoking Smoking is banned on all scheduled routes within the 48 contiguous states; within the states of Hawaii and Alaska; to and from the U.S. Virgin Islands and Puerto Rico; and on flights of less than six hours to and from Hawaii and Alaska. The rule applies to the domestic legs of all foreign routes but does not affect international flights.

On a flight where smoking is permitted, you can request a nonsmoking seat during check-in or when you book your ticket. If the airline tells you there are no seats available in the nonsmoking section on the day of the flight, insist on one: Department of Transportation regulations require U.S. carriers to find seats for all nonsmokers, provided they meet check-in time restrictions.

From the Airport to Center City All flights arrive at Lindbergh Field, just three miles northwest of downtown. **San Diego Transit** Route 2 buses leave every 20–30 minutes, from 5:30 AM–midnight, from the center traffic aisle at the East Terminal and at the traffic island at the far west end of the West Terminal. The buses go to 4th and Broadway, downtown. Fare is $1 per person. Bus fares are projected to rise in 1992. Taxi fare is $5–$6, plus tip, to most center-city hotels. **The Super Shuttle Airport Limousine** (tel. 619/278–5800 or 800/722–9455) will take you directly to your destination, often for less than a cab would cost. Numerous hotels and motels offer complimentary transportation to their guests. If you have rented a car at the airport, follow the signs to I-5 and go south for about three miles to downtown.

By Car

I-5 stretches from Canada to the Mexican border and bisects San Diego. I-8 provides access from Yuma, Arizona, and points east. Drivers coming from Nevada and the mountain regions beyond can reach San Diego on I-15. Avoid rush-hour periods when the traffic can be jammed for miles.

Car Rentals

A car is essential for San Diego's sprawling freeway system and for Baja California. Since the airport is a 5-minute drive from downtown and rates are equivalent in both areas, an airport rental may be your best bet. Major companies like Hertz (tel. 800/654–3131), Avis (tel. 800/331–1212), National (tel. 800/328–4567), and Budget (tel. 800/527–0700) have offices at the airport and near the downtown Hotel Circle.

Major budget companies serving San Diego are General (tel. 800/327–7607) and Alamo (tel. 800/327–9633). Local budget companies include Five Dollar Rent-A-Car (tel. 619/260–1781) and RPM (tel. 619/234–5566). At the other end of the price range is Presidential Exotic (tel. 619/291–2820), which rents upscale vehicles at a Hotel Circle location.

Daily rates for subcompacts with major rental firms average $40–$60, with 100 free miles. Rental companies are beginning to allow their cars to be taken across the Mexican border, but you must ask permission and purchase Mexico auto insurance. **Avis** (tel. 800/331–1212) and **Courtesy** (tel. 619/232–3191) offer this option.

Especially if you're driving into Mexico, carefully consider your collision-damage waiver options. Would the waiver still leave you responsible for damage incurred there? Does any personal, corporate, or supplemental insurance policy of yours, combined with Mexican insurance, make an $8–$11 daily collision-damage waiver surcharge unnecessary?

Three important suggestions for car rentals: No matter what company, get a reservation number; compare prices (ask about weekend and promotional rates); and be sure you understand all the provisions of an agreement before you sign it. Often you will have to pay extra for the privilege of picking up a car in one location and dropping it in another; know the difference in cost and know how important this privilege is to you. Different requirements for filling gas tanks can change the cost of the rental. Ask questions!

By Train

Amtrak trains (tel. 800/USA–RAIL) from Los Angeles arrive at Santa Fe Depot, at Kettner Boulevard and Broadway, near the heart of downtown. There are additional stations in Del Mar and Oceanside, both located in north San Diego County. Eight trains operate daily in either direction.

By Bus

Greyhound-Trailways (tel. 619/239–9171) operates frequent daily service between the downtown terminal at 120 W. Broadway and Los Angeles, connecting with buses to all major U.S. cities. Many buses are express or nonstop; others make stops at coastal towns en route.

Staying in San Diego

Important Addresses and Numbers

Tourist Information

The International Information Center is in Horton Plaza, at the corner of 1st Avenue and F Street, tel. 619/236–1212. Open daily 8:30–5. Closed Thanksgiving and Christmas.

Recorded visitor information (tel. 619/236–1212).

Mission Bay Visitor Information Center is located at 2688 East Mission Bay Drive, off I–5 at the Mission Bay side of the Clairemont Drive exit, tel. 619/276–8200. Open Mon.–Sat. 9–5, Sun. 9:30–4:30.

Balboa Park Information Center is at 1549 El Prado, in Balboa Park, tel. 619/239–0512. Open daily, 9:30–4.

Beach Report (tel. 619/225–9492).

Weather Forecast (tel. 619/289–1212).

Emergencies **Police, Ambulance,** and **Fire** departments can all be reached by dialing 911. For the **Poison Control Center,** call 619/543–6000.

Doctor Hospital emergency rooms, with physicians on duty, are open 24 hours. Major hospitals are **UCSD Medical Center** (225 Dickinson, tel. 619/543–6400), **Mercy Hospital and Medical Center** (4077 5th Ave., tel. 619/260–7000), **Scripps Memorial Hospital** (9888 Genesee Ave., La Jolla, tel. 619/457–6150), **Veterans Administration Hospital** (3350 La Jolla Village Dr., La Jolla, tel. 619/453–7500).

Getting Around

Many attractions, such as the Gaslamp Quarter, Balboa Park, and La Jolla, are best seen on foot. A variety of public transportation can be incorporated to reach any major tourist and shopping area, but it is best to have a car for exploring more remote coastal and inland regions. The International Information Center in Horton Plaza, at the corner of 1st Avenue and F Street, provides maps of the city.

By Bus Fares on **San Diego Transit** buses are $1, $1.25 on express buses; senior citizens pay 50¢ on any bus. Bus fares are expected to rise in 1992. A free transfer is included in the fare, but it must be requested upon boarding. Buses to most major attractions leave from 4th or 5th and Broadway. San Diego Transit Information Line (tel. 619/233–3004) is open daily, 5:30 AM–8:30 PM. Call for precise details on getting to any location. The **Day Tripper Transit Pass** is good for unlimited trips within the same day on buses and the trolley for $3; passes are available at the **Transit Store** (449 Broadway, tel. 619/234–1060). If ordering by mail, include the dates of your trip and 50¢ for postage and handling.

Regional bus companies that service areas outside the city are **National City Transit** (tel. 619/474–7505), for National City; **Chula Vista Transit** (tel. 619/233–3004), for Bonita and Chula Vista; **The Strand Route** (tel. 619/232–8505), for Coronado, the Silver Strand, and Imperial Beach; **Northeast County Rural Bus System** (tel. 619/765–0145) or **Southeast County Rural Bus System** (tel. 619/478–5875), for access to rural county towns; and **North County Transit District** (tel. 619/233–3004), for the area bound by the ocean, east to Escondido, north to Camp Pendleton, and south to Del Mar.

By Taxi Taxi fares are regulated at the airport—all companies charge the same rate. Fares vary between companies on other routes, however, including the ride back to the airport. Cab companies that serve most areas of the city are **Yellow Cab** (tel. 619/234–6161), **Orange Cab** (tel. 619/291–3333), **La Jolla Cab** (tel. 619/453–4222), **Co-op Silver Cabs** (tel. 619/280–5555), **Coast Cab** (tel. 619/226–8294), and **Coronado Cab** (tel. 619/435–6211).

By Trolley The **San Diego Trolley** travels from downtown to within 100 feet of the United States–Mexican border, stopping at 21 suburban stations en route. Basic fare is 50¢–$1.50, one way (expected to rise in 1992). The trolley also travels from downtown to La Mesa and El Cajon in East County. Ticket vending machines, located at each station, require exact change. Tickets must be purchased before boarding. Trolleys operate daily, approximately every 15 minutes, 5 AM–1 AM. The new Bayside line serves the Convention Center and Seaport Village; a line to Old Town is under construction.

By Train Amtrak (tel. 800/USA–RAIL) makes eight trips daily, each direction, between San Diego, Del Mar, and Oceanside. One-way fare from San Diego to Del Mar is $6; from San Diego to Oceanside, $9; from Del Mar to Oceanside, $5.75. Seats are nonreserved, but tickets should be purchased before boarding.

By Ferry The San Diego–Coronado Ferry leaves from the Broadway Pier daily, every hour on the hour, 10 AM–10 PM. Fare is $1 each way. **The Harbor Hopper** (tel. 619/229–8294) is a water-taxi service that shuttles passengers from one side of the San Diego Harbor to another, with 87 possible pick-up points. The fare is $5 each way.

By Limousine Limousine companies provide chauffeured service for business or pleasure. Some offer airport shuttles and customized tours. Rates vary and are per hour, per mile, or both, with some minimums established. Companies offering a range of services include **A Touch of Class** (tel. 619/698–6301), **Olde English Livery Service** (tel. 619/232–6533), **La Jolla Limousines** (tel. 619/459–5891), and **Presidential Limousine** (619/291–2820).

By Horse-Drawn Carriage **Cinderella Carriage Co.** (tel. 619/239–8080) will take parties of 2–4 persons through the Gaslamp Quarter and Seaport Village. Cost: $35 for a half-hour ride, $60 for a full hour.

From Center City to the Airport The average taxi fare from downtown to Lindbergh Field is $5–$6. San Diego Transit Route 2 departs 4th and Broadway, daily, every 20 to 30 minutes, 5:30 AM–midnight. Buses stop at both East and West terminals. Many hotels and motels operate a courtesy shuttle service for their guests. By car, take I-5 to the Laurel Street exit and follow signs to the airport.

Guided Tours

Orientation Tours Both **Gray Line Tours** (tel. 619/491–5011) and **San Diego Mini Tours** (tel. 619/234–9044) offer daily four-hour sightseeing excursions. Gray Line uses 45-passenger buses; San Diego Mini Tours uses 25-passenger tour buses. Cost: $20–$50 depending on the length of the tour and the attractions visited.

Champagne Cowboy Tours (tel. 619/283–0220) escorts smaller groups of 12 in minibuses or vans. Each of the companies provides pickup at major hotels. Tour prices start at $20.

Old Town Trolley (tel. 619/298–8687) travels to almost every attraction and shopping area on open-air trackless trolleys. Drivers double as tour guides. You can take the full 90-minute, narrated city tour or get on and off as you please at any of the 10 stops. An all-day pass costs only $14 for adults, $7 for children 5–12. The trolley carries 34 passengers and operates daily 9–5.

Free one-hour bus tours of the downtown redevelopment area, including the Gaslamp Quarter, are hosted by **Centre City Development Corporation** (tel. 619/696–3215). Groups of 43 passengers leave from 119 W. F Street, downtown, every Saturday at 10 AM. Reservations are necessary. The tour may be cancelled if there aren't enough passengers.

Special-Interest Tours **Golflink** (tel. 800/356–4653) arranges golf tournaments and golf-related tours.

Holidays on Horseback (tel. 619/445–3997) offers horseback riding excursions in the back country.

Pied Piper Tours (tel. 619/224–7455) offers customized shopping trips for individuals or groups, specializing in excursions to the Los Angeles garment district.

Flight Trails Helicopters also known as Civic Helicopters (tel. 619/438–8424) has helicopter tours starting at $65 per person per ½ hour.

National Air (tel. 619/440–7752) has round-trip flights to Catalina Island, the Grand Canyon, and other destinations.

San Diego Harbor Excursion (tel. 619/234–4111) and **Invader Cruises** (tel. 619/234–8687) sail with more than 100 passengers on narrated cruises of San Diego harbor. Both vessels have snack bars. One-hour cruises depart several times daily from the Broadway Pier. San Diego Harbor Excursion offers a two-hour tour each day at 2 PM. Reservations are not necessary for any of the tours. Cost: $9 for a one-hour tour; $12 for a two-hour tour. **Mariposa Sailing Cruises** (tel. 619/542–0646) offers morning and afternoon sailing tours of the harbor and San Diego Bay on the 35-foot cutter, *Mariposa.*

Balloon Tours Six-passenger hot-air balloons lift off from San Diego's north country. Most flights are at sunrise or sunset and are followed by a traditional champagne celebration. Companies that offer daily service, weather permitting, are **A Beautiful Morning Balloon Co.** (tel. 619/481–6225), **California Dreamin'** (tel. 619/438–3344), and **Pacific Horizon Balloon Tours** (tel. 619/756–1790). Balloon flight costs start at $75 for a half-hour ride.

Whale-Watching Tours The California gray whale migrates south to Mexico and back north from mid-December to mid-March. Up to 200 whales pass the San Diego coast each day, coming within yards of tour boats. Some tour companies will give a free second trip to any passenger who fails to sight a whale.

The Avanti (tel. 619/222–0391), a 70-foot, luxury motor yacht, and California Cruisin's 180-passenger *Fast Cat* (tel. 619/235–8600), are two of the fastest boats in the harbor. Both offer 2½-hour narrated tours twice a day during the week, three times a day on weekends. **H&M Landing** (tel. 619/222–1144) and **Seaforth Boat Rentals** (tel. 619/223–1681) have daily whale-watching trips in large party boats.

An intimate tour is conducted by **Sail San Diego** (tel. 619/548–4227) on a 38-foot Bristol sailing yacht. A full lunch and an informative lecture are provided for a maximum of six persons. Early booking is recommended because of space limitations.

Walking Tours The **Gaslamp Foundation** (410 Island Ave., tel. 619/233–5227) leads 1½-hour guided walks of the restored downtown historic district, highlighting the Victorian architecture. Groups meet at the foundation office, near Horton Plaza, Saturday at 10 AM and 1 PM. A donation is requested. Self-guided tour brochures are available at the office weekdays 8:30–5.

Free walking tours exploring the gardens, architecture, and history of Balboa Park are given every Saturday at 10 AM by **Offshootours** (tel. 619/525–8200). Also offered are guided botanical tours through more than 7,000 species of exotic fauna and flora at the San Diego Zoo. The tour is free with zoo admission and is offered on the last Sunday of each month.

Old Town Walking Tours (tel. 619/296–1004) leads strolls through 200 years of history in San Diego's original city center. Groups leave from 3977 Twiggs St., daily, on the hour, 10–5. Cost: $1, and reservations are suggested.

Personal Guides **Orange Cab Custom Tours** (tel. 619/291–3333) are available daily for private excursions in five-passenger sedans or seven-passenger station wagons. You can choose from one of the customized tours or, for an hourly rate, be taken wherever you like. **Hector Lam y Asociados** (011–52/688–3364) offers bilingual tours of Tijuana.

2 Exploring San Diego

Introduction

*by Maribeth
Mellin*

Exploring San Diego is an endless adventure, limited only by time and transportation constraints, which, if you don't have a car, can be considerable. San Diego is more a chain of separate communities than a cohesive city. Many of the major attractions are 15 miles or so away from each other—a half-hour or more apart under the best circumstances. The streets are fun for getting an up-close look at how San Diegans live, and if you've got a car, be sure to drive through Mission and Pacific beaches along Mission Boulevard for a good view of the vibrant beach scene. But true Southern Californians use the freeways, which crisscross the county in a sensible fashion. Interstate 5 runs a direct north–south route through the county's coastal communities to the Mexico border. Interstates 805 and 15 do much the same inland, with Interstate 8 as the main east–west route. Highways 163, 52, and 94 act as connectors.

If you are going to drive around San Diego, study your maps before you hit the road. The freeways are convenient and fast most of the time, but if you miss your turnoff or get caught in commuter traffic, you'll experience a none-too-pleasurable hallmark of Southern California living—freeway madness. Southern California drivers rush around on a complex freeway system with the same fervor they use for jogging scores of marathons each year. They particularly enjoy speeding up at interchanges and entrance and exit ramps. Be sure you know where you're going before you join the freeway chase. Better yet, use public transportation or tour buses from your hotel and save your energy for walking in the sun.

If you stick with public transportation, plan on taking your time. San Diego's bus system covers almost all the county, albeit slowly. Since many of the city's major attractions are clustered along the coast, you'll be best off staying there or in the Hotel Circle/Mission Valley zone. Downtown and Fashion Valley Shopping Center in Mission Valley are the two major transfer points, and there are plenty of commuters and friendly bus drivers who can help you along your route. Some buses have bicycle racks in the back, and a bike is a great mode of transportation here. The bike path system, though never perfect, is extensive and well marked. Taxis are expensive, given the miles between various sights, and are best used for getting around once you're in a given area.

We have divided San Diego into eight exploring sections, organized around neighborhoods. (*See* the Exploring San Diego map for the location of each tour.) No matter how you arrive, use your feet for transportation once you get within each section. Downtown's main thoroughfares are Harbor Drive, running along the waterfront, Broadway, through the center of downtown, and Sixth Avenue to Balboa Park. The numbered streets run roughly north–south; the lettered and named streets (Broadway, Market, Island, and Ash) run east–west. Only Broadway, Market, and Island have two-way traffic. The rest alternate one-way directions.

There are large, reasonably priced ($3–$7 per day) parking lots along Harbor Drive, Pacific Highway, and lower Broadway and Market. Meters cost 50¢ an hour and usually are good for two hours. Don't plan on beating a ticket by rushing back and throwing quarters in your meter every so often. The space is

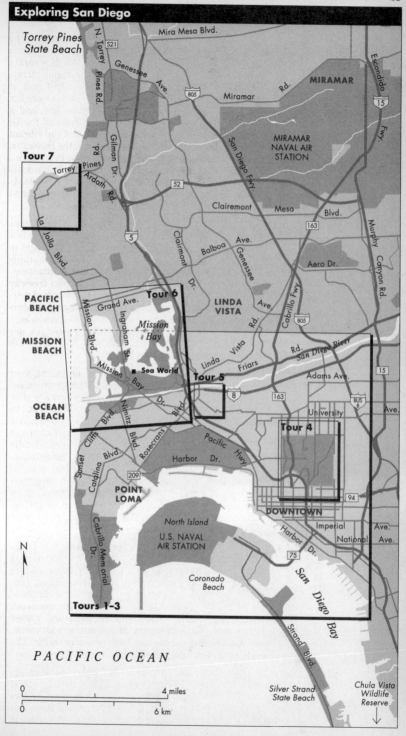

Exploring San Diego

limited to two hours—if you stay longer, no matter how much money is in your meter, you can get a ticket.

Balboa Park, Sea World, Cabrillo National Monument, and Mission Bay all have huge parking lots, and it is rare not to find a space, though it may seem you've parked miles away from your destination. Parking is more of a problem in La Jolla and on Coronado. Basically, you've got to resort to the cruising system, using your passengers as parking-place spotters, or pay a hefty per-hour charge in a lot. Cruising gives you a chance to see a little more than you'd see on foot.

Following the eight exploring sections are sections listing museums and historic sites, parks and gardens, and other places of interest, as well as sections suggesting things to do and see in San Diego for free and with children. The last section in this chapter describes some of the neighborhoods you might visit if you want to get off the beaten track in San Diego.

Highlights for First-time Visitors

Seaport Village, Tour 1: Downtown and the Embarcadero

Horton Plaza, Tour 1: Downtown and the Embarcadero

Hotel Del Coronado, Tour 2: Coronado

Cabrillo National Monument, Tour 3: Point Loma, Shelter Island, and Harbor Sound

Ruben H. Fleet Space Theater and Science Center, Tour 4: Balboa Park

San Diego Zoo, Tour 4: Balboa Park

Bazaar del Mundo, Tour 5: Old Town

Sea World, Tour 6: Mission Bay and Sea World

La Jolla Cove, Tour 7: La Jolla

Scripps Institute of Oceanography Aquarium, Tour 7: La Jolla

Tour 1: Downtown and the Embarcadero

Numbers in the margin correspond with points of interest on the Tours 1–3: Central San Diego map.

Downtown San Diego, just three miles south of the international airport, is changing and growing rapidly, gaining status as a cultural and recreational center for the county's residents and visitors alike. This is the city that brought you the 1988 Super Bowl, merely a harbinger of the tourism boom the city expects to enjoy for years to come. San Diego had 12.4 million overnight guests in 1989, with over $3.1 billion spent by tourists, making tourism the city's third-largest industry.

San Diego's politicians and business leaders have made a concerted effort to draw San Diegans downtown, which has long been ignored by the local populace. Many of the 10,000 or so newcomers who move to San Diego County each year settle in minicities that crop up along the freeways like sagebrush. These communities usually include research and industrial parks and shopping centers and recreation areas, so many residents never need to visit downtown.

But that scenario is changing. A downtown redevelopment project that has been in the works for more than a decade is nearing completion, and the center city has become a place to see. Boosters are counting on it also being a place to stay, whether for the night or the rest of your life. Much attention has been paid to retaining San Diego's character as a healthy, outdoors kind of place. Even the business district, divided into perfect rectangles by an easily managed gridwork of numbered and lettered streets, seems more like a park than a dungeon for workday drones. New mirrored office and banking towers reflect the nearly constant blue skies and sunshine; a view of the harbor or Balboa Park from your office window is a sign of true success.

Downtown's natural attributes were easily evident to its original booster, Alonzo Horton, who arrived in San Diego in 1867. Horton looked at the bay and the acres of flatland surrounded by hills and canyons and knew he had found San Diego's center. Though Old Town, under the Spanish fort at the Presidio, had been settled for years, Horton knew it was too far away from the water to take hold as the commercial center of San Diego. He bought 960 acres along the bay at 27½¢ per acre and literally gave away the land to those who would develop it or build houses. Within months, he had sold or given away 226 city blocks of land, and settlers were camping on their land in tents as their houses and businesses rose. In 1868, Horton and other city fathers staked out 1,400 acres surrounding a mesa overlooking the harbor and created a permanent greenbelt overlooking downtown. That acreage officially became Balboa Park in 1911.

The transcontinental train arrived in 1885, and the grand land boom was on. The population soared from 5,000 to 35,000 in less than a decade—a foreshadowing of San Diego's future. In 1887, the tile-domed Santa Fe Depot was constructed at the foot of Broadway, two blocks from the water. Freighters chugged in and out of the harbor, and by the early 1900s, the navy had discovered this perfect West Coast command center. Today, the navy has a strong presence in the harbor and on Point Loma and Coronado Island and is an integral part of the cityscape.

As downtown grew into San Diego's transportation and commercial hub, residential neighborhoods blossomed along the beaches and inland valleys. Downtown's business district gradually moved farther away from the original heart of downtown, at Fifth and Market, past Broadway, up toward the park. Downtown's waterfront fell into bad times during World War I, when sailors, gamblers, prostitutes, and boozers were drawn like magnets to each other and the waterfront bars.

But Alonzo Horton's modern-day followers, city leaders intent on prospering while preserving San Diego's natural beauty, have reclaimed the waterfront. Replacing old shipyards and canneries are hotel towers and waterfront parks, which surround the new San Diego Convention Center. The $160 million, 760,000-square-foot center hosted its first events in early 1990, and since then downtown has been lively even when the offices and banks are closed. Hotels, restaurants, shopping centers, and housing developments are rising on every square inch of available space as downtown San Diego comes of age.

❶ Your first view of downtown, no matter what your mode of transportation, will likely include the **Embarcadero,** a waterfront walkway lined with restaurants and cruise-ship piers along Harbor Drive. Though the entire waterfront has become a major tourist attraction, as yet there is no tourist office on the Embarcadero.

❷ Your closest access to maps and brochures is at the recently restored **Santa Fe Depot,** just two blocks away, at the corner of Broadway and Kettner Boulevard. There is a tourist information booth inside the station, with bus schedules, maps, and a Traveler's Aid booth. The depot's unmistakable blue tile dome will soon be overshadowed by the Great American Plaza, a massive office tower under construction that will include a transit center linking the train, trolley, and bus systems. For now, the depot is the city's transit hub. Tour buses to Mexico depart from here, and the Greyhound bus station is just a few blocks away at 120 West Broadway.

❸ The bright red **San Diego Trolley** departs a block from the depot, at the corner of India and C streets. The trolley runs through San Diego's south coastal communities—Chula Vista, National City, and Imperial Beach—to the Tijuana border. The fare for the 40-minute ride to the border is $1.50. Once you cross into Mexico, there are plenty of taxis waiting to shuttle you to the shopping and sightseeing districts. The trolley is recognized worldwide as an innovative, self-supporting solution to commuter gridlocks on the road. There is also a trolley line to East County, and the Bayside Line that travels along downtown's waterfront to the Convention Center.

Begin your Embarcadero tour at the foot of Ash Street on Harbor Drive, where the harbor's collection of houseboats, ferries, cruise ships, naval destroyers, tour boats, and a fair share of seals and seagulls begins. The *Star of India*, a beautiful windjammer built in 1863, is docked at the foot of Grape Street on Harbor Drive, across from the Spanish-style San Diego County Administration Center. The *Star of India* is part of the
❹ **Maritime Museum,** a collection of three ships that have been restored and are open for tours. *The Maritime Museum headquarters is located in the* Berkeley *paddle-wheeler boat by the B Street Pier, tel. 619/234–9153. Admission: $5 adults, $4 senior citizens and students, $10 families. Ships open daily 9–8.*

The *Star of India*'s high wooden masts and white sails flapping in the wind have been a harbor landmark since 1926. The ship, made at Ramsey on the Isle of Man, made 21 trips around the world in the late 1800s, when it traveled the East Indian trade route, shuttled immigrants from England to Australia, and served the Alaskan salmon trade. Once retired in the San Diego harbor, she languished, virtually ignored until 1959. Then a group of volunteers, organized by the Maritime Museum, stripped her wooden decks, polished her figurehead, and mended her sails. On July 4, 1976, the *Star of India* commemorated the bicentennial by setting sail in the harbor, after 50 years of neglect.

The *Berkeley*, headquarters for the Maritime Museum, is an 1898 riverboat that served the Southern Pacific Railroad at San Francisco Bay until 1953. The boat's most important days were during the great San Francisco earthquake of 1906, when it carried thousands of passengers across the San Francisco Bay to Oakland. Its carved wood paneling, stained-glass windows, and plate-glass mirrors have been faithfully restored, and its main deck serves as a floating museum, with exhibits on oceanography and naval history.

The steam yacht *Medea* was owned by a wealthy Scot who used it for fishing off the Scottish isles. In World War I, the *Medea* was used to scout for submarines off the English coast. The *Medea* was built of iron, with a deck of imported teak and English oak.

A cement pathway runs from the *Star of India* along the water, past restaurants and fish markets to the docks for harbor tour boats and whale-watching trips (which are scheduled in January and February during the grand migration of the gray whales from the Pacific Northwest to southern Baja).

This section of the Embarcadero, at Harbor Drive and the foot of Broadway, has become a tourists' gathering spot. A cluster of streetfront windows sell tickets for tours; those waiting for their boats grab a beer or ice cream at the diner-style Bay Cafe and sit on the upstairs patio or on benches along the busy pathway and watch the sailboats, paddle-wheelers, and yachts vie for space.

Time Out The Anthony Ghio family got a handle on feeding the Embarcadero's visitors long before anyone else, and they dominate the waterfront north of Broadway. First is the gourmet **Anthony's Star of the Sea** restaurant in a low wooden building perched on stilts over the water. **Anthony's Harborside,** across Harbor Drive, has an upstairs dining room looking out to the harbor and the waterfront's most popular drinking and dancing lounge downstairs. **Anthony's Fish Grotto and Fishette** are more casual. Take a break from touring and grab a beer and some fresh fish-and-chips from the Fishette and sit on one of the outside stools, watching the boats as you eat. **The Bay Cafe,** by B Street Pier, is the place to get ice cream cones, sandwiches, and beer, and there are plenty of benches along the way for sitting and snacking.

---

❺ The pink and blue **B Street Pier** has become a central loading zone for catamaran trips to the island of Catalina, about three hours northeast, and cruise trips to Ensenada, Mexico's harborfront city about 80 land miles south of San Diego. Ships from major cruise lines use San Diego's pier as both a port of call and a departure point for cruises to San Juan, Vancouver, and the Panama Canal. The cavernous pier building has a cruise-information center and a small, cool bar and gift shop. There is a huge public parking lot ($3 a day) along the south side of the pier building. Since much of the parking along Harbor Drive is limited to two-hour meters, this lot is good if you're planning to tour the harbor for the day.

One of the newest, yet most traditional, boat trips is the **Bay Ferry** to Coronado Island, which runs hourly from 10 AM to 10 PM. Ten years ago, Coronado could be reached only by boat from downtown. Then the magnificent blue arc of the 2.2-mile San Diego–Coronado Bridge rose over the harbor, providing spectacular views for the drivers commuting from the island's close community and busy naval base. The ferry lost its appeal

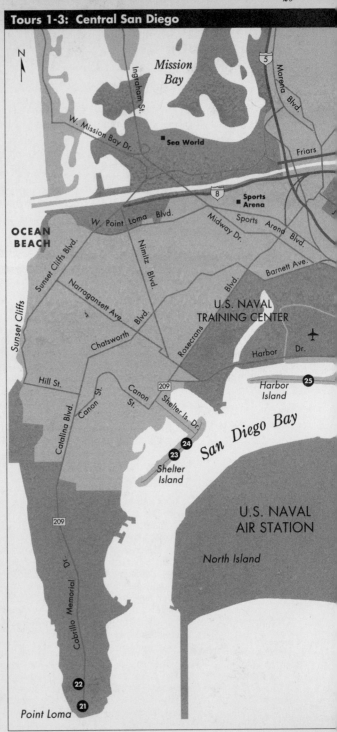

Tours 1-3: Central San Diego

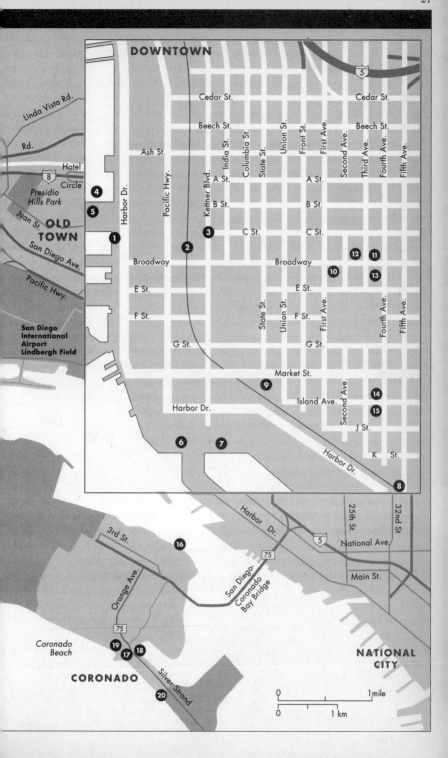

DOWNTOWN

Cedar St.
Cedar St.
Beech St.
Beech St.
Ash St.
A St.
A St.
B St.
B St.
C St.
C St.
Broadway
Broadway
E St.
E St.
F St.
F St.
G St.
G St.
Market St.
Island Ave.
J St.
K St.

Linda Vista Rd.
Rd.
Hotel
Circle
Presidio
Hills Park
Juan St.
OLD
TOWN
San Diego Ave.
Pacific Hwy.

San Diego
International
Airport
Lindbergh Field

Harbor Dr.
Pacific Hwy.
Kettner Blvd.
India St.
Columbia St.
State St.
Union St.
Front St.
First St.
Second Ave.
Third Ave.
Fourth Ave.
Fifth Ave.
First Ave.
State St.
Union St.
Second Ave.
Fourth Ave.
Fifth Ave.

Harbor Dr.
Harbor Dr.

3rd St.
Orange Ave.
Harbor Dr.
25th St.
32nd St.
National Ave.
Main St.

San Diego-Coronado Bay Bridge

NATIONAL
CITY

Coronado
Beach
CORONADO
Silver Strand

0   1 mile
0   1 km

and disappeared. But Coronado is undergoing its own building boom, and its harborfront shores are filling up with luxury condominium towers and waterfront restaurants and shops. The trip across is delightfully picturesque, particularly at sunset.

Back along the Embarcadero are other traditional craft, some housing gift shops, some awaiting restoration. The navy's Eleventh Naval District has control of the next few waterfront blocks, and a series of destroyers, submarines, and carriers cruise in and out, some staying for weeks at a time. The navy occasionally offers tours of these floating cities.

A steady stream of joggers, bicyclists, and serious walkers pick up speed where the Embarcadero pathway passes the Tuna Harbor, where San Diego's tuna boats once gathered. A new Fish Market Restaurant has opened over the water at the end of the pier, offering spectacular views of the harbor and downtown.

❻ Seaport Village (tel. 619/235–4013) is next. It was a wise developer who saw the good fortune in this stretch of prime waterfront that now connects the harbor with the newly rising hotel towers and convention center. Seaport Village is a privately developed and operated 14-acre shopping, dining, and recreational outdoor mall of sorts. The village's clapboard and stucco buildings house a seemingly unending series of specialty shops, snack bars, and restaurants—each with an independent theme. Seaport Village spreads from Harbor Drive to the waterfront. The village is expanding across Market Street to the old San Diego Police Department, a complex of hacienda-style buildings now deserted. The addition will include a multitiered parking garage and a Night Court with clubs, restaurants, and bars. The parking lots along Harbor Drive fill up quickly, but there is additional parking up Market Street and Kettner Boulevard. Stay away from parking meters if you're planning to stay for a while, since they are patrolled frequently. Seaport Village's shops are open daily from 10 to 9, with restaurants closing closer to midnight.

The **Broadway Flying Horses Carousel,** whose handcarved animals rose and fell at Coney Island during the turn of the century, is surrounded by inexpensive ethnic cafes and takeouts and a video parlor for those who prefer their fun in the shade. The carousel was moved to the village from Salisbury Beach in Massachusetts, and faithfully restored. The handcarved, handpainted unicorns and stallions are beautiful, and as many adults as children enjoy riding them. This section is food central of sorts, with take-out stands offering pizza, egg rolls, hot dogs, sandwiches, and Greek salads.

Picnic tables are scattered under shade trees around the restaurants, but the best seats are on the patio behind the Greek Islands Cafe. Jerry G. Bishop, a popular local TV talk-show host, owns and runs this restaurant with a friendly flair, and the Greek specialties are excellent. The tables here fill up quickly, but there is a long concrete wall by the water where you can sit and dine alfresco. Beside the wall is Seaport Village's official symbol, the 45-foot-high Mulkilteo Lighthouse, modeled after an 80-year-old lighthouse in Everett, Washington. The San Diego Pier Cafe, an on-the-water seafood restaurant, occupies the lighthouse. The best seats are along the outdoor walkway or upstairs inside the lighthouse, overlooking the boats in the harbor.

Seaport Village has over 65 specialty shops. Upstart Crow bookstore has a coffeehouse atmosphere and serves fancy coffee drinks (nonalcoholic) and great pastries and cakes. A long bar faces the espresso machine, and there is an upstairs reading lounge with tables and couches and photographs of famous writers. The selection of books on San Diego is excellent, and there is a nice children's section. There is a teddy bear shop, a clown shop, and one solely devoted to items for left-handed people. The hammock shop has beautiful hammocks from Mexico and South America, and lounging is encouraged.

Snacking is a must in Seaport Village. The Fudge House has huge slabs of fudge in a variety of flavors, made on the premises. Warm croissants and lavish French pastries are available at A La Francaise, and popcorn pops in red vendor wagons along the paths.

Full-scale restaurants include Papagayo, specializing in Latin American seafood, and the Harbor House, a seafood restaurant with a large upstairs deck and an indoor lounge with live music in the evenings. The Jolly Roger, at the far end of the village, is popular with families who prefer hearty breakfasts and burgers.

Seaport Village's center reaches out on a long grassy point into the harbor, where kite fliers, roller skaters, and picnickers hang out in the sun. On summer evenings, the San Diego Symphony presents its annual Summer Pops concert series on the lawn, where seasonal celebrations, replete with live music and fireworks, are held throughout the year. Even when nothing special is planned, the village is filled with clowns, mimes, musicians, and magicians in a shopper's paradise.

7 The mirrored towers of the **San Diego Marriott Hotel and Marina** mark the end of Seaport Village. The waterfront walkway continues past the hotel's marina, where hotel guests moor their enormous, extravagant yachts. Farther on is a large park with a fishing pier and walking paths.

8 Just past the Marriott is the new **San Diego Convention Center,** designed by Arthur Erickson. The architecture is striking, especially against the blue sky and sea. The Center often holds trade shows that are open to the public. Tours of the building are available.

To reach the heart of downtown, walk up Market Street from Seaport Village or up Broadway from the B Street Pier. The **9** **Olde Cracker Factory,** at Market and State streets, houses antiques and collectibles shops. Turn left here and go two blocks to G Street, where many of San Diego's new residential developments are clustered around the pretty **Pantoja Park.**

Walking up Broadway, you'll pass the Santa Fe Depot and a dwindling collection of dive bars and tattoo parlors. Lower Broadway has long been a headache for downtown's boosters, but several high-rise office buildings have been erected in the area, and more are in the planning stages. A few blocks farther, at the corner of First and Broadway, is where downtown comes **10** alive. Here you'll pass the **Spreckels Theater,** a grand old stage that now presents pop concerts and touring plays. Arts-Tix, a discount theater ticket outlet, is in the Spreckels's Lobby.

⓫ The grand **U.S. Grant Hotel**, built in 1910, is across the street. Far more elegant and formal than most San Diego hotels, the U.S. Grant has massive marble lobbies, with gleaming chandeliers and hospitable doormen. The Grant Grill, closed for two years during the hotel's refurbishing, is the prime watering **⓬** hole for San Diego's old guard. One block away is the **Westgate Hotel**, another deluxe hostelry for visiting celebrities and royalty. The Westgate is French Provincial in style and has a nice piano bar on the main floor and an elegant French restaurant, Le Fontainebleau, at the top.

The theme of shopping in adventureland carries over from Sea- **⓭** port Village to downtown San Diego's centerpiece, **Horton Plaza.** Completed in August 1985, this shopping, dining, and entertainment mall fronts Broadway and G Street from First to Fourth avenues and covers more than six city blocks. Designed by Jon Jerde, whose touch you might have seen in views from the 1986 Summer Olympics in Los Angeles, Horton Plaza is far from what one imagines a shopping center, or city center, to be. It rises in uneven, staggered levels to six floors and has great views of all downtown, from the harbor to Balboa Park and beyond. The 450-room Omni Hotel is connected to Horton Plaza and often hosts special events in conjunction with the plaza.

The **International Visitor Information Center** was opened in Horton Plaza by the San Diego Convention and Visitors Bureau in 1985, and it has become the traveler's best resource for information on all San Diego. The staff members and volunteers who run the center speak an amazing array of languages and are well acquainted with the myriad needs and requests of tourists. They dispense information on hotels, restaurants, and tourist attractions, including Tijuana. Photos of San Diego's landmarks decorate the walls, and a wealth of brochures and pamphlets in many languages are neatly arrayed by the counters. *11 Horton Plaza, street level at the corner of First and F Sts., tel. 619/236–1212. Open daily 8:30–5:30.*

Horton Plaza was designed to be an architectural surprise in itself, a collage of pastel colors with elaborate, colorful tilework marking benches and stairways, cloth banners waving in the air, and modern sculptures marking the entrances. Horton Plaza's innovative architecture has strongly affected the rest of downtown's development, and new apartment and condominium complexes along G and Market streets mimic the pastel-colored towers and cupolas of the plaza. Horton Plaza was a massive gamble, dependent on downtown workers and tourists for its success until those living five, 10, 15, and 50 miles away could be convinced to come to town. Thus far, it seems to be paying off.

The plaza has a large, multilevel parking garage, and the first three hours are free with validation (you needn't purchase anything to get a shop to validate your ticket). To encourage people to stay downtown at night, parking is free after 5 PM. The long lines of cars in search of a place to land show just how successful Horton Plaza has become. If you park here, be sure to remember where you leave your car. The lot is notoriously confusing, with levels that don't quite match up with the levels the shops are on.

Robinson's, Nordstrom, the Broadway, and Mervyn's department stores anchor the shopping sections, with an eclectic assortment of 120 clothing, sporting goods, jewelry, book, and
gift shops. A movie theater complex, major restaurants, and a
long row of take-out ethnic food shops and dining patios line the
uppermost tier. The San Diego Repertory Theater, one of the
longest-burning and brightest lights in San Diego's explosive
theater scene, has two stages below ground level. Most of the
shops close at 9 PM on weekdays, and 6 PM on Saturday and Sunday, but the restaurants and theaters are open later.

Horton Plaza filled an essential gap for downtown workers and
residents, who had few places to shop for essentials in the past.
On the lowest level, facing First Street, is the Horton Plaza
Farmers Market, an upscale grocery of sorts, with fresh, gourmet meats, seafood, and produce. The salad bar and deli counter are popular during lunch breaks, when office workers swarm
to the plaza and enjoy a few minutes of fresh air at the sidewalk
patio. The take-out places on the highest tier are equally popular. It's downright impossible to stroll past the shops selling
fragrant cinnamon rolls, cheese-covered french fries, French
pastries, and Mexican tacos without eating something.

Downtown's sidewalk merchants felt a nasty pinch when
Horton Plaza first opened. Those closest to Horton ended up
facing four levels of parking lot—the plaza's biggest drawback
to accessibility for the rest of downtown. But shoppers, diners,
and strollers are roaming farther, and prosperity seems to be
spreading. Restaurateurs close to the plaza who succeeded are
branching out to the surrounding blocks, creating pockets of
culinary culture.

Time Out   It's fun to wander outside the enclave and go authentically,
pleasantly ethnic at **Greektown,** near Fourth and E, and at **Ath-
ens' Market,** on the other side of the plaza at First and E. In the
Gaslamp Quarter, the **Golden Lion Tavern,** at Fourth and F, is a
popular after-work spot. **Croce's,** at the corner of Fifth and F,
is owned and operated by the widow of the late Jim Croce, of
pop music fame. Ingrid Croce has created a combination Continental restaurant and jazz club that is gaining ground as a lively nightlife spot. **Java,** at Ninth and G, is the happening
coffeehouse.

Dining options at Horton Plaza itself are extensive—everything from sweet cinnamon rolls to pungent burritos to Peking
duck. **La Salsa,** on the uppermost dining level, has wonderful
marinated pork tacos and blue corn chips—darker in color and
stronger in flavor than traditional corn chips. **Marie Callender's**
specializes in pies, serving minipies for one—the strawberry is
particularly grand. **Galaxy Grill** is a fifties-style diner with
great burgers and shakes.

Long before Horton Plaza became the bright star on downtown's redevelopment horizon, the **Gaslamp Quarter** was gaining attention and respect. A 16-block National Historic
District, centered on Fifth and Fourth avenues, from Broadway to Market Street, the quarter contains most of San Diego's
Victorian-style commercial buildings from the late 1800s, when
Market Street was the center of early downtown. At the farthest end of the redeveloped quarter, the **Gaslamp Quarter Association** is headquartered in the William Heath Davis house

(410 Island Ave., tel. 619/233–5227), a restored 19th-century saltbox house. Walking tours of the historic district leave from here on Saturdays at 10 and 1. A $2 donation is suggested. If you can't make the tour, stop by the house and pick up a brochure and map.

The William Heath Davis house is located in the heart of Alonzo Horton's New Town, so-called to distinguish it from Old Town. In the late 1800s, businesses thrived in this area. But at the turn of the century, downtown's business district moved farther west, toward Broadway, and many of San Diego's first buildings fell into disrepair. During the early 1900s, the quarter became known as the Stingaree district, where hookers picked up sailors in lively taverns and dance halls. Crime flourished here, and the blocks between Market Street and the waterfront were considered to be seedy, dangerous, and best left alone. As the move for downtown redevelopment emerged, there was talk about destroying the buildings in the quarter, literally bulldozing them and starting from scratch.

In 1974, history buffs, developers, architects, and artists formed the Gaslamp Quarter Council. Bent on preserving the district, they gathered funds from the government and private benefactors and began the tedious, expensive task of cleaning up the quarter, restoring the finest old buildings, and attracting businesses and the public back to the heart of New Town. Fifteen years later, their efforts have paid off. Beaten down flophouses have become choice office buildings. The brick sidewalks are lined with trees and benches, and the shops and restaurants tend toward individuality. The battle to combat the quarter's image as a sleazy, scary place has been a long, slow one, but there is a growing movement among artists and entrepreneurs to turn this south side of Broadway into a neighborhood of galleries, artists' lofts, and historical landmarks.

Across the street from the Gaslamp Quarter Association's headquarters, at the corner of Island and Third streets, is the **①⑤** 100-year-old **Horton Grand Hotel,** restored and operated in turn-of-the-century style. The hotel's central courtyard has become a popular wedding and party site. The 110 rooms are decorated with period furnishings, lace curtains, and gas fireplaces—some even have legendary ghosts. A small Chinese Museum serves as a tribute to the surrounding Chinatown district, which is nothing more than a collection of modest homes that once housed Chinese laborers and their families.

Many of the quarter's landmark buildings are located on Fourth and Fifth avenues, between Island and Broadway. Among the nicest are the Backesto Building, the Keating Building, the Louis Bank of Commerce, and the Mercantile Building, all on Fifth. The Golden Lion Tavern, at the corner of Fourth and F, is a magnificently restored turn-of-the-century tavern with a 12-foot mahogany bar and a spectacular stained-glass domed ceiling.

The section of G Street between Sixth and Tenth avenues is becoming an art gallery district. The three-story brick Pannikin Building, at the corner of Seventh and G, houses the International Gallery and a coffee importer and roasting plant. The groundfloor Pannikin shop sells a large selection of freshroasted coffees, imported candies and coffee, and teapots and cups. Java, at the corner of Ninth and G, is a coffeehouse that is popular with the artists and actors who live in the area.

Tour 2: Coronado

Coronado Island is a charming, peaceful community, essentially left alone for decades to grow at its characteristically slow pace. It is a city unto itself, ruled by its own municipal government. Longtime residents live in grand Victorian homes handed down by their families for generations. North Island Naval Air Station was established in 1911 on the island's north end, across from Point Loma, and was the site of Charles Lindbergh's departure on his flight around the world. Today, high-tech air- and seacraft arrive and depart continuously from North Island, providing a real-life education in military armament. Coronado's long relationship with the navy has made it an enclave of sorts for retired military personnel.

The streets are wide, quiet, and friendly, with lots of neighborhood parks where young families mingle with the island's many senior citizens. Grand old homes face the waterfront and the Coronado Municipal Golf Course, with its lovely setting under the bridge, across the water from Seaport Village. Community celebrations, live band concerts, and the Fourth of July fireworks take place in the park next to the golf course. The Spaniards called the island "Los Coronados," or "the Crowned Ones," in the late 1500s. The name stuck, and today's island residents tend to consider their island to be a sort of royal encampment, safe from the hassles and hustle of San Diego proper.

Coronado is visible from downtown and Point Loma and accessible via the arching blue 2.2-mile-long San Diego–Coronado Bridge, a landmark just beyond downtown's skyline. There is a $1 toll for crossing the bridge into Coronado, but cars carrying two or more passengers may enter through the free car-pool lane. The bridge handles more than 20,000 cars each day, and rush hour tends to be slow, which is fine, since the view of the harbor, downtown, and the island is breathtaking, day and night. Until the bridge was completed in 1969, visitors and residents relied on the Coronado Ferry, which ran across the harbor from downtown. When the bridge was opened, the ferry closed down, much to the chagrin of those who were fond of traveling at a leisurely pace. In 1987, the ferry returned, and with it came the island's most ambitious development in decades.

16 The Bay Ferry runs from the B Street Pier at downtown's Embarcadero to the **Old Ferry Landing,** which is actually a new development on an old site. Its buildings resemble the gingerbread domes of the Hotel Del Coronado, long the island's main attraction. The Old Ferry Landing is similar to Seaport Village, with small shops and restaurants and lots of benches facing the water. Nearby, the elegant Le Meridien Hotel accommodates many wedding receptions and gala banquets. The Bay Ferry is located at the B Street Pier, at Broadway and Harbor Drive. Boats depart hourly from 10 to 10. The fare is $1.50 each way.

A trackless trolley runs from the landing down Orange Avenue, the island's version of a downtown, to the Hotel Del Coronado. Coronado's residents and commuting workers have quickly adapted to this traditional mode of transportation, and the ferry has become quite popular with bicyclists who shuttle their bikes across the harbor and ride the island's wide, flat boulevards for hours.

⑰ The **Hotel Del Coronado** is the island's most prominent landmark. Selected as a National Historic Site in 1977, the Del (as natives say) celebrated its 100th anniversary in 1988. Celebrities, royalty, and politicians marked the anniversary with a weekend-long party that highlighted the hotel's colorful history. *1500 Orange Ave., tel. 619/435–6611. Free guided tours from the lobby Sat. 1 PM.*

The hotel is integral to the island's history. In 1884, two wealthy financiers, Elisha Spurr Babcock, Jr., and H. L. Story, stopped hunting grouse and rabbits on the undeveloped island long enough to appreciate the long stretches of virgin beaches, the view of San Diego's emerging harbor, and the island's potential. They decided to build a luxurious resort hotel, formed the Babcock-Story Coronado Beach Company and purchased the 4,100-acre land parcel for $110,000 in 1885. Prospective investors were invited to a lavish Fourth of July celebration in 1886, with free ferry rides across the bay and a free shuttle ride up Orange Avenue to the hotel site. Visitors were regaled with tales of the prospective hotel's grand future as a hunting and fishing resort. By November, orange trees had been planted along Orange Avenue, olive trees on Olive Avenue, and palms on Palm Avenue. Home lots were cleared and ready for development. The 6,000 visitors who swarmed to the island on the weekend of November 13 and 14, 1886, quickly bought up the lots and shares in the new hotel, and Babcock and Story had an ample return on their investment.

It took only one year to build the 400-room main hotel, though it was a mighty effort that employed hundreds of Chinese laborers racing against the clock. All materials and laborers had to be ferried to the island and transported up Orange Avenue on the Babcock-Story Railroad, which was capable of transporting private railroad cars popular with industrial tycoons. The hotel was completed in 1888, and Thomas Edison himself threw the switch as the Del became the world's first electrically lighted hotel. It has been a dazzling sight ever since.

The hotel's gingerbread architecture is recognized all over the world, for it has served as a set for many movies, political meetings, and extravagant social happenings. The Duke of Windsor met Wally Simpson here. Eight presidents have stayed here. The film *Some Like It Hot*, starring Marilyn Monroe, was filmed here. The hotel's underground corridors are lined with historic photos from the days when the hotel was first built. Of particular interest are the photos of the enormous tent city that was built during a major remodeling project in 1902. The tent city was so popular with guests that it was reerected every summer until 1939.

Huge cupolas and towers rise from the Hotel Del Coronado's bright red roof, and though closed to the public, one can easily imagine the views from the tiny windows and balconies in their peaks. A red carpet leads up the front stairs to the main lobby, with its grand oak pillars and ceiling, and out to the central courtyard and gazebo. To the right is the Crown Room, a cavernous room with an arched ceiling, of notched sugar pine, constructed without nails. Sunday, an elaborate brunch is laid out on serving tables scattered through the room, and pianists and harpists play soothing melodies from the curved balconies. Enormous chandeliers sparkle overhead.

The Grand Ballroom looks out to the ocean and the hotel's long white beach. The patio surrounding the sky-blue swimming pool is a great place to sit back and imagine what the bathers looked like during the twenties, when the hotel rocked with good times. More rooms have been added on in high-rise towers beside the original building, which is still the most charming place to stay. The hotel is well worth a visit even if you're staying elsewhere.

Coronado's other main attraction is its 86 historic homes and sites. Many of the homes are turn-of-the-century mansions. **⑱** The **Glorietta Bay Inn,** across the street from the Del, was the home of John Spreckels, original owner of North Island and the property on which the Hotel Del Coronado now stands. Nearby is the **Boat House,** a small replica of the hotel that once served as the launching point for deep-sea fishing craft, which now houses a Chart House restaurant. The Boat House is a great spot for watching the sails in the harbor and watching the sun set over downtown.

The **Coronado Historical Association** offers walking tours of the island's historic highlights along Ocean Boulevard and the surrounding streets. These mansions, a few of which are open **⑲** to the public, are truly spectacular. **Star Park,** on Loma Avenue, acts as a hub for five streets all designated as historic sites. Among the homes here is the Meade House, where L. Frank Baum wrote *The Wizard of Oz.* Coronado Touring (tel. 619/435–5892 or 619/435–5993) has historical tours of the homes that leave from the Glorietta Bay Inn on Tuesday, Thursday, and Saturday mornings at 11; the cost is $5 per person.

⑳ **Silver Strand Beach State Park** runs along Silver Strand Boulevard from the Del to Imperial Beach. The view from the beach to Point Loma is lovely, and the long, clean beach is a perfect family gathering spot, with fire rings, rest rooms, and lifeguards. Across from the strand is the Coronado Cays, an exclusive community, popular with yacht owners and celebrities.

| **Time Out** | The most popular meal on the island is the lavish brunch in the Crown Room at the Hotel Del Coronado (tel. 619/435–1600). Though the room can seat over 1,000 diners, it is wise to make reservations in advance if you are dining with a group, particularly on holidays. Brunch is served from 9 to 2 and costs $20.95 for adults, $16.95 children 6–10. |

Tour 3: Point Loma, Shelter Island, and Harbor Island

Point Loma curves around the San Diego Bay west of downtown and the airport, protecting the center city from the Pacific's tides and waves. Though its main streets are cluttered with hotels, fast-food shacks, and military installations, Point Loma is an old and wealthy enclave of stately family homes for military officers, successful Portuguese fishermen, and political and professional leaders. Its bayside shores front huge estates, with sailboats and yachts packed tightly in private marinas.

㉑ **Cabrillo National Monument,** named after the Portuguese explorer Juan Rodríguez Cabrillo, sits at the very tip of Point Loma. Cabrillo was the first European to discover San Diego, which he called San Miguel, in 1542. In 1913 the monument grounds were set aside to commemorate his discovery. Today his monument is one of the most frequently visited of all National Park Service sites.

In the past few years Cabrillo Monument has undergone subtle development that simultaneously serves tourism and protects the 144-acre preserve's rugged cliffs and shores. Visitors are now charged $3 to park at the monument's center or $1 to visit on foot. Your pass lasts a week, and discounts are available for seniors and those with the National Park Service's Golden Eagle pass. There is a shuttle service for disabled visitors who are unable to hike around. *Tel. 619/557–5450. Open daily 9–5:15.*

Begin your tour at the Visitor Center, where films and lectures about the monument, the sea-level tidal pools, and the gray whales migrating offshore are presented frequently. The center has an excellent shop with an interesting selection of books about nature, San Diego, and the sea; maps of the region, posters of whales, flowers, and shells, and the requisite postcards, slides, and film are also on sale.

Signs along the walkways that edge the cliffs explain the views, with posters picturing the various navy, fishing, and pleasure craft that sail into and fly over the bay. Looking directly south across the bay from the Visitor Center, you see the North Island Naval Air Station on the west end of Coronado Island. Directly left on the shores of Point Loma is the Naval Ocean Systems Center and Ballast Point, where nuclear-powered submarines are docked where Cabrillo's small ships anchored in 1542.

A new statue of Cabrillo overlooks downtown from the next windy promontory, where visitors gather to admire the stunning panorama over the bay, from the snow-capped San Bernardino Mountains, some 200 miles northeast, to the hills surrounding Tijuana. Rest rooms and water fountains are plentiful along the paths that climb to the monument's various view points, but there are no food facilities. Exploring the grounds consumes time and calories; bring a picnic and rest on a bench overlooking the sailboats headed to sea.

Hardier types looking for a good workout will enjoy the two-mile Bayside Trail winding through cliffside chaparral. The trail curves under the clifftop lookouts, bringing you ever closer to the bayfront scenery, below the clouds and haze. You cannot reach the beach from this trail and must stick to the path to protect the cliffs from erosion and yourself from poisonous plants. Along the way, you'll see prickly pear cactus and yucca, black-eyed Susans, fragrant sage, and maybe a lizard or a hummingbird. The climb back is long but gradual, leading up to the old lighthouse.

The oil lamp of the **Old Point Loma Lighthouse** was first lit in 1855. The light, sitting in a brass and iron housing above a painstakingly refurbished white wooden house, shone through a state-of-the-art lens from France and was visible from the sea for 25 miles. Unfortunately, it was too high above the cliffs to guide navigators trapped in Southern California's thick off-shore fog and low clouds. In 1891 a new lighthouse was built on the small shore under the slowly eroding 400-foot cliffs. The old lighthouse is open to visitors, and the Coast Guard still uses the newer lighthouse and a mighty foghorn to guide boaters through the narrow channel leading into the bay.

The western and southern cliffs of Cabrillo Monument are prime whale-watching territory. A sheltered viewing station offers a tape-recorded lecture describing the great gray whales' migration from the Bering Sea to Baja, and high-powered viewers help you focus on the whales' waterspouts. The whales are visible on clear days in January and February, mostly in early morning.

More accessible sea creatures can be seen in the tidal pools at the foot of the monument's western cliffs. To reach the pools, drive north from the Visitor Center to the first road on the left, which winds down to the coast guard station and the shore. When the tide is low (check with the ranger) you can walk on the rocks around saltwater pools filled with starfish, crabs, anemones, octopus, and hundreds of other sea creatures and plants. The pools are protected by law, so leave the creatures alone.

22 Over 40,000 white headstones in **Fort Rosecrans National Cemetery** overlook both sides of the point just north of the monument as you head back into the neighborhoods of Point Loma. The navy has various centers along Rosecrans Street, which also leads to the U.S. Marine Corps Recruit Depot.

23 **Shelter Island** sits in the narrow channel between Point Loma's eastern shore and the west coast of Coronado. In 1950 the port director thought there should be some use for the soil dredged to deepen the ship channel. Why not build an island?

His hunch paid off. Shelter Island's shores now support towering mature palms, a cluster of mid-range resorts, restaurants, and side-by-side marinas. It is the center of San Diego's yacht-building industry, and boats in every stage of construction are visible in the yacht yards. A long sidewalk runs from the land-

24 scaped lawns of the **San Diego Yacht Club** (tucked down Anchorage Street off Shelter Island Drive), past boat brokerages to the hotels and marinas, which line the inner shore, facing Point Loma. On the bay side, fishermen launch their boats or simply stand on shore and cast. Families relax at picnic tables along the grass, where there are fire rings and permanent barbecue grills, while strollers wander to the huge Friendship Bell, given to San Diegans by the people of Yokohama in 1960.

Scott Street, which runs along Point Loma's waterfront from Shelter Island to the Marine Corps Recruiting Center on Harbor Drive, is lined with deep-sea fishing charters and whale-watching boats. This is a good spot to watch fishermen (and women) haul marlin, tuna, and puny mackerel off their boats.

25 **Harbor Island,** made from 3.5 million tons of rock and soil from the San Diego Bay, forms a peninsula adjacent to the airport. Again, hotels and restaurants line the inner shores, but here, the buildings are many stories high, and the views from the bayside rooms are spectacular. The bay shore has pathways and gardens and picnic spots for sightseeing or working off the calories from the island restaurants' fine meals. On the west point Tom Ham's Lighthouse restaurant has a coast guard-approved beacon shining from its tower.

Sunset Cliffs Park is at the western side of Point Loma near Ocean Beach. The cliffs are aptly named, since their main attraction is their vantage point as a fine sunset-watching spot. The dramatic coastline here seems to have been carved out of ancient rock. Certainly the waves make their impact, and each year more sections of the cliffs sport caution signs. Don't climb around on the cliffs when you see these signs. It's easy to lose your footing and slip in the crumbling sandstone, and the surf can get very rough. Small coves and beaches dot the coastline and are popular with surfers drawn to the pounding waves and locals from the neighborhood who name and claim their special spots. The homes along Sunset Cliffs Boulevard are lovely examples of Southern California luxury, with pink stucco mansions beside shingle Cape Cod-style cottages. To reach the cliffs from Cabrillo Monument, take Catalina Boulevard to Hill Street. Turn left and drive straight to the cliffs. Sunset Cliffs Boulevard intersects Hill Street and runs through Ocean Beach to Interstate 8.

Time Out
The freshest and tastiest fish to be found along Point Loma's shores comes from **Point Loma Sea Foods** at Emerson and Scott streets, behind the Vagabond Hotel, by the sportfishing boats. The fish market sells shark, shrimp, lobster, crab, and a dozen other local specialties fresh from the boat. The adjacent takeout counter has simple seafood cocktails and salads and great ceviche (a marinated cocktail of fish, tomatoes, onions, and cilantro pickled in lime juice). The crab and shrimp sandwiches on freshly baked sourdough bread are sublime. Fresh lemonade, beer, and wine go well with the fried calamari, and the homemade chocolate chip cookies make a great dessert. PLSF (as the natives say) is open daily Mon.–Sat. 9–6:30, Sun. noon–6:30. Parking is tight, but people come and go quickly as they pick up their picnic and barbecue supplies or eat in the sheltered patio by the pier.

Point Loma and the islands are at their nicest before noon and near sunset. On Shelter Island, **Humphrey's** (2303 Shelter Island Dr., tel. 619/224–3411) has a lavish weekend champagne brunch and jazz and pop concerts on the lawn by the marina on summer nights. The **Red Sails Inn** (2614 Shelter Island Dr., tel. 619/223–3030) is where the saltier seafarers hang out. Harbor Island is more upscale, and the sunset view is particularly pleasing from the **Sheraton's Reflections Lounge** (1590 Harbor Island Dr., tel. 619/291–6400). Both islands have a good representation of chain restaurants, ranging from seafood to Mexican fare.

Tour 4: Balboa Park

Numbers in the margin correspond with points of interest on the Tour 4: Balboa Park map.

If it were on the ocean, Balboa Park would encompass all that is wonderful about San Diego. But you can see the ocean, or the bay at least (Balboa Park straddles two mesas overlooking downtown), from many points in the park's 1,400 acres of cultural, recreational, and environmental delights.

Many of the park's ornate Spanish-Moorish buildings were intended to be temporary structures housing exhibits for the Panama–California International Exposition of 1915. Fortunately, city leaders realized the buildings' value and incorporated them in their plans for Balboa Park's acreage, which had been set aside by the city founders in 1868. The Spanish theme first instituted in the early 1900s was carried through in new buildings designed for the California Pacific International Exposition of 1935–36. El Prado, the courtyard and walkway first created for the 1915 exposition, now passes through San Diego's central museum district, with pathways forking off to other attractions.

Most of San Diego's museums are located in the park, making it San Diego's cultural center. The newest additions are the **Automotive Museum** and the **Museum of San Diego History.** All the museums have excellent gift shops, with a good selection of books and posters dealing with the museum's focus. The shops are open during museum hours. The museums offer free admission on a rotating basis on Tuesdays.

The Laurel Street Bridge, also known as Cabrillo Bridge, is the park's official gateway, leading over a vast canyon, filled with downtown commuter traffic on Highway 163, to El Prado which, beyond the art museum, becomes the park's central pedestrian mall. At Christmas the bridge is lined with colored lights; bright pink blossoms on rows of peach trees herald the coming of spring. The 100-bell carillon in the California Tower tolls the hour. Figures of California's historic personages decorate the base of the 200-foot spire, and a magnificent blue-tiled dome shines in the sun.

❶ **The Museum of Man** sits under the California Tower and houses the extensive collection of archaeological and anthropological exhibits first assembled for the 1915 exposition. One of that fair's primary cultural highlights was the "Story of Man Through the Ages" display, with artifacts culled from expeditions throughout the world. Over the years the museum has amplified that original theme and is now one of the finest anthropological museums in the country.

Exhibits focus on Southwestern, Mexican, and South American cultures, and the museum sponsors expeditions and research in South America. The "Lifestyles and Ceremonies" exhibit uses high-tech gadgetry for displays on biology, reproduction, and culture, and includes a display of the costumes and rituals of San Diego's many ethnic communities. The Chapel of St. Francis is a model of a typical early California hacienda chapel that was constructed for the 1915 exhibition and recently renovated. The museum underwent a $2 million renovation in the late 1980s that included the complete restoration of the Administration Building, which had served as the entrance to the 1915 exposition; offices are now located in this building, freeing up space for exhibits. *Tel. 619/239–2001. Admission: $3 adults, $1 children 13–18. Open daily 10–4:30.*

The **Simon Edison Center for the Performing Arts** (tel. 619/239–2255) sits beside the Museum of Man under the California Tower. It includes the Cassius Carter Centre Stage, the Lowell Davies Festival Theatre, and the Old Globe. The Globe originally

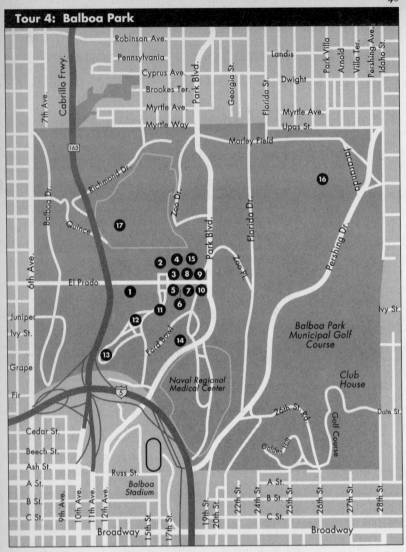

Tour 4: Balboa Park

was a Shakespearean theater, but now holds first-rate productions by other playwrights, too. All three theaters are small and intimate, and evening performances on the outdoor stages are particularly enjoyable during the summer. Beside the center is the **Sculpture Garden,** an outdoor exhibit of traditional and modernistic sculptures. The Sculpture Garden Cafe, with tables set amid the art, is open for lunch.

2 The **San Diego Museum of Art** faces the central parking lot, where an empty parking space is rarer than any painting. Traffic is diverted from the rest of El Prado here, with the roadway leading toward the park's southern circle of museums. Be sure to check out the Museum of Art's special shows, which can be quite adventurous. Recent shows have included the paintings of Dr. Seuss and Maurice Sendak, giving the kids something to appreciate while the grownups admire the old masters. *Tel. 619/232–7931. Admission: $5 adults, $4 seniors, $2 children 6–18. Open Tues.–Sun. 10–4:30.*

3 The **Timken Art Gallery,** next to the museum, is a private gallery housing works of European masters and a collection of Russian icons. The Putnam Foundation operates the gallery, which is the only privately owned building in the park. *Tel. 619/239–5548. Admission free. Open Tues.–Sat. 10–4:30, Sun. 1:30–4:30. Closed Sept.* Across the Prado, **The San Diego Art Institute** (tel. 619/239–5946) has occasional shows of students' work.

The action gets lively in the next section of El Prado, where mimes, jugglers, and musicians perform on long lawns beside **4** the Lily Pond, in front of the graceful **Botanical Building.** Built for the 1915 exposition, the latticed, open-air nursery houses over 500 types of tropical and subtropical plants. The orchid collection is stunning, and there are benches beside cool, miniature waterfalls for resting away from the sun. The Lily Pond is filled with giant koi fish and blooming water lilies and is a popular spot for taking photographs. *Admission free. Open Tues.–Sun. 10–4:30.*

The **Park Information Center** (tel. 619/239–0512), open daily 9– **5** 4:30, is located in the **House of Hospitality,** across El Prado from the pond. The office, staffed by volunteers, has maps and booklets on Balboa Park, and sells the Passport to Balboa Park, which offers reduced-price coupons to the museums. Many of the city's cultural groups also have offices in this building, which surrounds a peaceful patio and Spanish fountain. Next door, the Cafe Del Rey Moro serves drinks, lunch, and dinner. The flowering grotto, hidden by eucalyptus trees behind the restaurant, is a favorite spot for weddings.

6 The **Hall of Champions,** a sports museum with a vast collection of memorabilia, paintings, and photographs honoring local athletes and sports history, is next in line. San Diego, sometimes called the Sports Center of the United States, has nurtured the talents of many famous athletes, including Archie Moore, Gene Littler, and Maureen Connolly. *Tel. 619/234–2544. Admission: $2 adults, 50¢ children 6–17. Open daily 10–4:30.*

7 The **Museum of Photographic Arts,** in the **Casa de Balboa,** is one of few museums in the country dedicated solely to photography. It celebrated its fifth anniversary in 1988. MOPA exhibits the works of world-renowned and relatively obscure photographers, ranging from themes that highlight human tragedies to celebrations. MOPA has garnered a loyal following and a strong base of volunteers who lead tours through the changing exhibits. The museum's director hopes to open an annex to MOPA downtown in the next few years that will concentrate on film and video as artistic media. *Tel. 619/239–5262. Admission: $2.50. Open daily 10–5, Thurs. 10–9.*

Below MOPA in the basement of the Casa de Balboa is the **San Diego Model Railroad Museum.** The room is filled with the sounds of chugging engines, screeching brakes, and shrill whistles when the six model-train exhibits are in operation. *Tel. 619/ 696–0199. Admission: $1 adults, 50¢ children. Open Wed.– Fri. 11–4, weekends 11–5.*

The **Museum of San Diego History** opened in 1990 in the Casa de Balboa under the auspices of the San Diego Historical Society. Rotating exhibits focus on local history after California became part of the United States. The society's research library is in the basement. *Tel. 619/232–6203. Donation requested. Open Wed.–Sun. 10–4:30.*

⑧ Across the street, the **Casa del Prado** (tel. 619/232–5762) houses classes, group meetings, and special events. The San Diego Floral Association has a small gift shop, research library, and offices here. Be sure to wander through—you may chance upon a show of orchids, bonsai, or ikebana, the Japanese art of flower arranging.

The short flight of steps leading to the park's main fountain is another gathering spot for talented street performers. On one side of the fountain is the **Natural History Museum,** with displays on the plants and animals of Southern California and Mexico. Children seem particularly impressed by the dinosaur bones, while amateur geologists, gemologists, and jewelers admire the collection of gems, including beautiful rose-colored tourmaline crystals mined in San Diego County. The Foucault Pendulum, near the museum entrance, is a 185-pound brass ball suspended on a 43-foot cable, demonstrating the rotation of the earth. The museum has an active public participation policy and frequently schedules nature walks, films, and lectures. *Tel. 619/232–3821. Admission: $5 adults, $1 children 6–18. Open daily 10–4:30.*

⑩ The **Reuben H. Fleet Space Theater and Science Center** is on the other side of the fountain. The Omnimax theater has a domed overhead screen on which fantastic films about nature, space, and life seem to lift the viewer into the action. Films are shown regularly throughout the day, and are informative and exhilarating. The science center is like a giant laboratory playground, where clever interactive exhibits teach children and adults about basic and complex scientific principles. The center's gift shop is akin to a museum, with toys and gadgets that inspire the imagination. The Laserium has laser shows set to rock music at night. Shows change frequently, so call ahead if you have a particular show in mind. *Tel. 619/238–1168. Science Center admission: $2.25 adults, $1 children 5–15 or included with price of theater ticket. Theater tickets: $5.50 adults, $3 children 5–15; laser shows: $6 adults, $3.50 children 6–17. Open Sun.–Thurs. 9:30–9:30, Fri.–Sat. 9:30 AM–10:30 PM.*

El Prado ends in a bridge that crosses over Park Boulevard to a perfectly tended rose garden and a seemingly wild cactus grove. From here you can see across the canyon to even more parkland, with picnic groves, sports facilities, and acres of ranging chaparral. Back along El Prado, roads and pathways lead to even more sights.

The main road off El Prado goes south from the parking lot by the Museum of Art. A long island of flowers divides the road ⑪ curving around the **Organ Pavilion** and the 5,000-pipe Spreckels Organ, believed to be the largest outdoor organ in the world. Much of the time it is locked up on a stage before rows of benches where wanderers rest and regroup. Concerts are sometimes given on Sunday afternoons, and the organ is amazing to hear. On summer evenings local military bands, gospel groups, and barbershop quartets give concerts in the pavilion. At Christmas the park's massive Christmas tree and life-size nativity display turn the Organ Pavilion into a seasonal wonderland.

⑫ The **House of Pacific Relations,** across from the pavilion, is really a cluster of stucco cottages representing various foreign countries. The buildings are open on Sunday, and individual cottages often present celebrations on their country's holidays. A large parking lot sits just behind the pavilion and is a good place to find a space, particularly if you're attending an evening cultural event.

⑬ This southern road ends at the Pan American Plaza and the **San Diego Aerospace Museum and International Aerospace Hall of Fame.** The building is unlike any other in the park. The Ford Motor Company commissioned the building for the 1935 exposition, when sleek, streamlined design was all the rage. A thin line of blue neon outlines the round building at night, giving it the appearance of a landlocked UFO. Exhibits about aviation and aerospace pioneers line the rotunda, and a collection of real and replicated aircraft fill the center. *Tel. 619/234–8291. Admission: $4 adults, $1 children 6–17. Open daily 10–4:30.*

Beside the museum, the Starlight Bowl (tel. 619/544–7800) presents live musicals during the summer on its outdoor stage, where actors freeze in their places when planes roar overhead on their way to Lindbergh Field. The Federal Building, also in the Pan American Plaza, is the home of the U.S. Olympic Volleyball Team, and the Municipal Gymnasium is used by amateur basketball and volleyball teams. The Palisades Building houses the park's Puppet Theater (tel. 619/236–5717), where performances are given on summer afternoons.

Next to the Palisades Building is one of the newest museums in Balboa Park, the **San Diego Automotive Museum.** It maintains a large collection of classic cars and has an ongoing restoration program. *Tel. 619/231–2886. Admission: $3.50 adults, $1 children 6–16. Open daily 10–4:30.*

President's Way leads from the plaza to Park Boulevard, the main thoroughfare from the park to downtown. Pepper Grove, along the boulevard, has lots of picnic tables and a playground. ⑭ The **Centro Cultural de la Raza** (tel. 619/235–6135), by the grove, is an old water tower converted into a cultural center focusing on Mexican arts. The tower's exterior is covered with an elaborate mural depicting Mexican history.

⑮ North of El Prado is the **Spanish Village Art Center,** between the Natural History Museum and the zoo. Built for the 1935 exposition, the village houses are now used as arts and crafts studios, with individual artists renting space and displaying their wares on weekends. Behind the village, the **Balboa Park Railroad** is a 48-passenger train running a half-mile loop through eucalyptus groves. Nearby, riders on the antique carousel stretch from their seats to grab the brass rings suspended an arm's length away and earn a free carousel ride.

For those interested in exploring the outdoors, Balboa Park has a wealth of natural wonders. The **Alcazar Garden,** across El Prado from the Museum of Man, was designed to replicate the gardens surrounding the Alcazar Castle in Seville. The flower beds are ever-changing horticultural exhibits, with bright orange and yellow poppies blooming in the spring and deep rust and crimson chrysanthemums in the fall. The benches by the tiled fountains are a nice place to rest. The Japanese Friendship Garden, behind the House of Hospitality, will eventually be a 6.5-acre tea garden with ponds, benches, and bonsai exhibits.

The parklands across the Cabrillo Bridge, at the west end of El Prado, are set aside for picnics and athletics. Roller skaters perform along Balboa Drive, leading to Marston Point, overlooking downtown. Ladies and gents in spotless white outfits meet regularly on summer afternoons for lawn-bowling tournaments at the green beside the bridge. Dirt trails lead into pine groves with secluded picnic areas.

The far east end of Balboa Park, across Park Boulevard and Florida Canyon on Morley Field Drive, is the park's athletic
16 center. **Morley Field** has an unusual Frisbee Golf Course, with challenging holes (which really are wire baskets hung from metal poles) where players toss their frisbees over canyons and treetops to reach their goal. Morley Field also has a public swimming pool, tennis courts, a casting pool, playgrounds, and a velodrome used for bicycle races.

17 The **San Diego Zoo** is Balboa Park's most famous attraction. It ranges over 100 acres fronting Park Boulevard and is surely one of the finest zoos and tropical gardens in the world. Over 3,200 animals of 777 species roam in expertly crafted habitats that spread down into, around, and above the natural canyons. Equal attention has been paid to the flora and the fauna, and the zoo is an enormous botanical garden with one of the world's largest collections of subtropical plants. From the moment you walk through the entrance and face the swarm of bright pink flamingos and blue peacocks, you know you've entered a rare pocket of natural harmony.

Exploring the zoo fully takes the stamina of a healthy hiker, but there are open-air trams running throughout the day on a three-mile tour of 80% of the zoo's exhibits. The animals are attuned to the buses, and they are quite willing to show off for special treats. The bears are particularly fine performers, waving and bowing to their admirers. The Skyfari ride soars 170 feet above ground, giving a good overview of the zoo's layout and a marvelous panorama of the park, downtown San Diego, the bay, and the ocean, far past the Coronado Bridge.

Still, the zoo is at its best when you can wander the paths that climb through the huge enclosed Scripps Flight Cage, where brightly colored tropical birds swoop between branches just inches from your face. The Gorilla Tropics exhibit, beside the bird cage, is the zoo's latest venture into bioclimatic zone exhibits, where animals live in enclosed environments modeled after their native habitats. Throughout the zoo walkways wind over bridges and past waterfalls ringed with tropical ferns, and giant elephants roam in a sandy plateau so close you're tempted to pet them. The San Diego Zoo houses the only koalas outside Australia and three rare golden monkeys among its impressive collection of endangered species; the zoo frequently hosts special exhibits, such as the 1987 display of the two giant pandas from China.

The Children's Zoo is worth a visit, no matter what your age. Goats and sheep beg to be petted and are particularly adept at snatching bag lunches, while bunnies and guinea pigs seem willing to be fondled endlessly. In the nursery windows, you can see baby lemurs and spider monkeys playing with Cabbage Patch kids, looking much like the human babies peering from strollers through the glass. The exhibits are geared in size and style for four-year-old children, but that doesn't deter kids of all ages from having fun. Even the rest rooms are child-size. The hardest part of being in the Children's Zoo will be to get your family to move on.

The Wedgeforth Bowl, a 3,000-seat amphitheater, holds various animal shows throughout the day, occasionally hosted by the zoo's ambassador of goodwill, Joan Embery, called "the most widely known inhabitant of the zoo." Embery's frequent appearances on television talk shows, usually with some charming critter to entertain the host, have made the San Diego Zoo a household name among late-night TV viewers.

The zoo's Tiger River exhibit opened in spring 1988. A simulated Asian rain forest, Tiger River is really a collection of 10 exhibits with more than 35 species of animals. As spectacular as the tigers, pythons, and water dragons are, they seem almost inconsequential among the $500,000 collection of exotic trees and plants. The mist-shrouded trails winding down a canyon into Tiger River pass by fragrant jasmine, ginger lilies, and orchids, giving the visitor the feeling of descending into a South American jungle. In Sun Bear Forest playful cubs constantly claw apart the trees and shrubs that serve as a natural playground for climbing, jumping, and general rowdiness. Throughout the zoo plans are underway to remodel exhibit areas into closer facsimilies of the animals' natural habitats.

The zoo rents strollers, wheelchairs, and cameras. The one indoor restaurant serves breakfast and lunch, and there are many outdoor restaurants and snack shops.

Tel. 619/234–3153. Admission (including unlimited access to the Skyfari ride and the Children's Zoo): $10.75 adults, $4 children 3–15. Deluxe package (bus tour, Skyfari ride, and Children's Zoo): $13.75 adults, $6.50 children. Gates open daily 9–4; visitors may remain until 5 PM. Summer hours are 9–5; visitors may remain until 6.

Time Out   Perhaps the most pleasant way to take a break from museum hopping is by sipping a cup of freshly brewed coffee or a glass of California chardonnay in the **Sculpture Garden Cafe.** Located on El Prado by the San Diego Museum of Art, the cafe serves a small selection of expensive but tasty gourmet lunches and frequently hosts meetings of the various museums' boards and volunteers.

The outside patio behind the **Cafe del Rey Moro** in the House of Hospitality is another great place to grab a margarita or meal while staying out amid the park's lush vegetation. The restaurant also sells box lunches, so you can hold your picnic wherever you wish. Ice cream and hot dog vendors are found throughout the park for quick snacks. The zoo is not known for its culinary wonders, though there are plenty of food stands selling popcorn, pizza, and enormous ice cream cones. The best restaurant in the zoo is the **Peacock and Raven,** serving sandwiches, salads, and light meals. The **Safari Kitchen** serves reasonably good fried chicken, and warm chocolate chip cookies. Be sure to visit the zoo's two gift shops for unusual souvenirs and postcards.

Tour 5: Old Town

Numbers in the margin correspond with points of interest on the Tour 5: Old Town San Diego map.

San Diego's Spanish and Mexican history and heritage are best evident in Old Town, just north of downtown at Juan Street, near the intersection of interstates 5 and 8. It wasn't until 1968 that Old Town became a state historic park. Fortunately, private efforts kept the area's history alive until then, and many of San Diego's oldest structures remain in good shape.

Though Old Town is often credited as being the first European settlement in Southern California, the true beginnings took place overlooking Old Town from atop Presidio Park (*see* below). There, Father Junipero Serra established the first of California's missions, called San Diego de Alcalá, in 1769. San Diego's Indians, called the San Diegueños by the Spaniards, were forced to abandon their seminomadic lifestyle and live at the mission. They were expected to follow Spanish customs and adopt Christianity as their religion, but resisted these impositions fiercely. Poor planning and the need to serve as a lookout caused the mission to be built on a hill without an adequate water supply, and food was scarce as more and more Indians and Spanish soldiers occupied the site.

In 1774 the hilltop was declared a Royal Presidio, or fortress, and the mission was moved to its current location along the San Diego River, six miles east of the original site. The Indians lost more of their traditional grounds and ranches as the mission grew along the riverbed. In 1775 the Indians attacked and burned the mission, destroying religious objects and killing Franciscan Padre Luis Jayme. Their later attack on the presidio was less successful, and their revolt was short lived. By 1800, around 1,500 Indians were living on the mission's grounds, receiving religious instruction and adapting to the Spanish way of life.

The pioneers living within the presidio's walls were mostly Spanish soldiers, poor Mexicans, and mestizos of Spanish and Indian ancestry, all unaccustomed to farming San Diego's arid land. They existed marginally until 1821, when Mexico gained independence from Spain, claimed its lands in California, and flew the Mexican flag over the presidio. The Mexican government, centered some 2,000 miles away in Monterrey, stripped the Spanish missions of their landholdings, and an aristocracy of landholders began to emerge. At the same time, settlers were beginning to move down from the presidio to what is now called Old Town.

A rectangular plaza was laid out along today's San Diego Avenue to serve as the settlement's center. In 1846, during the war between Mexico and the United States, a detachment of marines raised the U.S. flag over the plaza on a pole said to have been a main ship mast. The flag was torn down a time or two, but within six months, Mexico had surrendered California, and the U.S. flag remained. In 1850 San Diego became an incorporated city, with Old Town as its center.

➊ Old Town's historic buildings are clustered around the main plaza, called **Old Town Plaza,** with a view of the presidio from behind the cannon by the flagpole. The plaza today serves much the same purpose as it did when it was first laid out. It is a pleasant place to rest and regroup as you plan your tour of Old Town and watch other visitors stroll by. Art shows often fill the lawns around the plaza, and lounging and strolling are encouraged. San Diego Avenue is closed to traffic here, and the cars are diverted to Juan and Congress streets, both of which are lined with shops and restaurants. There are plenty of free parking lots on the outskirts of Old Town, which is best seen by foot. Shopping and eating are essential for a true Old Town tour, so bring your wallet and an appetite.

➋ The **Old Town State Historic Park** office is located in the **Robinson-Rose House,** on the south side of the plaza. Free guided tours of the park are available from here at 2 PM daily, and there is a good booklet for sale that provides a brief history and self-guided tour map for the 12-acre park. The Robinson-Rose House was the original commercial center of old San Diego, housing railroad offices, law offices, and the first newspaper press; one room has been restored and outfitted with period furnishings. Park rangers now show films and distribute information from the living room. *San Diego Ave. and Mason St., tel. 619/237–6770. Open 10–5 daily. Free walking tour of the park at 2 PM daily.*

➌ The historic section of Old Town includes a collection of adobe and log houses in a subdued Mexican-colonial style. **La Casa de Pedrorena,** a hacienda-style home built in 1869, is currently ➍ closed for renovation. La Casa de Altamirano serves as the **San Diego Union Newspaper Historical Building.** A wood-frame structure prefabricated in Maine and shipped around Cape Horn in 1851, the building has been restored to replicate the newspaper's offices of 1868, when the first edition of the *San Diego Union* was printed.

➎ **La Casa de Estudillo,** across Mason Street from the plaza, is an original Old Town adobe built in 1827. The house has been restored to its former grandeur as the home of the prestigious ➏ Estudillo family, and it is now open for tours. The **Seeley Stables** became San Diego's stagecoach stop in 1867 and was the hub of Old Town until near the turn of the century, when the tracks of the Southern Pacific Railroad passing by the south side of the settlement became the favored route. The stables now house a collection of horse-drawn vehicles, Western memorabilia, and Indian artifacts. There is a $1 admission fee to tour

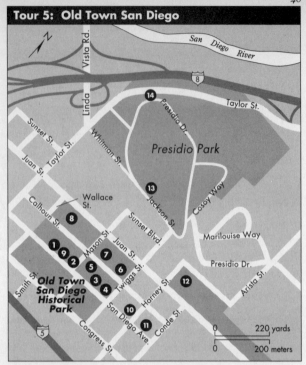

Tour 5: Old Town San Diego

the stables, where a slide show on San Diego history is presented three times a day.

7 **La Casa de Bandini,** next to the stables, is one of the loveliest haciendas in San Diego. Built in 1829 by a Peruvian, Juan Bandini, the house served as Old Town's social center during Mexican rule. After Bandini lost his financial, political, and social standing through various political and business schemes, he lost the house in the 1850s. Albert Seeley, the stagecoach entrepreneur, purchased the home in 1869, built a second story, and turned it into the Cosmopolitan Hotel, a comfortable way station for travelers on the day-long trip south from Los Angeles. Surely it must have been a lovely hotel, with rooms overlooking the huge central gardens and patio. Casa Bandini's colorful gardens and main-floor dining rooms now house a good Mexican restaurant run by the owners of other highly successful Old Town businesses.

8 The unofficial center of Old Town is the **Bazaar del Mundo,** a shopping and dining enclave built to represent a colonial Mexican square. The central courtyard is always in blossom with magenta bougainvillaea, scarlet hibiscus and irises, poppies, and petunias in season. Ballet Folklorico and flamenco dancers perform in the outdoor gazebo on weekend afternoons, and the bazaar frequently holds arts and crafts exhibits and Mexican festivals in the courtyard. Colorful shops specializing in Latin American crafts and unusual gift items border the courtyard, beyond a shield of thick bushes and huge birdcages with cawing macaws and toucans.

Geppetto's, an imaginative toy store with an unusual display of inexpensive toys as well as outrageously expensive dolls, model trains, and baby clothes, is a great place to take the kids for a souvenir. The bookstore Los Libros has a good selection of books on Southern California and Mexico. The Gallery Shop has changing displays of Southwestern, Mexican, and Mideastern jewelry. Four restaurants, a candy shop, and a bakery offer excellent Mexican treats and meals, somewhat subdued to please tourists' tastes. Casa de Pico's outdoor patio is the most popular dining spot, and lines of people waiting for a table often stretch past the courtyard. Hamburguesa, which sits between the main plaza and the bazaar, is a good spot for those hesitant to dive into tacos and burritos. The hamburgers, with dozens of toppings to choose from, are quite good.

Old Town's boundaries and reputation as a combination historic attraction and shopping/dining center have spread in the past few years. One of the original shopping enclaves was **⑨ Squibob Square,** on San Diego Avenue beside the state park headquarters. The center is currently being reconstructed and when reopened it will be called Dodson's Corner. Farther away from the plaza, art galleries and expensive gift shops are interspersed with curio shops, restaurants, and open-air stands selling inexpensive Mexican pottery, jewelry, and blankets. San Diego Avenue continues on as Old Town's main drag, with an ever-changing array of shopping plazas constructed in mock Mexican plaza style. The best of these is the Old Town Esplanade (2461 San Diego Avenue between Harney and Conde streets). Several shops display Mexican and South American folk art, and there's a Haagen Dazs ice-cream shop for refueling.

Historic sites punctuate the lineup of ice cream and souvenir **⑩** shops. The **Whaley House,** a two-story brick building considered to be a mansion when built in 1856, served as the county courthouse and government seat during the 1870s. It also was the site where the Yankee Jim Robinson, convicted of stealing a boat, was sentenced to hang. The gallows were too short, and Robinson was strangled instead. His ghost, it is said, still in- **⑪** habits the place. **El Campo Santo,** an old adobe-walled cemetery, was the burial place for some of Old Town's founders and the gamblers and bandits who passed through town during the rowdy days of the early 1900s.

⑫ Heritage Park, up the Juan Street hill east of the Seeley Stables, is the headquarters for SOHO, the Save Our Heritage Organization. The climb up to the park is a bit steep, but the view of the harbor is great. SOHO has moved several grand Victorian homes and a temple from other parts of San Diego to the park, where they have been restored. The homes are now used for offices, shops, and restaurants. The Heritage Park Bed & Breakfast Inn is housed in a particularly fine Queen Anne mansion and is a peaceful spot to stay, away from traffic and noise.

⑬ Presidio Park, overlooking Old Town from the north end of Taylor Street, is a 40-acre park with rolling, grassy hillsides popular with picnickers. Unless you love to climb, you will prefer to drive to the top of Presidio Park, then wander around on foot. A new sport, grass skiing, has taken hold on these hills, where skiers glide over the grass on wheels. The park is surely one of San Diego's greenest, consisting primarily of these long stretches of lawns, where many bridal couples have taken their

⑭ vows. The **Junipero Serra Museum** is on the site of the original mission and fort, on a 160-foot-high hill above Old Town and Mission Valley. The museum has a fine research library and collection of artifacts from San Diego's history. *Library information, tel. 619/297–3258. Admission: $3 adults, free for children under 12. Open Tues.-Sat. 10–4:30, Sun. noon–4:30.*

Time Out The margarita is Old Town's premier drink. Made of tequila, lime juice, and Triple Sec or Cointreau, it is served as an icy slush with salt on the rim of the glass. When combined with tortilla chips and spicy salsa, it is the perfect refresher after a hard touring stint. **Casa de Pico** and **Casa de Bandini,** in the Bazaar del Mundo, are two of Old Town's most popular margarita spots. Both have large flowering patios and wandering mariachis—after one large, fishbowl-size margarita, you'd swear you were in Guadalajara. Both serve excellent *antijitos*, or Mexican appetizers, including flavorful guacamole and nachos. For teetotalers, both restaurants will prepare a virgin strawberry margarita, made with crushed frozen strawberries and coconut milk. Casa de Pico is best if you want to relax while the shoppers in your group are exploring. Casa de Bandini is a bit quieter, and the outdoor garden is larger than Pico's patio. In the summer, drinks are also served along the second-floor balcony, where you can keep an eye on the stragglers from your group while relaxing.

Also in the bazaar is **La Panaderia,** a take-out bakery with fresh, hot *churros,* long sticks of fried dough coated with cinnamon sugar. For a real sugar rush, have your churro with a cup of hot, fragrant Mexican chocolate, laced with cinnamon. On weekends, there are stands where women make and sell fresh corn tortillas near the Casa de Pico patio.

Old Town Mexican Cafe, on San Diego Avenue, is another great margarita stop, and a good place for *carnitas*, made with marinated roasted pork wrapped in fresh tortillas. Old Town Mex, as locals call the restaurant, is always busy; expect to wait in line. The shoppers in your group will be delighted to pass the time across the street at **Old Town Pottery,** a huge yard filled with birdbaths, flowerpots, fountains, and tables piled with Mexican dishes and glassware.

Tour 6: Mission Bay and Sea World

Numbers in the margin correspond with points of interest on the Tour 6: Mission Bay Area map.

Mission Bay is San Diego's monument to sports and fitness. Action and leisure are the main themes of this 4,600-acre aquatic park, 75% of which is public land. Admission to its 27 miles of bayfront beaches and 17 miles of ocean frontage is free. All you need for a perfect day is a bathing suit, shorts, and the right selection of playthings.

When explorer Juan Rodriguez Cabrillo first spotted the bay in 1542, he called it "Baja Falso." The ocean-facing inlet led to acres of swampland, inhospitable to boats and inhabitants. In the 1960s the city planners decided to dredge the swamp and build a man-made bay with acres of beaches and lawns for play. Only 25% of the land would be used for commercial property, and now just a handful of resort hotels break up the natural landscape. Drivers and train riders coming down to San Diego from Los Angeles get a good view of the action and the park's most popular spots. Kite flying has become a fine art on the lawns facing Interstate 5, where the sky is flooded with the bright colors of huge, intricately made kites.

❶ The **Visitor Information Center,** at the East Mission Bay Drive exit from Interstate 5, is an excellent tourist resource for the bay and all of San Diego. Leaflets and brochures for most of the area's attractions are provided free, and information on transportation, reservations, and sightseeing is offered cheerfully. The center is a gathering spot for the runners, walkers, and exercisers who take part in group activities. From the low hill outside the building, you can easily appreciate the bay's charms. *2688 E. Mission Bay Dr., tel. 619/276–8200. Open Mon.–Sat. 9–5, Sun. 9:30–4:30.*

A five-mile-long pathway runs through this section of the bay from the trailer park and miniature golf course, south past the high-rise Hilton Hotel to Sea World Drive. Playgrounds and picnic areas abound on the beach and low grassy hills of the park. Group gatherings, company picnics, and birthday parties are common along this stretch, where huge parking lots seem to expand to serve the swelling crowds on sunny days. On weekend evenings, the path is filled with a steady stream of exercisers jogging, speed walking, biking, and skating, releasing the stress from a day at the office. The water is filled with bathers, water-skiers, fishermen, and boaters, some in single-man kayaks, others in crowded powerboats. The San Diego Crew Classic, which takes place in April, fills this section of the bay with crew teams from all over the country and college reunions complete with flying school colors and keg beer. Swimmers should note signs warning about water pollution; certain areas of the bay are chronically polluted, and bathing is strongly discouraged.

❷ **Fiesta Island,** off Mission Bay Drive and Sea World Drive, is a smaller, man-made playground popular with jet- and water-skiers. In July the annual Over-the-Line Tournament, a local variety of softball, attracts thousands of players and oglers drawn by the teams' raunchy names and outrageous behavior.

Ingraham Street is another main drag through the bay, from ❸ the shores of Pacific Beach to Sea World Drive. **San Diego Princess Resort** on Vacation Isle is the focal point of this part of the bay, with its lushly landscaped grounds, model yacht pond, and bayfront restaurants. Ducks and cottontail bunnies are as common as tourists, and the village is a great family playground. Powerboats take off from Ski Beach, across Ingraham Street, which is also the site of the annual Miller High Life Thunderboat Regatta, held in September. The noise from these boats is absolutely deafening, and the beach is packed from dawn till dark with thrill seekers.

West Mission Bay Drive runs from the ocean beyond Mission Boulevard to Sea World Drive. The pathways along the Mission Beach side of the bay are lined with vacation homes, many for rent by the month. Those fortunate to live here year-round have the bay as their front yards, with wide sandy beaches, volleyball courts, and an endless stream of sightseers on the ❹ sidewalk. **Belmont Park,** once an abandoned amusement park at the corner of Mission Boulevard and West Mission Bay

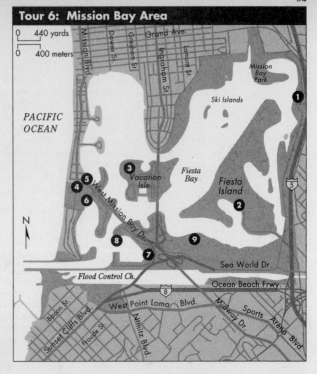

Tour 6: Mission Bay Area

Drive, is now a shopping, dining, and recreation area between the bay and the Mission Beach boardwalk. Twinkling lights outline the old, but recently refurbished Belmont Park roller coaster where screaming thrill-seekers can once again ride the coaster's curves. Nearby, younger riders enjoy the antique carousel, beside a stand selling fresh cotton candy. The Plunge, an indoor fresh-water swimming pool has also been renovated, and is open to the public making Belmont Park a focal point for the beach area.

⑤ The Bahia Hotel sits on the eastern shores of West Mission Bay Drive. The hotel owns and operates the ***Bahia Belle,*** a restored paddleboat that cruises the bay during sunset on weekend nights. The boat is often used for private parties. *998 West Mission Bay Dr., tel. 619/488–0551. Admission: $5 for unlimited cruising. The* Bahia Belle *departs Fri. and Sat. hourly from 7:30 PM to 12:30 AM, from Sept. to June; in July and Aug. the boat sails Tues.–Sat. on the same schedule.*

⑥ **Ventura Cove,** opposite the Bahia, is a good, quiet picnic spot.
⑦ The frontage road past the sportfishing marina leads to **Marina Village** (619/224–3125), the only shopping center on the bay, with specialty shops and bayview restaurants.

⑧ **Hospitality Point,** at the end of the frontage road, is one site for the annual Summer Pops concerts, with the San Diego Symphony playing popular tunes, ending with rousing Sousa marches accompanied by fireworks.

⑨ **Sea World** is Mission Bay's grandest attraction, on the shore along Sea World Drive. The world's largest marine-life park,

Sea World is an ocean-oriented amusement park set amid tropical landscaping along the bay. The Sky Tower's glass elevator takes you to the top, where the views of San Diego County from the ocean to the mountains are nicest in early morning and late evening. A gigantic Christmas tree of lights, stretching from the tower's peak to the ground, is a seasonal landmark.

The traditionally favorite exhibit is the Shamu show, with giant killer whales performing in a newly constructed stadium. The Penguin Encounter has a moving sidewalk passing by a glass-enclosed arctic environment, where hundreds of emperor penguins slide over glaciers into icy waters. The shark exhibit, with fierce-looking sharks of a variety of species, is especially popular with imaginative youngsters. True children are entranced by Cap'n Kids' World, an enclosed playground with trampolines, swinging wood bridges, towers for climbing, and giant tubs filled with plastic balls, perfect for diving. The playground is a good stop for when the kids are getting bored and the grownups are tired of pushing strollers. In fact, Cap'n Kids' World is so popular that many San Diegans buy yearlong passes to the park just so they can bring their kids to the playground regularly.

Places of Learning, a new Sea World exhibit, has a gigantic map of the United States painted on the ground, where visitors can walk among the states. City Streets resembles an inner-city neighborhood, with stairs down to the subway stops and candy and ice cream shops in brownstones along the sidewalks. There is a fantastic skateboard and bicycle show here, complete with daredevil teenagers riding their boards and bikes up and down stairs, leaping over trash cans and other obstacles.

More traditional sea-life exhibits include buildings filled with saltwater aquariums, with colorful, unusual fish swimming among beautiful coral formations. A hands-on tidal pool exhibit gives visitors a chance to explore San Diego's indigenous marine life with a guide well versed in the habits of these creatures. Dolphin, seal, and sea lion petting pools give visitors a chance to feed and feel these docile mammals. The Japanese Pavilion has a pearl-diving show, with divers fetching valuable oysters for their customers.

Sea World spreads over 100 acres of bayfront land, where a cool breeze seems always to rise off the water. A sky tram travels between Sea World and the Atlantis Hotel across Mission Bay. During summer 1988, Sea World began a series of summer evening concerts, and fireworks are regularly scheduled just after sunset.

Sea World is located on Sea World Dr. at the western end of I–8, tel. 619/226–3901. Admission: $22.95 adults, $16.96 children 3–11. Gates open 9–3; park open until 5 PM and later during summer.

Time Out Food and drink are secondary activities in Mission Bay, where more active enterprises are encouraged. The Hilton Hotel's **Cargo Bar** is a drinking and dancing spot, and the **Hyatt Islandia** has an excellent Sunday brunch. Sea World has plenty of snack shops and take-out restaurants. Picnics and barbecues are popular at the bay, where many picnic areas have stationary barbecue grills. **Sportsmen's Sea Foods,** at 1617 Quivira Road in Mission Bay, serves good fish-and-chips and seafood salads to eat on the inelegant but scenic patio (by the marina, where sportfishing boats depart daily) or to take out to your chosen picnic spot.

Tour 7: La Jolla

Numbers in the margin correspond with points of interest on the Tour 7: La Jolla map.

La Jollans have long considered their village to be the Monte Carlo of California, and with good cause. Its coastline curves into natural coves backed by verdant hillsides and covered with lavish homes, now worth millions as housing values soar. Though La Jolla is considered part of San Diego, it has its own postal zone and a coveted sense of class. Movie stars and royalty frequent established hotels and private clubs, and the social scene is the stuff gossip columns are made of.

The Indians called it "La Hoya," meaning "the cave," referring to the caves dotting the shoreline. The Spaniards changed the name to La Jolla, meaning "the jewel," and its residents have cherished the name and its allusions ever since. Though development and construction have radically altered the town's once-serene and private character, it remains a haven for the elite, a playground for those who can afford lavish luxuries.

To reach La Jolla from Interstate 5, take the Ardath Road exit if you're traveling north and drive slowly down this long hill so you can appreciate the breathtaking view. Traveling south, take the La Jolla Village Drive exit. If you enjoy meandering, the best way to reach La Jolla from the south is to drive through Mission and Pacific beaches on Mission Boulevard, past the crowds of roller skaters, bicyclists, and sunbathers headed to the beach. The clutter and congestion eases up as the street becomes La Jolla Boulevard, where quiet neighborhoods with winding streets lead down to some of the best surfing beaches in San Diego. The boulevard here is lined with expensive restaurants and cafes and a few take-out spots.

➊ At the intersection of La Jolla Boulevard and Nautilus Street, turn toward the sea to reach **Windansea Beach,** where the surfing is said to be as good as in Hawaii. The beach is also known for its old pumphouse made famous by Tom Wolfe's book *The Pumphouse Gang.* Floodlights illuminate the waves at night, making the beach an eerie sight. The homes along this stretch are impressive examples of Southern California luxury and include famous spots designed by Frank Lloyd Wright and Irving Gill. The streets curve past neighborhood beaches, where the locals jealously guard their surf and challenge those who think they have the skills to ride these waves. Scenic road signs direct drivers and bicyclists past some of La Jolla's loveliest homes along Camino de la Costa toward the village.

➋ Nautilus Street east leads up to **Mount Soledad,** the highest point in La Jolla. From the cross on top of the mountain, you can see the coast, from the county's northern border south, far beyond downtown—barring smog and haze. It is an excellent spot for getting a true sense of San Diego's geography. Sunrise services are held here on Easter Sunday.

➌ La Jolla's coastal attraction is **Ellen Browning Scripps Park** at the **La Jolla Cove.** Towering palms line the sidewalk along Coast

Tour 7: La Jolla

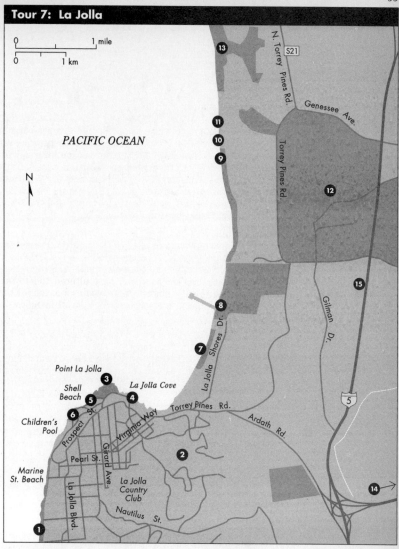

0 _____ 1 mile
0 _____ 1 km

PACIFIC OCEAN

N

Point La Jolla

Shell Beach

Children's Pool

Marine St. Beach

La Jolla Cove

Prospect St.

Virginia Way

Torrey Pines Rd.

Pearl St.

Girard Ave.

La Jolla Country Club

La Jolla Blvd.

Nautilus St.

Ardath Rd.

La Jolla Shores Dr.

Torrey Pines Rd.

N. Torrey Pines Rd.

S21

Genessee Ave.

Gilman Dr.

5

Children's Museum of San Diego, **15**

Ellen Browning Scripps Park, **3**

La Jolla Caves, **4**

La Jolla Shores, **7**

La Valencia Hotel, **5**

Mingei International Museum of World Folk Art, **14**

Mount Soledad, **2**

Salk Institute, **9**

San Diego Museum of Contemporary Art, **6**

Scripps Institute of Oceanography, **8**

Torrey Pines City Park, **11**

Torrey Pines Glider Port, **10**

Torrey Pines State Reserve, **13**

University of California at San Diego, **12**

Windansea Beach, **1**

Boulevard, where strollers in evening dress are as common as Frisbee throwers. The **Children's Pool**, at the south end of the park, is aptly named for its curving beach and shallow waters protected by a seawall from strong currents and waves. Each September the La Jolla Rough Water Swim takes place here, with hundreds of hardy swimmers plunging into the chilly waters and swimming one mile out into the sea.

Smaller beaches appear and disappear with the tides, which carve small private coves in cliffs covered with pink and yellow ice plant. Some of these cliffs are unstable, but there are plenty of pathways leading down to the beaches. Just be sure to keep an eye on the tide to keep from getting trapped once the waves come in. A long layer of sandstone stretching out above the waves provides a perfect sunset-watching spot, with plenty of tiny tidal pools formed in erosion pockets in the rocks. Starfish, sea anemones, and hermit crabs cluster in these pools when the tide is in. Again, keep an eye on the waves, for these rocks can get mighty slippery.

La Jolla Cove's most popular beach is at the north end, which is an underwater preserve and popular diving and snorkeling spot. On summer days, when the water visibility reaches 20 feet deep or so, the sea seems almost to disappear under the load of bodies floating face down, snorkels poking up out of the water. The small beach is literally covered with blankets, towels, and umbrellas, and the lawns at the top of the stairs leading down to the cove are staked out by groups of scuba divers putting on wet suits and tanks. If you're not there by noon, forget finding a parking spot or a small square of sand for your towel. But no matter what time you arrive, be sure to walk through the park, past the groves of twisted junipers to the cliff's edge. Perhaps one of the open-air shelters overlooking the sea will be free, and you can spread your picnic out on a table and watch the scenery.

❹ The **La Jolla Caves** are at the far northern point of the cove, under the La Jolla Cave and Shell Shop. A trail leads down from the shop into the caves, with some 133 steps down to the largest, Sunny Jim Cave. For claustrophobic types, there are photos of the caves in the shop, along with a good selection of shells and coral jewelry. *1325 Coast Blvd., tel. 619/454–6080. Admission to caves $1 adults, 50¢ children 3–11. Open Mon.–Sat. 10–5, Sun. 11–5.*

Prospect Street, La Jolla's main boulevard, overlooks the cove from one block up. The street is lined with excellent restaurants, expensive boutiques, and a recent proliferation of office buildings and two-story shopping complexes. Many of the restaurants on the west side of the street have great views of the cove. At the corner of Prospect and Girard streets sits the

❺ charming pink **La Valencia Hotel.** Its grand lobby with floor-to-ceiling windows overlooking the cove is a popular weding spot, and its Whaling Bar is the main hangout for La Jolla denizens. The hotel exudes a certain snobbish stuffiness, and as Prospect Street grows ever more crowded, lines of Mercedes and Jaguars crowd the valet stand at the hotel's entrance. Pretend you are visiting nobility and wander through the lobby to the outdoor balcony—the view is worth the deception.

Like Prospect Street, Girard Street is lined with expensive shops, where the wares are lovely to look at, even if they are unaffordable. The shopping and dining district has spread to Pearl and other side streets, with a steady parade of amblers and sightseers strolling about, chatting in many languages. Wall Street, a quiet tree-lined boulevard, was once the financial heart of La Jolla, but banks and investment houses can now be found throughout town. The nightlife scene is an active one here, with jazz clubs, piano bars, and watering holes for the elite younger set coming and going with the trends. Though the village has lost some of its charm and its close-knit community feeling, it has gained a cosmopolitan air that makes it a popular vacation resort for the international set.

❻ The **San Diego Museum of Contemporary Art** is the village's cultural center, housed in a remodeled Irving Gill home. The museum has a permanent collection of post-1950 art and often exhibits shows of contemporary art, furnishings, and design. Film series and lectures are held frequently in Sherwood Hall. An excellent bookstore adjacent to the museum has a good collection of art books and magazines. *700 Prospect St., tel. 619/ 454–3541. Admission: $4 adults, $2 children 12–18, $1 children under 12; free after 5 PM on Wed. Open Tues. and Thurs.– Sun. 10–5, Wed. 10–9.*

North of the cove on La Jolla Shores Drive is the La Jolla Beach
❼ and Tennis Club, host of many tennis tournaments. **La Jolla
❽ Shores'** beaches are some of the finest in San Diego, with long stretches allotted to surfers or swimmers. The **Scripps Institute of Oceanography,** up the hill from the shore, has a fine aquarium with more than 20 huge tanks filled with colorful saltwater fish and helpful exhibits on how tides affect the shoreline. The fish are most active during feeding time, at 1:30 on Wednesday and Sunday. An outdoor tidal-pool exhibit is filled with starfish, sea anemones, lobsters, crabs, and myraid sea creatures that inhabit the local shoreline. The bookstore has a nice selection of illustrated books and cards. There are paths leading down from the institution's buildings to the beaches at La Jolla Shores. The beach north of the Scripps Pier is a great tidal-pool spot, where you can find all sorts of sea creatures. If you plan to stay at the beach, be sure not to park at a meter. A new aquarium building is now under construction and scheduled to open in 1992. *8602 La Jolla Shores Dr., tel. 619/534–6933. Suggested admission by donation: $3 adults, $2 children 12–18, $1 children 3–11. Open daily 9–5.*

As La Jolla Shores Drive goes north, it curves onto Torrey
❾ Pines Road and the world-famous **Salk Institute** designed by Louis Kahn. The same road that leads to the institute ends at
❿ the **Torrey Pines Glider Port,** where hang gliders soar off high cliffs over the ocean. On days when the winds are just right, gliders line the clifftops, waiting for the right gust of wind to carry them into the sky. Seasoned hang gliders with a good command of the current can soar over the sea for hours, then ride the winds back to the cliffs. Less-experienced fliers sometimes land on the beach below, to the cheers and applause of the sunbathers who scoot out of their way. The view from atop the cliffs with the colorful gliders in the sky is spectacular.

⓫ The beach at the foot of the cliffs is called **Torrey Pines City Park,** though locals still refer to it as Black's Beach. Black's was for many years a clothing-optional beach, and though nudity is now prohibited by law, it is practiced whenever the authorities are out of sight. This is one of the most beautiful and secluded beaches in San Diego, with long stretches of pale sand backed by steep cliffs whose colors change with the light from the sun. There are no rest rooms, showers, or snack shops, though some hardy entrepreneurs do lug ice chests filled with sodas and beer down the cliffs to sell to the unprepared. The paths leading down to the beach are steep, and the cliffs are very unstable. Cliff rescues are not uncommon, particularly when daring explorers ignore the safety signs and strike out on uncharted trails. Stick to the well-traveled paths.

At the intersection of Torrey Pines Road and Genessee Avenue **⑫** is the entrance to the **University of California at San Diego.** The massive campus spreads over canyons and wooded lands, where students and faculty jog, bike, and roller-skate to class. A bit **⑬** farther north is **Torrey Pines State Reserve,** an 887-acre park overlooking the beaches of La Jolla. The preserve is home to ancient, twisted torrey pines and has some nice hiking trails and picnic spots.

La Jolla's newest enclave is the Golden Triangle, spreading through the Sorrento Valley east of Interstate 5. High-tech research-and-development companies, attracted to the area in part by the facilities of UCSD, Scripps, and Salk, have developed huge state-of-the-art compounds in areas that were not long ago populated solely by coyotes and jays. The area along La Jolla Village Drive and Genessee Avenue has become an architectural wonderland full of futuristic buildings. The most spectacular is Michael Graves' Aventine, visible from I–5 at the La Jolla Village Drive exit.

The first major establishment in the Golden Triangle was University Towne Center, a huge shopping mall with an indoor ice-**⑭** skating rink. The **Mingei International Museum of World Folk Art** is located here among the shops and restaurants. The museum has some wonderful creative shows of pottery, textiles, costumes, and gadgets from all over the world. *4405 La Jolla Village Dr., tel. 619/453–5300. Admission: $2. Open Tues.– Sat. 11–5, Sun. 2–5.*

⑮ Another museum amid the shops is the **Children's Museum of San Diego,** located in La Jolla Village Square. Hands-on exhibits with plenty of arts and crafts materials so kids can make their own art are the attractions here, and adults seem to get as much pleasure from the museum as do the kids. The gift shop has a great collection of educational toys and kits. *8657 Via La Jolla Dr., tel. 619/450–0767. Admission: $3. Open Wed.–Fri. noon–5, Sat. 10–5.*

Time Out   Cafes, takeouts, and restaurants proliferate along the streets of La Jolla village, and strollers always seem to be munching on something as they window-shop. **Haagen-Dazs** and **Swensen's** both have ice cream parlors on Prospect Street near the La Valencia Hotel, and the lines seem to stretch on forever on hot weekends.

Alfonso's, at 1251 Prospect Street, is La Jolla's original sidewalk cafe, with tables crowded together under a shady awning. The margaritas are excellent here, as are the chips, salsa, and huge carne asada burritos. **George's at the Cove** (1250 Prospect St.), across the street from Alfonso's, has a few outdoor tables on a patio just below street level. The food is excellent and expensive.

Near Windansea beach there is **Sluggo's,** at 6980 La Jolla Boulevard. Hot dogs are the specialty here—huge hot dogs with every topping imaginable. Pick up your lunch here and take it down to the beach. Across the street, **Windansea Natural Grocery,** at 6903 La Jolla Boulevard, is a nice natural foods store with great smoothies, juices, and Middle-Eastern treats like hummus and tabouleh.

The favorite gathering spot is the **Pannikin,** at 7467 Girard Avenue, where locals chat over cups of steaming fresh coffee and flaky croissants. There are only a few tables on the front porch patio, but you can get your coffee and wander around the shop while you wait for a spot.

Museums and Historic Sites

Children's Museum of San Diego. *See* Tour 7: La Jolla, above.

Junipero Serra Museum. *See* Tour 5: Old Town, above.

San Diego Museum of Contemporary Art. *See* Tour 7: La Jolla, above.

Maritime Museum. *See* Tour 1: Downtown and the Embarcadero, above.

Mingei International Museum of World Folk Art. *See* Tour 7: La Jolla, above.

Mission San Diego de Alcala. Established by Father Junipero Serra in 1769 on Presidio Hill, the mission moved to its present location in 1774. The Padre Luis Jayme Museum—named after California's first Catholic martyr, killed by Indians—features relics of early mission days. Sunday services in the original mission chapel. *10818 San Diego Mission Rd., tel. 619/281-8449. Open daily 9–5.*

Mission San Luis Rey. Father Fermin Lasuen, a successor to Father Junipero Serra, established the "King of the Missions." The most extensive collection of old Spanish vestments in the country is on display in the museum. *4050 Mission Ave., San Luis Rey, 4 mi east of I–5 in Oceanside, tel. 619/757–3651. Open Mon.–Sat. 10–4:30, Sun. 12–4:30 PM.*

Museum of Photographic Arts. *See* Tour 4: Balboa Park, above.

Reuben H. Fleet Space Theater and Science Center. *See* Tour 4: Balboa Park, above.

San Diego Aerospace Museum. *See* Tour 4: Balboa Park, above.

San Diego Hall of Champions. *See* Tour 4: Balboa Park, above.

San Diego Museum of Art. *See* Tour 4: Balboa Park, above.

San Diego Museum of Man. *See* Tour 4: Balboa Park, above.

San Diego Natural History Museum. *See* Tour 4: Balboa Park, above.

Timken Art Gallery. *See* Tour 4: Balboa Park, above.

Villa Montezuma. The Jesse Sheppard House, built in 1887, is a fine example of Victorian architecture with a California flair. The house has stained-glass windows with portraits of Shakespeare, Beethoven, Mozart, and Goethe. Redwood paneling and massive fireplaces decorate the living quarters, which have been restored by the San Diego Historical Society. The house is owned by the City of San Diego and is used for community meetings and social gatherings. *1925 K St., tel. 619/239–2211. Admission is free, though donations are appreciated. Open Wed.–Sun. 1–4:30 PM.*

Parks and Gardens

With its huge urban parks and vast expanses of wilderness, San Diego County is in many ways one big park (or parking lot if you're stuck on the freeway). The flowers bloom year-round here, with red and white poinsettias popping up like weeds at Christmastime, and candy-colored pink and yellow ice plant edging the roads year-round. The dry climate, which seems inhospitable to growing things, actually nurtures some amazing plants. The golden, bushy stalks of pampas grass grow in wild patches near Sea World. Bougainvillaea covers roofs and hillsides in La Jolla, spreading magenta blankets over whitewashed adobe walls. Towering palms and twisted junipers are far more common than maples or oaks, and fields of wild daisies and chamomile cover dry dusty lots.

When the orange, lemon, and lime trees blossom in spring, the fragrance of their tiny white blossoms is nearly overpowering. Citrus groves pop up in unlikely places, along the freeways and back roads. Be sure to drive with your windows down—you'll be amazed at the sweet, hypnotic scent. Jasmine seems to be the city's flower, blooming on bushes and vines in front yards and parking lots. Its smell, stronger than any perfume or oil, adds a certain sensuality to the air. Birds of paradise poke up straight and tall, tropical testimonials to San Diego's temperate climate.

Balboa Park is really a series of botanical gardens, with a verdant, tropical oasis in its midst at the San Diego Zoo. The animals are fascinating, for sure, but the zoo's real charm and fame come from its tradition of creating hospitable environments that resemble natural habitats as closely as possible. Botanists will particularly enjoy Tiger River, a new exhibit with a $500,000 collection of endangered tropical plants.

Cultivated and wild gardens are an integral part of all of Balboa Park, thanks to "The Mother of Balboa Park," Kate Sessions, who made sure both the park's developed and undeveloped acreage bloomed with the purple blossoms of the jacaranda tree and planted thousands of palms and trees throughout the park. Left alone, all Balboa Park would look like **Florida Canyon,** which lies between the main park and Morley Field, along Park Boulevard. Volunteers from the **Museum of Natural History** give guided walks through Florida Canyon from the parking lot below the tennis courts at 2 PM on Sundays. Their informative talks turn the canyon's dusty brown, scrub-covered hills into a fascinating natural wonderland, where lizards and birds live amid wild herbs. For information on weekday tours and special activities, call 619/232–3821.

The **Rose Garden** along Park Boulevard overlooking Florida Canyon has over 2,000 rose plants. The adjacent **Cactus Garden** has trails winding around prickly cactus and soft green succulents, many indigenous to the area. The **Spanish Alcazar Garden** off El Prado across from the Museum of Man has colorful flower beds where the blossoms never seem to die. **Palm Can-**

yon, near the Organ Pavilion, has over 60 varieties of palm trees along a shady bridge. Behind the House of Hospitality, a new Japanese Garden is under development. The redwood-lathed **Botanical Building,** built in 1915, houses a beautiful selection of tropical flowers and plants, with ceiling-high tree ferns shading tiny, fragile orchids and feathery bamboo.

Mission Bay Park is more of a playground than a botanical wonder, but its grassy lawns are a soothing sight for displaced East Coasters. **Old Town State Park,** though historic in focus, has some lovely small, grassy parks for resting and picnicking. The lawns between the historic district and Bazaar del Mundo, by the plaza, are particularly nice and often hold arts and crafts shows. **Presidio Park** has a nice private canyon surrounded by palms at the bottom of the hill, off Taylor Street just before it intersects with Interstate 8. **Torrey Pines States Reserve,** north of La Jolla atop an oceanside cliff, has beautiful trails amid the twisted pines.

Quail Botanical Gardens is located in Leucadia, in the heart of the county's commercial flower fields. Much of north San Diego County is agricultural land, with the coastal strips reserved for endless rows of flowers. The hillsides are literally covered with blossoms during the spring. Quail Botanical Gardens is a 30-acre bird and plant sanctuary specializing in native flora and fauna. Carefully planned gardens exhibit cactus and succulents and exotic plants from all over the world. *To reach Quail Botanical Gardens, take I–5 north to Encinitas Blvd. Go east 1 mi to the gardens. Tel. 619/436–3036. $1 parking fee. Open daily 8–5.*

Other Places of Interest

The **San Diego Wild Animal Park,** about 30 miles northeast of downtown San Diego, is an extension of the San Diego Zoo. The 1,800-acre preserve in the San Pasqual Valley is designed to protect endangered species of animals from around the world. Five exhibit areas have been carved out of the dry, dusty canyons and mesas to represent the animals' natural habitats in North Africa, South Africa, East Africa, Asian Swamps, and Asian Plains.

The best way to see these preserves is on the 50-minute, five-mile Wgasa Bushline Monorail. As you ride in front of the exhibits, the animals leap and run through prairies and mesas as they would in the wild. The trip is especially enjoyable in the early evening when the heat has subsided and the animals are active and feeding. Photographers with zoom lenses can get some spectacular shots of zebras, gazelles, and rhinos. Enemy species are separated from each other by deep moats, but only the truly predatory tigers, lions, and cheetahs are kept in isolation. More than 2,500 animals from some 250 species roam through the expansive grounds.

On summer nights the Wgasa Bushline Monorail travels through the exhibits after dark, when soft amber sodium-vapor lamps highlight the animals in action. The setting, far from civilization, with clear starry skies, is enthralling and nearly as exciting as the real thing.

The park is as much a botanical garden as the zoo, and botanists collect rare and endangered plants for preservation. The five-foot-tall desert cypress in the botanical garden is native to the Sahara. Only six such trees are still in existence in the Sahara.

The 1¼-mile-long Kilimanjaro Hiking Trail leads through some of the park's hilliest terrain in the East Africa section, with observation decks looking out over the elephants and lions. A 70-foot suspension bridge, made of Douglas fir poles, leads over a steep ravine to the final observation point and a panorama of the San Pasqual Valley and the Wild Animal Park.

The park's center is called Nairobi Village, where the sound of African drums provides a constant background safari noise. The ticket booths are designed to resemble the tomb of an ancient king of Uganda, and dancers regularly perform complex African tribal dances in the center of the village. In the Petting Kraal, deer, sheep, and goats affectionately tolerate tugs and pats and are quite adept at posing for pictures with struggling toddlers on their backs. At the Congo River Fishing Village, 10,000 gallons of water pour each minute over a huge waterfall into a large lagoon.

Ravens, vultures, hawks, and a great horned owl perform throughout the day at the Bird Show Amphitheater. Pancho, a Mexican yellow-headed parrot, sings quite a credible version of "I Left My Heart in San Francisco," and the hawks look as though they'll fly off into the wilderness, though they never do. All the park's animal shows are entertainingly educational. The gift shops have a wide assortment of African crafts and animal-oriented souvenirs and free-loan cameras are available.

To reach the San Diego Wild Animal Park, take I–15 to Via Rancho Pkwy. in Escondido, then follow the signs. Tel. 619/ 234–6541. Admission: $14.50 adults (over 16), $5.50 children 3–15. Gates open daily 9–4, park open 9–6, later in summer.

Torrey Pines State Reserve is a 1,750-acre sanctuary for the world's rarest pine tree, the *Pinus torreyana*. About 6,000 of these unusual pines, some as tall as 60 feet, grow on the clifftops above one of San Diego County's loveliest beaches. The torrey pine grows in only two places—the preserve and Santa Rosa Island, about 175 miles northwest of the reserve.

The reserve has several hiking trails leading to the cliffs, 300 feet above the ocean. Picnic areas are scattered in pine groves, and wildflowers grow profusely in the spring. The park station has maps of the reserve and guided walks through the trails.

The beach below the reserve, called Torrey Pines State Beach, is one of the loveliest in the county. If you walk south past the lifeguard towers, you can find a secluded spot under the golden brown cliffs and feel as if there is no one on the beach but you. When the tide is out, you can walk south all the way to Black's Beach, through arches and over rocky promontories carved by the waves.

North Torrey Pines Rd., also known as Old Hwy. 101, tel. 619/ 755–2063. Take the Genessee Ave. west exit off I–5, then turn right (north) on Old Hwy. 101. Open daily 9–sunset. Parking $6. There is a large parking lot by the beach and another up the hill by the park station.

A 52-mile **Scenic Drive** over much of central San Diego begins at the foot of Broadway. Road signs with a white seagull on a yellow-and-blue background direct the way through the Embarcadero to Harbor and Shelter islands, Point Loma and Cabrillo Monument, Mission Bay, Old Town, Balboa Park, Soledad Mountain, and La Jolla. The drive is outlined on some local maps and travels surface streets past the main thoroughfares. You are best off taking this three-hour drive on the weekend, when the commuters are off the road.

San Diego for Free

San Diego's main attractions are its climate and natural beauty, which are accessible to all, free of charge. The 70 miles of beaches are free—no boardwalks with admission fees, no high-priced parking lots. All you need is a swimsuit and a towel. You can easily while away a week or two just visiting a different beach community each day, from the opulence of La Jolla to the laid-back hippie style of Ocean Beach. (*See* Chapter 4 for more details.) Nearly all San Diego's major attractions in our Exploring section are situated amid huge parks, gardens, and waterfronts, with plenty of natural wonders to keep you amused.

Mission Bay is a massive playground for all ages, with beaches for sunning and swimming, playgrounds and picnic tables, and fire rings for nighttime bonfires. The endless parade of runners, bikers, and roller skaters is a constant delight, and a great way really to take in the Southern California lifestyle and gather some great anecdotes to take back home. The people-watching is best near the Information Center on East Mission Bay Drive and near the intersection of West Mission Bay Drive and Mission Boulevard in Mission Beach.

Balboa Park is similarly entrancing, with its gorgeous gardens and recreational areas. The lawns along the Lily Pond are filled on weekends with people passing the time reading a good book, visiting with friends, or watching the fire-eaters and jugglers practice their moves before setting up their impromptu stages. Behind the museums there are many trails leading down into the park's canyons, where small botanical gardens seem to appear out of nowhere in the midst of dusty chaparral. The walkway behind the Reuben H. Fleet Space Theater leads through oak and eucalyptus groves to Gold Gulch, where a Japanese garden is beginning to take shape. A path by the Organ Pavilion leads to a lush, tropical garden with 60 species of palms.

Balboa Park's museums offer free admission on Tuesdays on a rotating basis. Call 619/239–0512 for a schedule. Free organ concerts take place in the Organ Pavilion on Sunday afternoons, and a variety of choral groups and bands appear there on summer evenings, also for free. There is no charge to wander through the Botanical Building, an enclosed tropical paradise.

If you can trust your ability to keep your wallet in your pocket and don't want to pay the museum fees, visit their gift shops. Each has a selection of books, artwork, crafts, and toys as befit their themes, and the shops can actually give you a pretty good idea of what's beyond the museum doors.

Seaport Village hosts a popular series of pops concerts on summer nights, complete with fireworks displays, all for free. **Sea World** has fireworks as well, which are visible from Mission Bay and Ocean Beach.

Navy ships docked at the downtown Embarcadero are sometimes open for free tours. Walking tours through Old Town are
free, and the tour guides are great history teachers.

What to See and Do with Children

As if swimming, roller-skating, biking, and hiking weren't
enough, San Diego has plenty of additional activities to keep
kids happy. The **San Diego Zoo** and **San Diego Wild Animal
Park** both have children's petting zoos, where the animals are
content to play nicely with curious kids. The zoo's animal nursery is a lot of fun for the little ones, who can spot baby chimps
and antelopes playing with the same brightly colored plastic
toys that all kids enjoy.

Many of **Balboa Park's** museums have special exhibits for children. Kids seem particularly entranced by the Museum of
Man's "Lifestyles and Ceremonies" exhibit; teens delight in the
small collection of mummies. The Natural History Museum's
dinosaurs are always a hit. But best of all is the Science Center
at the Reuben H. Fleet Space Theater, where the gadgets and
hands-on experiments are fascinatingly clever and educational.
(*See* Tour 4: Balboa Park and Other Places of Interest, both
above.)

Sea World's Cap'n Kids' World is an imaginative, no-holds-
barred playground that captures kids and occupies their energy and time for hours on end. The play equipment is designed
for various ages—the little ones like tumbling in huge pools of
plastic balls, while older kids like racing all over the rope
swings and balconies. The playground is so popular that San
Diegans often get yearly passes to Sea World so they can bring
their kids and have some time to sit peacefully in the sun while
the kids play. The City Streets exhibit has shows with young
performers displaying some incredible stunts on bicycles and
skateboards—just in case the kids don't have enough daredevil
ideas of their own. (*See* Tour 6: Mission Bay and Sea World,
above.)

The **Children's Museum** in La Jolla Village Square has trunks
full of costumes for dress-up, plenty of arts and crafts supplies,
and even a model dentist's chair where kids can pretend to drill
their parents' teeth. The Tide Pool at **Scripps Institute of
Oceanography Aquarium** gives kids a chance to hold and pet
starfish and sea anemones. Once they get a glimpse of these sea
creatures, they'll enjoy exploring the natural tidal pools on the
beach much more. (*See* Tour 7, La Jolla, above.)

Mission Bay and many of the beaches have large playgrounds
by the water. The **Children's Pool** at La Jolla Cove is a shallow
cove protected from the waves, safe enough to let the kids try
snorkeling. In **Old Town,** Geppetto's toy store is a must-see for
its inexpensive gadgets imported from Europe. The carousels
at Balboa Park and the zoo are good for burning up some energy. **Belmont Park** in Mission Beach is a mini-amusement park
by the sea, with a renovated 1925 rollercoaster, a carousel, a
photo booth where you can pose on a surfboard inside a plastic
wave, and a life-size gyroscope ride.

Off the Beaten Track

Don't think you've finished seeing San Diego once you've hit all the main attractions. The real character of the place doesn't shine through until you've hit a few neighborhoods and mingle with the natives. Then you can say you've seen San Diego.

Mission Hills is an older neighborhood near downtown that has the charm and wealth of La Jolla and Point Loma, without the crowds. The prettiest streets are above Presidio Park and Old Town, where huge mansions with rolling lawns resemble eastern estates. Drive along Fort Stockton Drive up from the Presidio, or Juan Street past Heritage Park in Old Town to Sunset Boulevard to see these homes. Washington Street runs up a steep hill from Interstate 8 through the center of Mission Hills. Palmier's, at the corner of Washington Street and Goldfinch, is a French cafe and charcuterie with wonderful pâtés, pastries, and wines to eat there or to go. On Goldfinch, visit the Gathering, a neighborhood restaurant with great breakfasts and outdoor tables for reading the Sunday paper in the sun.

Hillcrest, farther up Washington Street beginning at First Avenue, is San Diego's Castro Street, the center for the homosexual community and artists of all types. University Avenue and Fourth and Fifth avenues are filled with cafes, boutiques, and excellent bookstores. The Guild Theater, on Fifth Avenue between University Avenue and Robinson, shows first-run foreign films and has nice balcony seating, unusual in this age of multiplexes. The Blue Door, next to the theater, is one of San Diego's best small bookstores, with a great collection of books on art, philosophy, and other erudite matters. The Corvette Diner, on Fourth Avenue between University Avenue and Washington Street, is an outrageous fifties-diner sort of place, with burgers and shakes and campy waitresses. Quel Fromage, a coffeehouse on University Avenue between Fourth and Fifth streets, has long been the place to go to discuss philosophical or romantic matters over espresso.

Like most of San Diego, Hillcrest has been undergoing massive redevelopment. The largest new project is the **Uptown District,** on University Avenue at Eighth Avenue. This self-contained residential/commercial center is meant to resemble an inner-city neighborhood, with shops and restaurants within easy walking distance of high-priced townhomes. Restaurants include Cane's, a trendy pasta cafe, and La Salsa, part of a chain of excellent Mexican take-out stands.

Washington Street eventually becomes Adams Avenue, San Diego's Antiques Row, with shops displaying an odd array of antiques and collectibles. Adams Avenue leads into Kensington and Talmadge, two lovely old neighborhoods overlooking Mission Valley. The Ken Cinema, at 4066 Adams Avenue, shows older cult movies and current art films.

Ocean Beach, the westernmost point of the United States, is considered to be a hippie haven, a holdover from its radical days in the sixties. Of all the mainland beach towns, OB is the most self-contained, with a mixed populace of young families, longtime residents, and drifters. The OB Pier is the best spot to get a real feel for the place, though you may find the crowd a bit unsavory. For the bikinied beauties on roller skates, visit the Mission Beach boardwalk, where the parade is never ending.

San Diego's large Vietnamese, Cambodian, and Korean communities congregate in **Linda Vista** and **North Park.** There are great neighborhood restaurants in these relatively nondescript areas. The Mexican-American community is centered in Barrio Logan, under the Coronado Bridge. Chicano Park, just under the bridge supports, has huge murals depicting Mexican history, painted by artists from all over California.

Bargain shoppers spend their weekend mornings at **Kobey's Swap Meet** in the Sports Arena Parking Lot of Sports Arena Boulevard, near Point Loma. The swap meet seems to expand every week, with sellers displaying everything from futon beds to fresh strawberries from the farming communities. The back section with secondhand goods is a bargain-hunters' delight. Admission to the swap meet, which is open Thursday–Sunday from dawn to late afternoon, is $1.

3 Shopping

*by Marael
Johnson*

*A writer and
researcher on
many Fodor's
guides, Ms.
Johnson lives in
the San Diego
area.*

Most San Diego shops are open daily 10–6; department stores
and shops within the larger malls stay open until 9 PM on weekdays. Almost every store will accept traveler's checks, with
proper identification (driver's license, passport). Aside from
their own credit cards, major department stores usually accept
American Express, MasterCard, and Visa. Sales are adver-
tised in the daily *San Diego Union* and San Diego edition of the
Los Angeles Times and in the *Reader*, a free weekly that comes
out on Thursday.

Shopping Districts

San Diego's shopping areas are a mélange of self-contained
mega-malls, historic districts, quaint villages, funky neighborhoods, and chic suburbs.

Coronado Across the bay, Coronado is accessible by car or ferry. **Orange
Avenue**, in the center of town, has six blocks of ritzy boutiques
and galleries. The elegant Hotel Del Coronado, also on Orange
Avenue, houses exclusive (and costly) specialty shops. **Old
Ferry Landing**, where the new ferry lands, is a waterfront cen-
ter similar to Seaport Village.

Downtown **Horton Plaza**, in the heart of center city, is a shopper's Disneyland—visually exciting, multilevels of department stores, one-
of-a-kind shops, fast-food counters, classy restaurants, a farm-
er's market, live theater, and cinemas. Surrounding Horton Plaza is the 16-block Gaslamp Quarter, a redevelopment
area that features art galleries and antiques and specialty shops, housed in Victorian buildings and renovated warehouses.

Hotel Circle The Hotel Circle area, northeast of downtown near I–8 and
Freeway 163, has two major shopping centers. **Fashion Valley**
and **Mission Valley Center** contain hundreds of shops, as well as
restaurants, cinemas, and branches of almost every San Diego
department store.

Kensington/ These are two of San Diego's older, established neighborhoods,
Hillcrest situated several miles north and east of downtown. **Adams Avenue**, in Kensington, is Antiques Row. More than 20 dealers sell
everything from postcards and kitchen utensils to cut glass and
porcelain. **Park Boulevard**, in Hillcrest, is the city's center for
nostalgia. Small shops, on either side of University Avenue,
stock clothing, accessories, furnishings, and bric-a-brac of the
1920s–1960s. **Uptown District**, a new shopping center on University Avenue has the neighborhood's massive Ralph's grocery store, and several specialty shops.

La Jolla/ La Jolla, about 15 miles northwest of downtown, on the coast, is
Golden Triangle an ultrachic, ultraexclusive resort community. High-end and
trendy boutiques line Girard Avenue and Prospect Street.
Coast Walk, nestled along the cliffside of Prospect Street, offers several levels of sophisticated shops, galleries, and restaurants, as well as a spectacular ocean view. The Golden Triangle
area, several miles east of coastal La Jolla, is served by two
malls. **La Jolla Village Square**, just west of I–5, is an indoor
shopping complex; **University Towne Centre**, farther inland, between I–5 and Highway 805, is an open-air village. Both centers feature the usual range of department stores, specialty
shops, sportswear chains, restaurants, and cinemas.

Old Town North of downtown, off I–5, this popular historic district is reminiscent of a colorful Mexican marketplace. Adobe architecture, flower-filled plazas, fountains, and courtyards highlight the shopping areas of **Bazaar del Mundo, La Esplanade,** and **Old Town Mercado,** where you will find international goods, toys, souvenirs, and arts and crafts.

Seaport Village On the waterfront, a few minutes from downtown, **Seaport Village** offers quaint theme shops, restaurants, arts and crafts galleries, and commanding views of Coronado, the bridge, and passing ships.

Department Stores

I. Magnin (La Jolla Village Square, tel. 619/279–7803). Bullock's stocks exclusive, traditional fashions, accessories, and gift items for men and women.

Neiman-Marcus (Fashion Valley, tel. 619/692–9100). This Texas-based department store is world-famous for fine apparel, couture, furs, precious jewels, accessories, and gift items.

Nordstrom (Fashion Valley, tel. 619/295–4441; Horton Plaza, tel. 619/239–1700; University Towne Centre, tel. 619/457–4575). Up-to-the-minute, moderate-to-expensive clothing and accessories for men, women, and teens are found at these stores, noted for their extensive shoe department and customized service.

Saks Fifth Avenue (7600 Girard Ave., La Jolla, tel. 619/459–4123; Mission Valley Center, tel. 619/260–0030). Contemporary sportswear for men and women of all ages, designer apparel, lingerie, and accessories are featured.

Specialty Stores

Accessories **Bags 'n Belts** (7864 Girard Ave., La Jolla, tel. 619/459–3536). Here there are discounted designer handbags, belts, costume jewelry, and accessories.

Pomegranate (1152 Prospect Ave., La Jolla, tel. 619/459–0629). Here you'll find very fine accessories and exceptional antique jewelry.

Antiques **Maidhof Bros.** (1891 San Diego Ave., in Old Town, tel. 619/574–1891). This is one of California's oldest and largest dealers in genuine nautical and brass items.

The Olde Cracker Factory (448 Market St., in the Gaslamp Quarter, tel. 619/232–7961). There are three floors of specialty shops in a converted brick warehouse.

Unicorn Company Arts & Antiques Mall (310 5th Ave., in the Gaslamp Quarter, tel. 619/232–1696). This is the largest antiques complex in San Diego.

Art Galleries **African Accents** (1250 Prospect Ave., La Jolla, tel. 619/454–9983). Paintings and sculptures by African artists are surrounded by woven baskets, garish masks, and congo drums.

Gallery of Two Sisters (1298 Prospect St., La Jolla, tel. 619/459–7119). It has a large selection of area- and ocean-related art by California artists.

Knowles Gallery (7422 Girard Ave., La Jolla, tel. 619/454–0106). See paintings and sculpture by 50 San Diego artists.

Sue Tushingham McNary Art Gallery (Hotel Del Coronado Arcade, Coronado, tel. 619/435–1819). Paintings, lithographs,

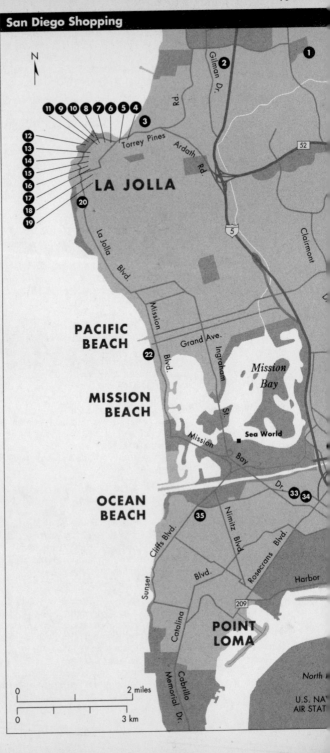

San Diego Shopping

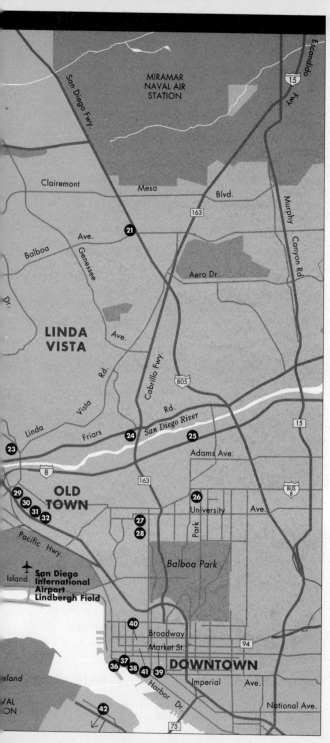

etchings, miniatures, and prints of San Diego scenes are displayed.

Bargains **Clothing Clearance Center** (Fashion Valley, tel. 619/291–5580). Here you'll find designer and major-label men's suits and separates at highly discounted prices.

The Garment Center (1911 San Diego Ave., in Old Town, tel. 619/297–4944). This is the place for end-of-season merchandise from East and West Coast manufacturers, discounted up to 60%.

Nordstrom Rack (Mission Valley Center, tel. 619/296–0143). Top-of-the-line, end-of-season collections from Nordstrom Department Store, at about 50% discount, are featured.

Beachwear **Latitudes** (Seaport Village, tel. 619/233–5005; University Towne Centre, tel. 619/455–5960). Here you'll find name-brand women's swimwear and other sports attire.

La Jolla Surf Systems (2132 Avenida de la Playa, La Jolla, tel. 619/456-2777). This boutique carries swimsuits, cruise and resort wear.

Pilar's Beach Wear (3745 Mission Blvd., Mission Beach, tel. 619/488–3056) has one of California's largest selections of imported and American major-label swimsuits, offering mix-and-match and split sizes.

Bookstores **Blue Door** (3823 Fifth Ave., in Hillcrest, tel. 619/298–8610). This store has an extensive selection of hard-to-find literary paperbacks, poetry, and magazines.

John Cole's Book Shop (780 Prospect St., La Jolla, tel. 619/454–4766) is in a 1904 cottage with loads of character and a fascinating selection of books on art and architecture.

The White Rabbit (7755 Girard Ave., La Jolla, tel. 619/454–3518). Here are books for prereaders through junior high school age.

Boutiques for Men **Custom Shirts of La Jolla** (7643 Girard Ave., La Jolla, tel. 619/459–6147). It stocks fine slacks, jackets, and sportswear. Shirts are made to order from more than 300 fabrics.

Polo Ralph Lauren (7830 Girard Ave., La Jolla, tel. 619/459–0554). This is the place for Polo and Ralph Lauren classic collections.

Raspini (Fashion Valley, tel. 619/296–8388; 1224 Prospect St., La Jolla, tel. 619/456–2077). This store stocks European designer suits, sportswear, and leather jackets.

Boutiques for Women **Capriccio** (6919 La Jolla Blvd., La Jolla, tel. 619/459–4189) is a *Women's Wear Daily* recommendation for super high-end European and designer ensembles and elegant evening wear.

Judy's (Fashion Valley, tel. 619/291–7088) has the latest fashions for the trendiest dressers.

La Plage by Kippy's (1147 Prospect St., La Jolla, tel. 619/459–7022; The Promenade at Pacific Beach, tel. 619/272–4337). There are contemporary, trend-setting fashions for beach to evening, as well as exquisite designer sunglasses.

Crafts Galleries **Brushworks Gallery** (425 Market St., tel. 619/238–4381) features contemporary crafts.

Gallery Eight (7464 Girard Ave., La Jolla, tel. 619/454–9781) is a showcase for fine crafts and wearable art.

International Gallery (643 G St., in the Gaslamp Quarter, tel. 619/235–8255) carries fine gifts, crafts, and folk, primitive, and native art from around the world.

Food **Horton Plaza Farmers Market** (Horton Plaza, tel. 619/696–7766). Here you'll see spectacular displays of gourmet foods, including cheeses, meats, produce, and deli specialties.
Ocean Beach People's Food Co-op (4765 Voltaire St., Ocean Beach, tel. 619/224–1387). This is where you'll find San Diego's largest selection of organic grains, beans, and produce.

Jewelry **Ben Bridge Jeweler** (Horton Plaza, tel. 619/696–8911; Mission Valley Center, tel. 619/294–2808; University Towne Centre, tel. 619/453–9996) offers fine watches, diamonds, repairs, and custom work.
The Collector (1274 Prospect St., La Jolla, tel. 619/454–9763) is a world-renowned source for colored gemstones and contemporary pieces designed by international jewelers and resident goldsmiths.
J. Jessop & Sons (Horton Plaza, tel. 619/239–9311) has been in business for nearly a century, specializing in diamonds, gems, and fine watches.

Luggage **John's Fifth Avenue Luggage** (3849 Fifth Ave., in Hillcrest, tel. 619/298–0993; Fashion Valley, tel. 619/574–0086) has a large selection of luggage, attaché cases, and travel accessories.
Le Travel Store (Horton Plaza, tel. 619/544–0005) stocks luggage, totes, travel packs, luggage carts, and travel accessories.

Perfume **The House of Versailles** (Hotel Del Coronado Arcade, Coronado, tel. 619/435–1010) is a world-famous perfumery offering custom blending and pH and fragrance compatibility analysis.

Seashells **La Jolla Cave and Shell Shop** (1325 Coast Blvd., La Jolla, tel. 619/454–6080) stocks specimen and decorative shells, coral, and nautical gifts.
Shell World International (3146 Sports Arena Blvd., tel. 619/222–5500) has everything from scallop shell nightlights to shell encrusted toilet seats.
Silver Sea of Old Town (2527 San Diego Ave., in Old Town, tel. 619/291–0274) sells specimen and decorative shells, coral, jewelry, and gift items.

Sporting Goods **Ocean Enterprises** (7710 Balboa Ave., tel. 619/565–6054) stocks high-quality wet suits, dry suits, and skin- and scuba-diving equipment.
Oshman's Sporting Goods (Mission Valley Center, tel. 619/299–0701) has all types of athletic and camping equipment, including athletic shoes and sportswear.
The Runner's Store Discount Outlet (1735 University Ave., tel. 619/260–8155) has a large assortment of well-priced running shoes, clothing, and accessories.

Swap Meets **Kobeys Swap Meet.** This is a large open-air market selling many different kinds of new and collectible merchandise. *3500 Sports Arena Blvd., near Midway and Rosecrans, tel. 619/226–0650. Open Thurs.–Sun. 7 AM–3 PM.*

T-shirts **Pacific Eyes & T's** (1241 Prospect St., La Jolla, tel. 619/454–7532; La Jolla Village Square, tel. 619/535–0365; 2461 San Diego Ave., tel. 619/692–0059). You'll find T-shirts in every price category.
Pro Jersey of Mission Valley (Mission Valley Center, 1288 Camino del Rio N, tel. 619/290–9711) carries T-shirts, jerseys, jackets, and caps, personalized with authentic NFL and major-league logos. You will get a better reception in the San Diego

area if you do not sport the jerseys of the rival Los Angeles Raiders or the Denver Broncos.

TNT T-Shirts (4373 La Jolla Village Dr., tel. 619/454–7244) offers photo and custom transfers on a variety of stock and styles, while you wait.

Toys   **Toys R Us** (1240 W. Morena Blvd., in Mission Bay area, tel. 619/276–7094) is a supermarket of toys, stuffed animals, and games for all ages.

4 Beaches

by Kevin Brass

A freelance writer, and long-time North County resident, Kevin Brass is a regular contributor to the San Diego edition of the Los Angeles Times, San Diego *magazine, and other publications.*

Like the magnificent mountains of Switzerland or the moors of Scotland, the beaches are San Diego's greatest natural attraction. But, alas, not all beaches are created equal. For example, some are best suited for surfing or swimming, while others are ideal for volleyball and Frisbee games.

Overnight camping is not allowed on any of the beaches, but there are campgrounds at some state beaches. Lifeguards are stationed at city beaches (from Sunset Cliffs to Black's Beach) in the summertime, but coverage in winter is erratic. It should be noted that few beaches in San Diego are ideal for dogs, although exceptions are noted below and it is rarely a problem on unpatrolled, isolated beaches, especially during the winter. Glass is prohibited on all beaches, and fires are allowed only in fire rings or barbecues. A year-long ban on alcoholic beverages—including beer—on all city beaches went into effect in April 1991. The public outcry of protest, however, was so strong and so immediate that there is some doubt that the ban will last for the intended 12 months. The measure is likely to become a hot political topic and will probably go before the public for a voter referendum. So, before you hit the beach with a six-pack or some wine coolers, find out the status of this law. Pay attention to signs listing illegal activities; the police often patrol the beaches undercover, carrying their ticket books in coolers. For a general beach and weather report, call 619/225–9494.

Beaches are listed from south to north. For information on Mission Bay, see Tour 6: Mission Bay and Sea World, Chapter 2.

South Bay

Border Field State Beach. The southernmost San Diego beach is different from most California beaches. Located just north of the Mexican border, it is a marshy area with wide chaparrals and wildflowers, a favorite of horse riders and hikers. Frequent sewage contamination from Tijuana makes the water unpleasant—if not downright dangerous—for swimming. There is ample parking and there are rest rooms and fire rings. *Exit I–5 at Dairy Mart Rd. and head west along Monument Rd.*

South Beach. One of the few beaches where dogs are free to romp, this is a good beach for long, isolated walks. The often-contaminated water and rocky beach tend to keep away crowds. The downside: There are few facilities, such as rest rooms. *Located at the end of Seacoast Dr. Take I–5 to Coronado Ave. and head west on Imperial Beach Ave. Turn left onto Seacoast Dr.*

Imperial Beach. A classic Southern California beach, where surfers and swimmers congregate to enjoy the water and waves, the Imperial Beach Municipal Pier was closed for several years due to storm damage and reopened in summer 1988. It provides a pleasant backdrop for the Frisbee games of the predominantly young crowd. Imperial Beach is also the site of the U.S. Open Sand Castle Competition every July. There are lifeguards on duty during the summer, parking lots, food vendors nearby, and rest room facilities. *Take Palm Ave. west from I–5 until it hits water.*

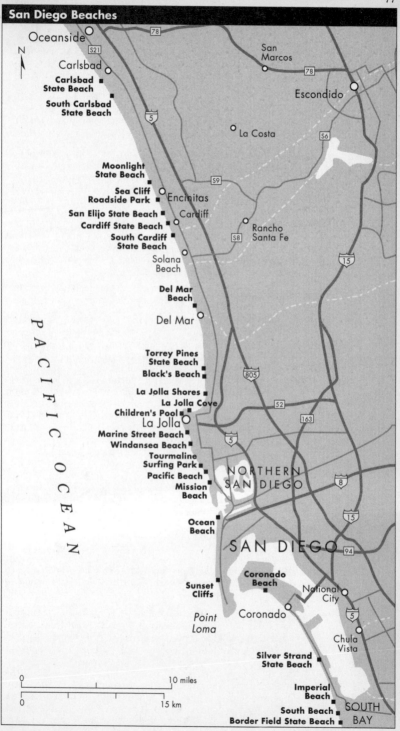

San Diego Beaches

Oceanside

Carlsbad

**Carlsbad
State Beach**

**South Carlsbad
State Beach**

La Costa

San
Marcos

Escondido

**Moonlight
State Beach**

**Sea Cliff
Roadside Park**

Encinitas

Cardiff

San Elijo State Beach

Cardiff State Beach

**South Cardiff
State Beach**

Solana
Beach

Rancho
Santa Fe

**Del Mar
Beach**

Del Mar

**Torrey Pines
State Beach**

Black's Beach

La Jolla Shores

La Jolla Cove

Children's Pool

La Jolla

Marine Street Beach

Windansea Beach

**Tourmaline
Surfing Park**

Pacific Beach

**Mission
Beach**

NORTHERN
SAN DIEGO

**Ocean
Beach**

SAN DIEGO

**Coronado
Beach**

National
City

**Sunset
Cliffs**

Coronado

*Point
Loma*

Chula
Vista

**Silver Strand
State Beach**

**Imperial
Beach**

South Beach

Border Field State Beach

SOUTH
BAY

PACIFIC OCEAN

0   10 miles

0   15 km

Coronado

Silver Strand State Beach. Farther north on the isthmus of Coronado (commonly mislabeled an island), Silver Strand was set aside as a state beach in 1932. The name is derived from the tiny silver seashells found in abundance near the water. The water is relatively calm, making it ideal for families. Four parking lots provide room for more than 1,500 cars. Parking costs $6 per car. There is also an RV campground and a wide array of facilities. *Take the Palm Ave. exit from I–5 west to State Hwy. 75; turn right and follow the signs.*

Coronado Beach. With the famous Hotel Del Coronado as a backdrop, this wide stretch of sandy beach is one of the largest in the county. It is surprisingly uncrowded on most days, since the locals go to the less touristy areas to the south or north. It's a perfect beach for sunbathing or games of Frisbee and Smash Ball (played with paddles and a small ball). Parking can be a little difficult on the busiest days, but there are plenty of rest rooms and service facilities, as well as fire rings. The view (even for a brief moment) as you drive over the Coronado Bridge makes it a worthwhile excursion. *From the bridge, turn left on Orange Ave. and follow the signs.*

Point Loma

Sunset Cliffs. Back on the mainland, beneath the jagged cliffs on the west side of Point Loma peninsula, is one of the more secluded beaches in the area, popular primarily with surfers and locals. The tide goes out each day to reveal tide pools teeming with life at the south end of the peninsula, near Cabrillo Point. Farther north, the waves attract surfers and the lonely coves attract sunbathers. Stairs are available at the foot of Bermuda and Santa Cruz avenues, but much of the access is limited to treacherous cliff trails. Another negative: There are no available facilities. *Take I–8 west to Sunset Cliffs Blvd. and head south.*

Northern San Diego

Ocean Beach. The northern end of this beach, past the second jetty, is known as Dog Beach, the only beach within San Diego city limits that allows dogs to romp around without a leash. The southern end of Ocean Beach, near the pier, is a hangout for surfers and transients. Much of the area, though, is a haven for local volleyball players, sunbathers, and swimmers. Limited parking, fire rings, and food vendors are available. *Reach Ocean Beach by taking I–8 west to Sunset Cliffs Blvd. and heading south. Turn right on Voltaire St., West Point Loma Blvd., or Newport Ave.*

Mission Beach. It's not Atlantic City, but the boardwalk stretching along Mission Beach is a popular spot for strollers, roller skaters, and bicyclists. The south end is a popular spot for surfers, swimmers, and volleyball players. It tends to get extremely crowded, especially on hot summer days. Toward the north end, near the old Belmont Park roller coaster, the beach narrows and the water grows rougher—and the crowd gets even thicker. The newly refurbished Belmont Park is now a shopping and dining complex. Parking can be a challenge, but there are plenty of rest rooms and restaurants in the area. *Exit*

I–5 at Garnet Ave. and head west to Mission Blvd. Turn south and look for parking.

Pacific Beach. The boardwalk turns into a sidewalk, but there are still bike paths and picnic tables running along the beachfront. The beach is a favorite for local teens, and the blare of rock music can be annoying. Parking, too, can be a problem, although there is a small lot at the foot of Ventura Place. *Same directions as for Mission Beach, except go north on Mission Blvd.*

La Jolla

Tourmaline Surfing Park and **Windansea Beach.** Immortalized in Tom Wolfe's 1965 book, *The Pumphouse Gang,* these La Jolla beaches are two of the top surfing spots in the area. Tourmaline has a better parking area. *Take Mission Blvd. north (it turns into La Jolla Blvd.) and turn west on Tourmaline St. (for the surfing park) or Nautilus St. (for Windansea Beach).*

Marine Street Beach. This is a classic stretch of sand for sunbathing and Frisbee games. *Accessible from Marine St. off La Jolla Blvd.*

Children's Pool. For the tikes, a shallow lagoon with small waves and no riptide provides a safe, if crowded, haven. *It can be reached by following La Jolla Blvd. north. When it forks, take the left choice, Coast Blvd.*

La Jolla Cove. Just north of the Children's Pool is La Jolla Cove, simply one of the prettiest spots in the world. A beautiful, palm-tree-lined park sits on top of cliffs formed by the incessant pounding of the waves. At low tide the tidal pools and cliff caves provide a goal for explorers. Seals sun themselves on the rocks. Divers explore the underwater delights of the San Diego–La Jolla Underwater Park, an ecological reserve. The cove also is a favorite of rough-water swimmers. Buoys mark distances for them. The beach below the cove is almost nonexistent at high tide, but the cove is still a must-see. *Follow Coast Blvd. north to the signs, or take the La Jolla Village Dr. exit from I–5, head west to Torrey Pines Rd., turn left and drive down the hill to Girard Ave. Turn right and follow the signs.*

La Jolla Shores. This is one of the most popular and overcrowded beaches in the county. On holidays such as Memorial Day, all access routes are usually closed. The lures are a wide sandy beach, relatively calm surf, and a concrete boardwalk paralleling the beach. There are also a wide variety of facilities, from posh restaurants to snack shops, within easy walking distance. Go early to get a parking spot. *From I–5 take La Jolla Village Dr. west and turn left onto La Jolla Shores Dr. Head west to Camino del Oro or Vallecitos St. Turn right and look for parking.*

Black's Beach. Once this was the only legal nude beach in the country, before nudity was outlawed in the late 1970s. But that doesn't stop people from braving the treacherous cliff trails for a chance to take off their clothes. Above the beach, hang gliders and sail-plane enthusiasts launch from the Torrey Pines Glider Port. Because of the difficult access, the beach is always relatively uncrowded. The waves make it a favorite haunt for surfers. *Take Genessee Ave. west from I–5 and follow the signs to the glider port.*

Del Mar

Torrey Pines State Beach. This is one of the easiest and most comfortable beaches to deal with in the area. A large parking lot (admission: $6) is rarely full. Lifeguard service is year-round, and there are fire rings for beach parties. Torrey Pines tends to get crowded during the summer, but more isolated spots under the cliffs are within a short walk in either direction. *Take the Carmel Valley Rd. exit west from I–5.*

Del Mar Beach. The numbered streets of this quaint little city, from 15th to 29th, end at a wide, sandy beach, a popular spot for volleyball players, surfers, and sunbathers. Although parking can be a problem on the busiest days, access is relatively easy, and the beach and water are both extremely comfortable. During the annual summer meeting of the Del Mar Thoroughbred Club, horse bettors can be seen sitting on the beach in the morning working on the *Daily Racing Form*, before heading across the street to the track in the afternoon. *Take the Via de la Valle exit from I–5 west to Old Hwy. 101 (also known as Camino del Mar in Del Mar) and turn left.*

Solana Beach

Most of the beaches of this little city are tucked away under cliffs with access limited to private stairways. At the west end of Lomas Santa Fe Drive, there is a beach area known to the locals as Pillbox, owing to the bunkerlike structures on top of the cliffs. However, there are a large parking lot, rest room facilities, and easy access to a small cove beach. During low tide, it is an easy walk to the beaches under the cliffs usually reserved for the residents. *From I–5 take Lomas Santa Fe Dr. west to its end.*

Cardiff

The area along Old Highway 101 north of Solana Beach is blessed with three state beaches. A small parking lot immediately to the north of the cliffs of Solana Beach marks **South Cardiff State Beach.** A reef break makes it extremely popular with surfers, which is also true of **Cardiff State Beach,** a mile to the north. A full campground with store and shower facilities can be found at **San Elijo State Beach,** a little farther to the north. Parking at state beaches is $6 per car. For camping reservations at San Elijo call 900/444–PARK. *From I–5, turn west on Lomas Santa Fe Dr. to Old Hwy. 101 and turn right.*

Encinitas

Undoubtedly one of the most picturesque spots in the county is **Sea Cliff Roadside Park,** known to the locals as Swami's, off Old Highway 101 on the south end of Encinitas. Palm trees and the golden domes of the nearby Self Realization Fellowship earned the beach its nickname. It is also considered to be one of the top surfing spots in the area. The only access to the beach is by a long stairway leading down from the clifftop park. *The park is at the south end of Encinitas, off Old Hwy. 101.*

Tucked into a break in the cliffs a mile to the north is **Moonlight State Beach,** with large parking areas and full facilities. *Take* *the Encinitas Blvd. exit from I–5 and head west until you hit the Moonlight parking lot.*

Carlsbad

The winter storms of the past few years have decimated some of the southern Carlsbad beaches, particularly **South Carlsbad State Beach,** which lost large amounts of sand. Still it is an excellent swimming spot and there is overnight camping (tel. 619/729–8947). There is no overnight camping allowed at **Carlsbad State Beach,** farther to the north, but there are a fishing area and a parking lot. Farther north, a new boardwalk running below the cliffs has eased access and enhanced desirability of Carlsbad beaches. *Exit I–5 at La Costa Ave. and head west to Old Hwy. 101. Turn north and follow the coastline.*

Oceanside

Two miles of wide, sandy beaches are extremely popular with swimmers, surfers, and the marines from nearby Camp Pendleton. The area around the Oceanside Pier at the foot of Sixth Avenue is a hangout for surfers. The exceptionally sandy beaches are ideal for almost all beach sports. *Take Vista Way west from I–5 to Hill St. (Old Hwy. 101) and turn right. Best access points are from Cassidy St. and the Oceanside Harbor area.*

5 Sports and Fitness

Participant Sports

by Kevin Brass

At least one stereotype of San Diego is true—it is an active, outdoors-oriented community. People recreate more than spectate. It is hard not to, with such a wide variety of choices available.

Basketball

Municipal Gym in Balboa Park (tel. 619/525-8264) is the best spot to find a high-quality pickup basketball game. Other popular congregating points for hoopsters include **Robb Field** (tel. 619/224-7581) in Ocean Beach, the **Mira Mesa Recreation Center** (tel. 619/566-5141), the **University of San Diego** (tel. 619/260-4600), and the **University of California at San Diego** (tel. 619/534-4037).

Bicycling

On any given summer day, Old Highway 101, from La Jolla to Oceanside, looks like a freeway for cyclists. Never straying more than a quarter-mile from the beach, it is easily the most popular and scenic ride around. Although the roads are narrow and windy, experienced cyclists like to follow Lomas Santa Fe Drive in Solana Beach east into beautiful Rancho Santa Fe, perhaps even continuing east on Del Dios Highway, past Lake Hodges, to Escondido. For more leisurely rides, Mission Bay, San Diego Harbor, and the Mission Beach boardwalk are all flat and scenic. San Diego even has a velodrome in Balboa Park, for those who like to race on a track. Call the Velodrome Office at 619/296-3345 for more information.

Bikes can be rented at any number of bike stores, including **Alpine Rent A Bike** in Pacific Beach (tel. 619/273-0440), **Hamel's Action Sports Center** in Mission Beach (tel. 619/488-5050), and **California Bicycle** in La Jolla (tel. 619/454-0316). A free comprehensive map of all county bike paths is available from the local office of the **California Department of Transportation** (tel. 619/688-6699).

Bocce Ball

The popular Italian version of lawn bowling is played on Monday, Wednesday, and Friday, from 1 to 5 PM on courts located in the Morley Field section of Balboa Park. The games are open to the public, and there are usually bocce balls at the courts. Call 619/692-4919 for more information.

Diving

Enthusiasts from all over the world flock to La Jolla to skindive and scuba dive in the areas off the La Jolla Cove that are rich in ocean creatures and flora. The area marks the south end of the **San Diego–La Jolla Underwater Park,** an ecological preserve. Farther north, off the south end of Black's Beach, **Scripps Canyon** lies in about 60 feet of water. Accessible by boat, the canyon plummets to more than 175 feet in some sections. Another popular diving spot is off Sunset Cliffs in Point Loma, where lobster and a wide variety of sea life are relatively close to shore, although the strong rip currents make it an area best enjoyed by experienced divers.

Diving equipment and boat trips can be arranged through **San Diego Divers** (tel. 619/224–3439), **Ocean Enterprises** (tel. 619/565–6054), or at the several **Diving Locker** locations throughout the area. It is illegal to take any wildlife from the ecological preserves in La Jolla or near Cabrillo Point. Spearfishing requires a license (available at most dive stores), and it is illegal to take out-of-season lobster and game fish out of the water. For general diving information, contact the San Diego City Lifeguards' office at 619/221–8884).

Fishing

Variety is the key. The Pacific Ocean is full of corbina, croaker, and halibut just itching to be your dinner. No license is required to fish from a public pier, such as the Ocean Beach pier. A fishing license from the state Department of Fish and Game, available at most bait and tackle stores, is required for fishing from the shoreline, although children under 15 won't need one.

There is also a wealth of well-stocked freshwater lakes in the area. Lake Jennings and Lake San Vicente in the East County are popular spots to catch trout and bass. Lakes Morena and Jennings offer both fishing and camping facilities. For general information on lakes, call 619/465–3474. Three freshwater lakes—Dixon, Hodges, and Wohlford—surround the North County city of Escondido. Camping is allowed at Wohlford at the Oakville Lodge (tel. 619/749–2895), and Dixon (tel. 619/741–3328). Boats can be rented at all the above-mentioned lakes, and a state fishing license is required. Contact the Department of Fish and Game (tel. 619/237–7311).

Several companies offer half-day, day, or multiday fishing expeditions in search of marlin, tuna, albacore, and other deepwater fish. **Fisherman's Landing** (tel. 619/229–0391), **H & M Landing** (tel. 619/222–1144), and **Seaforth Boat Rentals** (tel. 619/223–1681) are among the companies operating from San Diego. **Helgren's Sportfishing** (tel. 619/722–2133) offers trips from Oceanside Harbor.

Fitness

Why let a gluttonous vacation or strenuous business trip interrupt your training schedule? Several hotels offer full health clubs, at least with weight machines, stationary bicycles, and spas, including, in the downtown area, the **Omni San Diego** (910 Broadway Circle, tel. 619/239–2200) and the **U.S. Grant Hotel** (326 Broadway, tel. 619/232–3121). Other hotels with health clubs include: the **Hotel Del Coronado** (1500 Orange Ave., Coronado, tel. 619/435–6611), **Sheraton Grand** (1580 Harbor Island Dr., Harbor Island, tel. 619/291–2900), **Le Meridien** (2000 Second St., Coronado, tel. 619/435–3000), the **San Diego Hilton Beach and Tennis Resort** (1775 E. Mission Bay Dr., Mission Bay, tel. 619/276–4010), the **La Costa Hotel and Spa** (Costa del Mar Rd., Carlsbad, tel. 619/438–9111), and the **Olympic Resort Hotel** (6111 El Camino Real, Carlsbad, tel. 619/438–3330). Guests of the **Town and Country Hotel** (500 Hotel Circle, tel. 619/291–7131) and the **Hanalei Hotel** (2770 Hotel Circle, tel. 619/297–1101) have access to the tennis and racquetball courts,

weight room, saunas, and other facilities of the nearby **Atlas
Health Club** (901 Hotel Circle S., tel. 619/298–9321), in Mission
Valley. The dozen **Family Fitness Centers** in the area (including
centers in Mission Valley, tel. 619/281–5543; Sports Arena
area, tel. 619/224–2902; and La Jolla, tel. 619/457–3930) allow
nonmembers to use the facilities for a small fee. A company
called **Sweat 'N Smile Inc.** (320 Upas St., tel. 619/296–6776) offers fitness and recreation programs, including classes, volleyball, and baseball, geared toward travelers.

Frisbee Golf

This is just like golf, except it's played with Frisbees. A course
is laid out in the woods of Balboa Park. The course is open seven
days a week, from dawn to dusk, and there is no charge to play.
Rules are posted. From Highway 163, head east on Park Boulevard. Turn right on Zoo Place to Florida Drive; turn right and
follow Florida Drive to Pershing Drive. Turn left on Pershing
Drive. More information is available from the always-genial
Balboa Park Information Center (tel. 619/239–0512).

Golf

To list the more than 70 golf courses in San Diego County requires more space than we have here. Suffice it to say, the following is merely a sampling of the variety available. The
picturesque Torrey Pines Municipal Golf Course, perched on
the cliffs overlooking the ocean a few minutes north of La Jolla,
is the site of the annual Shearson-Lehman Brothers Open professional men's tournament, while the plush La Costa Country
Club hosts the pro tour's annual Tournament of Champions.
The Ladies Professional Golf Association tour stops at the
Stoneridge Country Club in April. Other courses worthy of
note in this area, sometimes known as "Golfland USA," are the
rolling hills of the Lomas Santa Fe Country Club and Whispering Palms Country Club in the Rancho Santa Fe area. One of
the nicest courses in the county is the Rancho Santa Fe Golf
Course, the original home of the Bing Crosby Clambake, but it
is open only to members of the Rancho Santa Fe covenant. Balboa Park, Mission Bay, Rancho Bernardo, Singing Hills, Torrey Pines, and Whispering Palms are among the most popular
public courses.

Public Courses   **Balboa Park Municipal Golf Course** (Golf Course Dr., San
Diego, tel. 619/232–2470), with 18 holes, 5,900 yards, has a
neighboring nine-hole course, driving range, equipment rentals, clubhouse, and restaurant.
Carmel Mountain Ranch Country Club (15010 Ave. of Science,
San Diego, tel. 619/487–9224), with 18 holes, 6,700 yards, offers a driving range and equipment rentals.
Carlton Oaks Lodge and Country Club (9200 Inwood Dr., Santee, tel. 619/448–4242), with 18 holes, 7,000 yards, honors
other memberships and has a driving range, equipment rentals, clubhouse, and lodge.
Castle Creek Country Club (8797 Circle R Dr., Escondido, tel.
619/749–2877), with 18 holes, 6,375 yards, honors other memberships, and reservations are not required; it has a driving
range and offers equipment rentals.
Coronado Golf Course (2000 Visalia Row, Coronado, tel. 619/
435–3121), with 18 holes, 6,700 yards, honors other member-

ships, and reservations are required; it has a driving range, equipment rentals, and a clubhouse.

Cottonwood Country Club (3121 Willow Glen Rd., El Cajon, tel. 619/442–9891), with 36 holes, honors other memberships, and reservations are required; it has a driving range and equipment rentals.

Lawrence Welk Village (8860 Lawrence Welk Dr., Escondido, tel. 619/749–3000), with 18 holes, 2,323 yards, honors other memberships, and reservations are not required; it offers equipment rentals and lodging.

Meadow Lake (10333 Meadow Glen Way East, Escondido, tel. 619/749–1620) is located near Lawrence Welk Village and has a par 72 championship 18-hole course.

Mission Bay Golf Course (2702 N. Mission Bay Dr., San Diego, tel. 619/273–1221), with 18 holes, 3,175 yards, honors other memberships, and reservations are required; it has a driving range and equipment rentals.

Oceanside Centre City Golf Course (1 Country Club La., Oceanside, tel. 619/443–8590), with 9 holes, 2,796 yards, offers equipment rentals; no reservations are required.

Pala Mesa Resort (2001 S. Hwy. 395, Fallbrook, tel. 619/728–5881) has 18 holes, 6,400 yards; reservations are required, and it offers a driving range, equipment rentals, and lodging.

Rancho Bernardo Inn and Country Club (17550 Bernardo Oaks Dr., tel. 800/487–0700) has 18 holes, 6,329 yards; reservations are required, and it offers a driving range, equipment rentals, and lodging.

Singing Hills Country Club (3007 Dehesa Rd., El Cajon, tel. 619/442–3425), with 54 holes, honors other memberships; reservations are required, and it offers a driving range, equipment rentals, and lodging.

Torrey Pines Municipal Golf Course (11480 N. Torrey Pines Rd., La Jolla, tel. 619/453–0380) has 36 holes; reservations are not required (but suggested), and it offers a driving range, equipment rentals, and lodging.

Whispering Palms Country Club (Via de la Valle, Rancho Santa Fe, tel. 619/756–2471), with 27 holes, honors other memberships; reservations are required, and it offers lodging.

Private Courses **Escondido Country Club** (1800 W. Country Club La., Escondido, tel. 619/746–4212), with 18 holes, 6,140 yards, honors other memberships; golf carts are mandatory, and a driving range is offered.

Fairbanks Ranch Country Club (15150 San Dieguito Rd., Rancho Santa Fe, tel. 619/259–8811), with 18 holes, 7,246 yards, offers a driving range and equipment rentals.

La Costa Hotel and Spa (Costa del Mar Rd., Carlsbad, tel. 619/438–9111 or 800/854–6564), with 36 holes and a driving range; reservations are required, golf carts are mandatory, and lodging is offered.

La Jolla Country Club (High Ave. Ext., La Jolla, tel. 619/454–9601), with 18 holes, 6,671 yards, offers a driving range and equipment rentals.

Pauma Valley Country Club (Hwy. 76, Pauma Valley, tel. 619/742–3721), with 18 holes, 7,004 yards, honors other memberships; a driving range and equipment rentals are offered.

Rancho Santa Fe Golf Club (La Granada, Rancho Santa Fe, tel. 619/756–3094) has 18 holes, 6,734 yards; equipment rentals are offered.

San Diego Country Club (88 L St., Chula Vista, tel. 619/422–8895) has 18 holes, 6,788 yards; a driving range is offered.
Handlery Hotel & Country Club (950 Hotel Circle, San Diego, tel. 619/298–0511), with 27 holes, honors other memberships and offers a driving range, equipment rentals, and lodging.
Stoneridge Country Club (17166 Stoneridge Country Club La., Poway, tel. 619/487–2117), with 18 holes, 6,407 yards, honors other memberships; golf carts are mandatory, and a driving range and equipment rentals are offered.

Hang Gliding

The **Torrey Pines Glider Port,** perched on the cliffs overlooking the ocean just north of La Jolla, is one of the most spectacular—and easiest—spots to hang glide in the world. However, it is definitely for experienced pilots only. Hang-gliding lessons are available from **Hang Gliding Center** (tel. 619/450–9008) and **Ultimate High Aviation** (tel. 619/748–1739), among others. For general information about the gliderport, contact the Torrey Pines Hang Gliders Association (tel. 619/457–9093).

Horseback Riding

Expensive insurance has severely cut the number of stables offering horses for rent in San Diego County. The businesses that remain offer a wide variety of organized excursions. **Holidays on Horseback** (tel. 619/445–3997) in the East County town of Descanso leads rides ranging from a few hours to a few days in the Cuyamaca Mountains. It rents special, easy-to-ride fox trotters to make it a little easier for beginners. **Rancho San Diego Stables** (tel. 619/670–1861) is located near Spring Valley. South of Imperial Beach, near the Mexican border, **Hilltop Stables** (tel. 619/428–5441), and **Sandi's Rental Stables** (tel. 619/424–3124) lead rides through Border Field State Park.

Hunting

It is illegal to hunt in most areas of San Diego County. For information about regulations, areas, limits, and seasons, contact the San Diego Division of the California Department of Fish and Game (1350 Front St., Room 2041, San Diego 92101, tel. 619/237–7311).

Jet Skis

Waveless Mission Bay and the small Snug Harbor Marina (tel. 619/434–3089), just east of the intersection of Tamarack Avenue and Interstate 5 in Carlsbad, are the favorite spots. Jet Skis can be launched from most beaches, though they need to be ridden beyond surf lines, and some beaches have special regulations. In the Mission Bay area, Jet Skis can be rented from **Jet Ski Rentals** (tel. 619/276–9200). **Seaforth Boat Rentals** (tel. 619/223–1681) rents Jet Skis for use in the South Bay Marina, and they are also available at Snug Harbor in Carlsbad.

Jogging

There is no truth to the rumor that San Diego was created to be one big jogging track. But it often seems that way. From downtown, the most popular run is along the Embarcadero, which stretches around the bay. There are nice, uncongested sidewalks through most of the area. The alternative for downtown visitors is to head east to Balboa Park, where a labyrinth of trails snake through the canyons. Mission Bay may be the most popular jogging spot, renowned for its wide sidewalks and basically flat landscape. Trails head west around Fiesta Island from Mission Bay, providing distance as well as a scenic route. The beaches, of course, are extremely popular with runners. But there is no reason to go where everyone else goes. Running is one of the best ways to explore San Diego, especially along the coast. There are organized runs almost every weekend; check any local sporting goods store for more information. Some tips: Don't run in bike lanes, and check the local newspaper's tide charts before heading to the beach.

Off-Road Vehicles

The 500,000 acres of the Anza-Borrego Desert State Park are now off-limits to off-road vehicles (in other words, these vehicles have to be kept on the roads), but the 14,000-acre Ocotillo Wells State Vehicular Recreation Area (tel. 619/767–5391) provides plenty of room to ride around in dune buggies and on motorcycles and three-wheel vehicles. It can be reached by following Highway 78 east from Julian.

Sailing

The city that spawned America's Cup winner Dennis Connor is perfect for sailing. The winds are consistent, especially during the winter. If you're bringing your boat to San Diego, there are several marinas that rent slips to the public, including the **Best Western Shelter Island Marina Inn** (2051 Shelter Island Dr., tel. 619/222–0561 or 800/325–5500), the **Dana Inn and Marina** (1710 W. Mission Bay Dr., tel. 619/222–6440 or 800/532–3737), the **Half Moon Inn** (2303 Shelter Island Dr., tel. 619/224–3411 or 800/854–2900), **Hyatt Islandia** (1441 Quivera Rd., tel. 619/224–1234), the **San Diego Marriott** (333 W. Harbor Dr., tel. 619/234–1500 or 800/351–3600), the **Kona Kai Club** (1551 Shelter Island Dr., tel. 619/222–1191), and the **Sunroad Resort Marina** (955 Harbor Island Dr. E, tel. 619/574–0736). Both the **San Diego Yacht Club** (1011 Anchorage La., tel. 619/222–1103) and the **Southwestern Yacht Club** (2702 Qualtrough Ave., tel. 619/222–0438) have reciprocal arrangements with other yacht clubs.

If you left the boat at home, boats of various sizes and shapes, from small paddleboats to sleek 12-meters, can be rented from the **Bahia Resort Hotel** (998 W. Mission Bay Dr., tel. 619/488–0551), the **Catamaran Resort Hotel** (3999 Mission Blvd., tel. 619/488–1081), **Harbor Sailboats** (2040 Harbor Island Dr., tel. 619/291–9568), the **Hotel Del Coronado** (1500 Orange Ave., Coronado, tel. 619/435–6611), the **Hyatt Islandia** (1441 Quivera Rd., tel. 619/224–1234), the **Mission Bay Sports Center** (1010 Santa Clara Pl., tel. 619/488–1004), and **Seaforth Boat Rental** (1641 Quivera Rd., tel. 619/223–1681).

If you are interested in leaving the sailing to others, charters with full crews can be arranged through **The Charter Connection** (7045 Charmant Dr., #2, tel. 619/552–1002), **Finest City Yacht Charters** (2742 Brant St., tel. 619/299–2248), **Fraser Charters, Inc.** (2353 Shelter Island Dr., tel. 619/225–0588), and **Hornblower Party Yachts** (Box 1140, Coronado, tel. 619/435–

2211). **Harbor Sailboats** (2040 Harbor Island Dr., Suite 118, San Diego, tel. 619/291–9568) and the **Mission Bay Sports Center** (tel. 619/488–1004) offer lessons. For general information, including tips on overnight anchoring, contact the Harbor Police (tel. 619/291–3900).

Skiing

Have breakfast on the beach and ski in the afternoon. Several ski resorts are within a two- to four-hour drive. In the Big Bear Lake area, in the San Bernardino Mountains east of Los Angeles, **Goldmine** (tel. 714/585–2517), **Snow Summit** (tel. 714/866–5753), and **Snow Valley** (tel. 714/867–2751 or 714/233–5307) usually have good snow December through April. Both are accessible by following Interstate 15 north to Interstate 10 east. Farther to the north, about an eight-hour drive away, **Mammoth Mountain** earns its name—it's one of the largest facilities in the west. Bus trips and junkets are constantly being organized to make the drive easier. Check with any of the local sporting goods stores, most of which will also offer equipment for rent.

Surfing

In San Diego, surfing is a year-round sport (thanks to wet suits in the winter) for people of all ages. Surprisingly, it's not hard to learn. Anyone can get on a board and paddle around. For the hardcore, some of the most popular surfing spots are the Ocean Beach pier, Tourmaline Surfing Park in La Jolla, Windansea Beach in La Jolla, South Cardiff State Beach, and Swami's (Sea Cliff Roadside Park) in Encinitas. (*See* Chapter 4 for directions.) Be aware that most public beaches have separate areas for surfers.

Many local surf shops rent boards, including **Star Surfing Company** (tel. 619/273–7827) in Pacific Beach and **La Jolla Surf Systems** (tel. 619/456–2777) and **Hansen's Sporting Goods** (tel. 619/753–6595) in Encinitas.

Swimming

If the ocean is too cold and salty, there are several public pools open for those interested in getting in a few laps. The most spectacular pool in town is the **Mission Beach Plunge,** (3115 Ocean Front Walk, tel. 619/488–3110), in Belmont Park, where the public can swim from 3:30 to 8 on weekdays and from 8 to 4 on weekends. Admission is $2. The **Copley Family YMCA** (3901 Landis St., tel. 619/283–2251) and the **Downtown YMCA** (500 W. Broadway Ave., tel. 619/232–7451) are both centrally located. The **Magdalena Ecke YMCA** (200 Saxony Rd., Encinitas, tel. 619/942–9622) is convenient for visitors to the North County.

Tennis

There are more than 1,300 courts spread around the county, most of them in private clubs. But there are a few public facilities. **Morley Field** (tel. 619/298–0920), in Balboa Park, has 25 courts, 12 of which are lighted. Nonmembers, however, cannot make reservations, so it's first come, first served. There is a nominal fee for use of the courts. The **La Jolla Recreation Center** (tel. 619/454–2071) offers nine public courts near downtown La Jolla, five of them lighted. Use of the courts is free. There are 12 lighted courts at **Robb Field** (tel. 619/224–7581) in Ocean Beach, with a small day-use fee.

The list of hotel complexes with tennis facilities includes the **Bahia Resort Hotel** (tel. 619/488–0551), the **Hotel Del Coronado** (tel. 619/435–6611), the **Kona Kai Beach and Tennis Resort** (tel. 619/222–1191), **Hilton San Diego** (tel. 619/276–4010), the **La Costa Hotel and Spa** (tel. 619/438–9111), and the **Rancho Bernardo Inn and Country Club** (tel. 619/487–1611). Intense tennis instruction is available at **John Gardiner's Rancho Valencia Resort** (tel. 619/756–1123 or 800/548–3664) in Rancho Santa Fe. Some of the larger private clubs are **Atlas Health Club** (tel. 619/298–9321), **San Diego Country Estates** (tel. 619/789–3826), **San Diego Tennis and Racquet Club** (tel. 619/275–3270), and **Tennis La Jolla** (tel. 619/459–0869).

Volleyball

Many of the community centers and local schools offer indoor volleyball programs. Contact the San Diego Parks and Recreation Department (tel. 619/236–5740) for more information. Ocean Beach, South Mission Beach, Del Mar, and Moonlight Beach are the most popular congregating points for beach volleyball enthusiasts. A warning: The competition can be fierce. Some of the best players in the world can show up on any given day.

Waterskiing

Mission Bay is one of the most popular waterskiing areas in Southern California. It is best to get out early when the water is smooth and the crowds are small. In Carlsbad, the **Snug Harbor Marina** (tel. 619/434–3089) is small, but off the beaten path. Boats and equipment can be rented from **Seaforth Boat Rentals** (1641 Quivera Rd., near Mission Bay, tel. 619/223–1681). The private **San Diego and Mission Bay Boat and Ski Club** (2606 N. Mission Bay Dr., tel. 619/276–0830) operates a slalom course and ski jump in Mission Bay's Hidden Anchorage. Permission from the club or the Mission Bay Harbor Patrol (tel. 619/224–1862) must be obtained to use the course and jump.

One of the few lakes in the county allowing waterskiing is **Lake San Vicente** (tel. 619/562–1042), located north of Lakeside off Interstate 8.

Windsurfing

Also known as sailboarding, this is a sport best practiced on smooth waters like Mission Bay or the Snug Harbor Marina at the intersection of Interstate 5 and Tamarack Avenue in Carlsbad. It is a tricky sport to learn, but it can be a lot of fun for novices as well as experts. Rentals and instruction are available at the **Bahia Resort Hotel** (998 W. Mission Bay Dr., tel. 619/488–0551), **California Pacific Sailing Sports** (2211 Pacific Beach Dr., tel. 619/270–3211), the **Catamaran Resort Hotel** (3999 Mission Blvd., tel. 619/488–1001), **Mission Bay Sports Center** (tel. 619/488–1004), the **San Diego Sailing Center** (1010 Santa Clara Pl., tel. 619/488–0651), and **Windsport** (844 W.

Mission Bay Dr., tel. 619/488–0612), all in the Mission Bay area. The **Snug Harbor Marina** (4215 Harrison St., Carlsbad, tel. 619/434–3089) also offers rentals and instruction. More experienced windsurfers will enjoy taking a board out on the ocean. Wave jumping is especially popular at the Tourmaline Surfing Park in La Jolla and in the Del Mar area.

Spectator Sports

San Diego doesn't have a professional basketball franchise, ever since the Clippers left for Los Angeles, but it has just about every other type of sporting team and event, including a few exclusive to the area. For information on tickets to any event, contact **Teleseat** (tel. 619/452–7328). **San Diego Jack Murphy Stadium** is located at the intersection of interstates 8 and 805.

Baseball

From April through September, the **San Diego Padres** (tel. 619/280–4494) slug it out for bragging rights in the National League West. Matchups with such rivals as the hated Los Angeles Dodgers and San Francisco Giants usually are the highlights of the home season at San Diego Jack Murphy Stadium. Tickets range from $4 to $9.50 and usually are readily available, unless the Padres are in the thick of the pennant race.

Basketball

No pro team, but the San Diego State University Aztecs (tel. 619/283–7378), under Coach Jim Brandenburg, are quickly gaining national prominence. The Aztecs, competing in the Western Athletic Conference with such powers as the University of Texas at El Paso and Brigham Young University, play at the San Diego Sports Arena (tel. 619/224–4171) December through March.

The University of San Diego (tel. 619/260–4600), playing in the West Coast Athletic Conference with schools like the University of San Francisco and the University of California at Santa Barbara, has earned trips to the NCAA national tournament and competes with the top teams in the country.

Dog Racing

The anorexic-looking greyhounds chase the electric bunny around the Agua Caliente track nightly, except Tuesday. The track offers a wide variety of gambling gimmicks, which keeps the action lively. Take Interstate 5 south to the border and follow the signs to Agua Caliente (tel. 706/685–1612).

Football

The **San Diego Chargers** (tel. 619/280–2111) have been one of the National Football League's most exciting teams since the merger with the American Football League. The Chargers were one of the original AFL franchises, originally based in Los Angeles. They fill San Diego Jack Murphy Stadium August through December. Games with AFC West rivals Los Angeles Raiders and Denver Broncos are always particularly intense.

Tailgating, partying in the parking lot before the game, is an accepted tradition.

The San Diego State University Aztecs compete in the exciting Western Athletic Conference. The biggest game of the year is always a showdown with Brigham Young University. The winner of the WAC plays in the **Holiday Bowl** (tel. 619/283–5808), always known as one of the most exciting bowl games, renowned for its exciting finishes. The big bowl game is played near the end of December in San Diego Jack Murphy Stadium, which is where the Aztecs play home games.

Golf

The La Costa Hotel and Spa (tel. 619/438–9111) hosts the prestigious **Tournament of Champions** in January, featuring the winners of the previous year's tournaments. The **Shearson-Lehman Brothers Open** brings the pros to the Torrey Pines Municipal Golf Course (tel. 619/453–0380). The Stoneridge Country Club (tel. 619/487–2117) hosts the **Ladies Professional Golf Association** in the spring.

Horse Racing

Begun 50 years ago by Bing Crosby, Pat O'Brien, and their Hollywood cronies, the annual summer meeting of the **Del Mar Thoroughbred Club** (tel. 619/755–1141), located on the Del Mar Fairgrounds—"Where the Turf Meets the Surf" in Del Mar— attracts a horde of Beautiful People, along with the best horses and jockeys in the country. The meeting begins in July and continues through early September, every day except Tuesday. But that is not the end of horse racing action in Del Mar. The Del Mar Fairgrounds also serves as a satellite wagering facility with betting on races on television from tracks throughout California. Take Interstate 5 north to the Via de la Valle Road exit (tel. 619/755–1161 for daily information).

Agua Caliente Racetrack (tel. 011/52–686–2002), in Tijuana, also offers pari-mutuel wagering on horse racing year-round on Saturday and Sunday. Horse players will tell you the quality of the horses and jockeys isn't as good as those at the California tracks, but the competition—and payoffs—are just as good. Enter Tijuana by following Interstate 5 south to the border and then follow the signs to Agua Caliente.

Jai Alai

Sort of like handball, with gunlike baskets used instead of hands, it is often called the world's fastest game. You can also bet on it. Some of the best players in Mexico compete at the Fronton Palacio on Avenida Revolución in Tijuana (tel. 011/52–685–1612) nightly, except Thursday, beginning at 8 PM.

Over-the-Line

As much a giant beach party as a sport, the game is a form of beach softball played with three-person teams. Every July, the world championships are held on Fiesta Island, with two weekends of wild beer drinking and partying. Some good athletes take part in the games, too. Admission is free, but parking and traffic around Mission Bay become unbearable. Call the Old

Mission Beach Athletic Club (tel. 619/688–0817) for more information.

Sailing

The **America's Cup XXVIII** races will be held in San Diego in May 1992. A series of competitions that began in January will decide which boat will defend the cup and which of the challengers will race it in the one-on-one finals. For information call 800/922–8792.

Soccer

The most successful professional franchise in town is the **San Diego Sockers** (tel. 619/224–GOAL) indoor soccer team. The team has dominated the game, which is a fast-paced combination of soccer and hockey, winning championships in the defunct North American Soccer League and the current Major Indoor Soccer League. Games are raucous, since San Diegans love to support their Sockers. The season runs October through May at the San Diego Sports Arena (tel. 619/224–4171). Take the Rosecrans exit from Interstate 5 west to Sports Arena Boulevard and turn right.

Volleyball

The U.S. men's and women's teams are based in San Diego. For information about competitions or practices, call 619/692–4162.

6 Dining

by David Nelson

A San Diego resident, David Nelson writes restaurant reviews for the San Diego edition of the Los Angeles Times.

San Diego certainly is a restaurant town in the sense that it offers one of the highest per capita ratios of dining places to population in the country; at last count, there were some 4,000 food-service establishments in San Diego County. But it is not yet an eating capital in the style of Los Angeles and New York, where good or excellent restaurant meals are taken for granted.

Almost any style of cooking can be found in San Diego, although quality varies. More and more good restaurants open every year, however, and a city that once stood solidly in the meat-and-potatoes camp now boasts Afghan, Thai, Vietnamese, and other exotic cuisines in addition to the more familiar French, Italian, and Chinese. Visitors naturally seek out Mexican restaurants, of which there are hundreds, but most of these serve California-style Mexican dishes, which have little to do with the excellent cuisine prepared south of the border. Take heart, though—there are good ones, and all are accessible, moderately priced, and informal.

The city's gastronomic reputation rests primarily on its seafood, which is so popular that even modest restaurants make a point of offering several fish specials daily. You are never more than a stone's throw from one or more seafood restaurants in San Diego. Bear in mind, though, that better restaurants offer better seafood dishes. As is true elsewhere, restaurants endowed with spectacular views—and there are many such in San Diego—often invest far more effort in washing the picture windows than in cooking.

The rules of dining out in San Diego are simple and pleasant. Most eateries serve lunch and dinner; breakfast is largely the province of hotels and coffee shops. Most restaurants accept reservations, but few require them, and waits are uncommon outside the beach areas. Dress codes, by and large, do not exist beyond simple shirt and shoes requirements, except at a handful of top restaurants that require men to wear jackets. City natives like to dine around 7:30 PM, and it is at that hour that restaurants will be the most crowded. Few restaurants offer seating past 9:30 or 10 PM.

A good *cheap* meal has become a rare commodity in San Diego. Cafeterias do not exist here, and except for chain establishments (the same places you will find in Boise, Buffalo, and Bangor), there are relatively few coffee shops or family-style places. The best areas in which to find well-prepared, inexpensive meals are in off-the-beaten-track neighborhoods, such as the Convoy Street district in Kearny Mesa, where virtually every sort of Oriental cuisine can be found.

The principal restaurant locations are in the renovated downtown area; in historic Old Town, site of the first settlement and close to the downtown area; in the beach neighborhoods; and in exclusive La Jolla, a lovely resort area that slopes from the top of Mt. Soledad to the sea and attracts jet-setters and trend setters from around the globe. Mission Valley, which remains a tourist center thanks to its concentration of hotels, sprouts restaurants like weeds, but is a virtual desert when it comes to high-quality cuisine. A similar caveat must be offered about the large, tourist-oriented eateries on Shelter and Harbor islands, which, in effect, rent out their enjoyable views and lively atmospheres by charging hefty prices for mediocre food.

Anthony's Star of the
Sea Room, **29**

Avanti, **8**

The Belgian Lion, **20**

Cafe Pacifica, **26**

Casa de Pico, **25**

Chart House at the
San Diego Rowing
Club, **39**

Croce's, **36**

Dobson's, **35**

El Crab Catcher, **11**

Firehouse Beach
Cafe, **14**

Fisherman's Grill, **4**

George's at the
Cove, **1**

Guadalajara Grill, **23**

Harbor House, **38**

Hard Rock Cafe, **6**

Hotel Del
Coronado, **41**

Issimo, **13**

Karinya, **17**

La Gran Tapa, **33**

La Valencia Hotel, **3**

L'Escargot, **12**

Manhattan, **7**

Marius, **42**

McCormick and
Schmick's, **15**

Old Columbia Brewery
& Grill, **32**

Old Town Mexican
Cafe, **27**

Pacifica Grill, **31**

Panda Inn, **34**

Peohe's, **40**

Piatti, **10**

Rainwater's, **30**

Rancho Valencia, **22**

Red Sails Inn, **28**

Salmon House, **19**

Salvatore's, **37**

Saska's, **18**

Spice Rack, **16**

The Spot, **9**

St. James Bar, **21**

Star of India, **5**

Top O' the Cove, **2**

Yakitori II, **24**

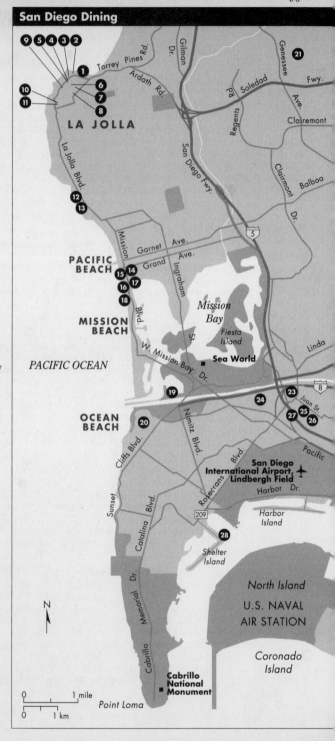

San Diego Dining

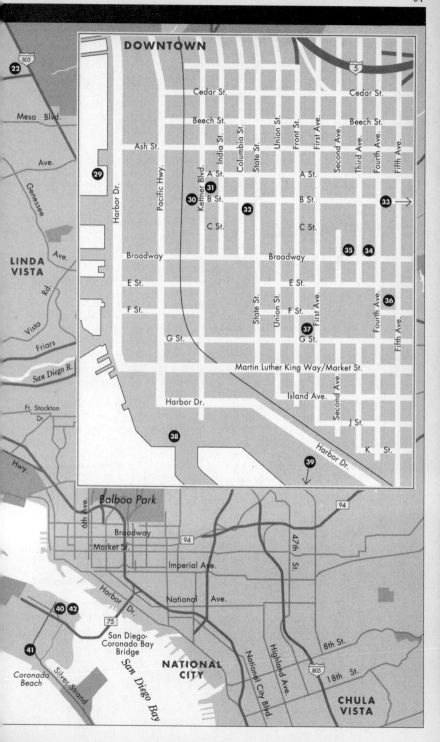

Restaurants are grouped first by location and then by type of cuisine. The most highly recommended restaurants in each price category are indicated by a star ★.

Category	Cost*
Very Expensive	over $35
Expensive	$25–$35
Moderate	$15–$25
Inexpensive	under $15

per person, without tax (6.5%), service, or drinks

The following abbreviations for credit cards have been used: AE, American Express; DC, Diner's Club; MC, MasterCard; V, Visa.

Downtown

American **Dobson's.** Consciously San Franciscan in style, Dobson's at-
★ tracts the city's power structure during the day and well-
heeled performing arts patrons at night. The menu changes
daily and is uniformly excellent, beginning with the always-
available mussel bisque and continuing with superb fish, veal,
fowl, and beef entrees. The service and wine list also approach
perfection. *956 Broadway Circle, tel. 619/231–6771. Reservations suggested. Dress: for success. AE, MC, V. No lunch Sat.
Closed Sun. Very Expensive.*

Chinese **Panda Inn.** Clean, graceful lines and fine works of art replace
★ the paper lanterns and garish dragons that decorate most Chinese eateries, but, better yet, this is a place to which you can
take visiting Chinese friends with utter confidence. Thanks to
superior kitchen and service staffs, this is not only the city's
best Chinese restaurant, but one of its best restaurants, period. Its location in Horton Plaza, downtown San Diego's shopping and entertainment hub, makes it a natural place to stop for
"burnt" pork, sensational hot and pungent chicken and shrimp,
succulent steamed dumplings, ridiculously delicious Szechuan-
style green beans, and first-rate Peking duck. *506 Horton Plaza, tel. 619/233–7800. Reservations accepted. Dress: casual.
AE, MC, V. Inexpensive.*

Continental **Croce's.** Thanks to its adjoining jazz cave, this rather funky bistro can be one of the liveliest restaurants in town. Situated in
the historic Gaslamp Quarter and operated by the widow of late
pop singer Jim Croce (the place is crammed with Croce memorabilia), this restaurant offers excellent pastas, good fish, and
several fine Russian-Jewish dishes, including a knockout
braised beef brisket with *tzimmes*, a casserole of sweet potatoes, and *kasha varnishkes*, buckwheat groats with bow-tie
noodles. Blintzes and similar fare are a specialty at lunch. *802
Fifth Ave., tel. 619/233–4355. Reservations unnecessary.
Dress: casual. MC, V. Inexpensive.*

Italian **Salvatore's.** Situated in the lush, luxurious Meridian tower,
★ Salvatore's makes the most of its surroundings and is a sophisticated milieu in which to lunch or dine. The Roman-born owners present a typically Roman menu, which is to say pan-
Italian, with regional specialties from the tip of the Italian boot

to the creamy, buttery pastas of the northernmost provinces. Presentations are spectacular; for a dish of edible beauty, try the Caterina di Medici salad or the excellent grilled swordfish, 100garnished to look like a pineapple. The pastas are uniformly superior. *750 Front St., tel. 619/544–1865. Reservations accepted. Dress for la dolce vita. AE, MC, V. No lunch Sat. Closed Sun. Expensive.*

Japanese   **Yakitori II.** Sidle up to the sushi bar and take a long gander at the display case filled with raw fish filets, cooked shrimp, eel and octopus, various exotic vegetables and seaweed, and order a sampler plate of freshly prepared, delicately seasoned tidbits. You, too, will find yourself saying, "I guess we're not in Kansas anymore!" But the sushi is just an optional opener to a traditional Japanese meal that can include the deep-fried morsels called tempura; teriyaki beef and chicken; and carefully grilled, delicately flavored salmon. *3740 Sports Arena Blvd., Point Loma, tel. 619/223–2641. Reservations accepted for large parties only. Dress: casual. AE, MC, V. No lunch Sun. Inexpensive.*

Mixed Menu   **Old Columbia Brewery & Grill.** As the first microbrewery in San Diego, Old Columbia can be somewhat forgiven for paying more attention to its house brews than to its menu, a well-written but perfunctorily executed listing of snacks, burgers, salads, and entrees. The draw is the beer, tapped directly from tanks in the adjacent brewing room. The nibbles to go along with the Gaslamp Gold ale or the Downtown After Dark lager are beer-battered fish and chips, hefty onion rings, and oversize hamburgers. Downtown mingles here when the sun sets, and the action runs late. *1157 Columbia St., tel. 619/234–2739. Reservations accepted. Dress: casual. MC, V. Inexpensive.*

Seafood   **Anthony's Star of the Sea Room.** This formal and admittedly stodgy restaurant occupies a choice location on the Embarcadero and looks across the water to the twinkling lights of Point Loma. For better or worse, the place specializes in cart service and turns in a good performance with its abalone dishes and the sole Admiral. The selection of fresh fish is admirable, but go with the simpler preparations. This restaurant remains a favorite with longtime San Diegans and visitors. *1360 N. Harbor Dr., tel. 619/232–7408. Reservations suggested. Jacket and tie required. AE, MC, V. Dinner nightly except major holidays. Very Expensive.*

Harbor House. This very popular eatery serves so much seafood that it is a wonder that the oceans have not been depleted in the years since it opened. Although the place could coast on its location in jammed Seaport Village, it turns in a good-quality performance with its shellfish appetizers, creamy chowder, and a long list of daily fish specials, the majority of which are simply grilled over mesquite. *831 W. Harbor Dr., tel. 619/232–1141. Reservations accepted. Dress: informal. AE, MC, V. Moderate.*

Southwestern–Nouvelle   **Pacifica Grill.** If you've never had *canarditas* (and you probably haven't), this is the place to visit for juicy chunks of slowly cooked duck, which one garnishes with any of a dozen spicy or savory condiments and then rolls inside fresh, hot, blue corn tortillas. Since switching to the new Southwestern style of cooking, this ever-trendy restaurant has seen its popularity soar almost as high as the atrium that lights this beautifully remodeled warehouse. The place also serves superior seafood and wildly imaginative pastas. *1202 Kettner Blvd., tel. 619/696–9226. Reservations accepted. Dress: to be noticed. AE, DC, MC, V. No lunch weekends. Moderate.*

Spanish   **La Gran Tapa.** Carefully modeled to recall the fabled tapas bars that line the principal streets in Madrid, this noisy, busy in-spot prints up a daily menu of classic Spanish snacks and appetizers, with more substantial dishes and even an excellent hamburger thrown in for those who prefer traditional dining. The best bet is to order two or three tapas per person and let the whole table share. Choices include *empanadas* (spicy filled pies) made with pork and olives, or spinach and cheese, or whatever the chef has dreamed up; tiny fried squid; miniature shrimp croquettes; shrimp in garlic sauce; fresh, hot potato chips, and much more. A good spot for late-night dining. *611 B St., tel. 619/234–8272. Reservations suggested. Dress: casual. AE, MC, V. No lunch Sat. Closed Sun. Moderate.*

Steak and Seafood   **Rainwater's.** San Diego's answer to New York's Palm, this
★   Eastern-style chophouse is the place to find oversize steaks, lobsters, veal and pork chops, prime ribs, and a rich, savory black bean soup accented with Madeira. Side dishes get as much attention as main events, so zero in on the wispy shoe-string potatoes, giant baked Idahos, steaming tangles of fried onion rings, and the rich, satisfying creamed corn, all served in gargantuan portions. The wine list is also excellent. The mood is masculine and expansive, which makes it a favorite with movers, shakers, and deal-makers. *1202 Kettner Blvd. (second floor), tel. 619/233–5757. Reservations accepted. Dress: formal. AE, DC, MC, V. Weekday lunch, Sun. brunch. Very Expensive.*

Chart House at the San Diego Rowing Club. This popular establishment, part of a countywide chain, serves the quintessential Southern California menu that formerly was typical of most waterside eateries. In other words, meals start with a "portable" salad bar, brought to the table and prepared with simple greens, garnishes, and dressings. The menu gives equal emphasis to seafood, steaks, and prime ribs, all of which are prepared competently, but without flair. This place gets its primary appeal from its premises, a renovated former boat house that sits over the water. *525 E. Harbor Dr., tel. 619/233–7391. Reservations suggested. Dress: informal. AE, DC, MC, V. Moderate.*

Old Town

Mexican   **Casa de Pico.** The centerpiece of the Bazaar del Mundo shopping and dining complex, this colorful eatery is a mecca for tourists who come to eat beans until they nearly burst. All the traditional American–Mexican foods, such as burritos, enchiladas, quesadillas, and tostadas vie for space on the menu, and if one wants "safe," moderately seasoned Mexican fare, this is one of the prime locations in which to find it. *2754 Calhoun St., tel. 619/296–3267. Reservations unnecessary. Dress: very casual. AE, DC, MC, V. Inexpensive.*

Guadalajara Grill. Noisy and boisterous, this place only partly succeeds in re-creating the carnival atmosphere that enlivens its parent Guadalajara Grill in Tijuana. Still, the atmosphere has a certain Mexican flavor, as do some of the dishes, most notably the *fajitas*, highly seasoned strips of steak or chicken, and the *cochinita pibil*, a spicy pork stew. The margaritas are just average. *4105 Taylor St., tel. 619/295–5111. Reservations unnecessary. Dress: casual. AE, MC, V. Inexpensive.*

Old Town Mexican Cafe. This old standby looks a touch seedy, but the burritos, enchiladas, and *carne asada*, thin slices of grilled, marinated steak, are sufficiently satisfying that lines are common even during the middle of the afternoon. Carnitas and shredded beef tacos are two of the dishes responsible for this restaurant's popularity with locals and visitors. This restaurant serves late, which makes it a good place at which to satisfy a midnight taco craving. *2489 San Diego Ave., tel. 619/297–4330. Reservations accepted for groups. Dress: casual. AE, MC, V. Inexpensive.*

Seafood **Cafe Pacifica.** The menu changes daily to reflect the market availability of a globe-spanning selection of fish and shellfish, most of which presumably are very pleased to place themselves in Cafe Pacifica's competent hands. The approach is moderately nouvelle, which means that light, interesting sauces and imaginative garnishes are likely to be teamed with simply cooked fillets of salmon, sea bass, swordfish, and so forth. Consider oysters and smoked fish as good opening courses, and don't miss the indulgent crème brûlée dessert. *2414 San Diego Ave., tel. 619/291–6666. Reservations accepted. Dress: thoughtfully informal. AE, DC, MC, V. No lunch weekends. Moderate.*

Beaches

American **Firehouse Beach Cafe.** The great attractions here are the casual beach ambience, the sun deck that allows a leisurely meal in full view of the nearby Pacific, and an acceptably prepared menu of sandwiches, seafood, steaks, and other simple American fare. *722 Grand Ave., tel. 619/272–1999. No reservations. Wear anything that fits reasonably well. AE, MC, V. Inexpensive.*

Spice Rack. A longtime beach favorite for its hearty breakfasts and home-baked rolls and pastries, this restaurant offers a pleasant, if viewless, patio for lunching on San Diego's many sunny days. The lunch and dinner menus run to complicated sandwiches and formal beef, chicken, and fish entrees, but regard the Spice Rack as a good bet for omelets and other egg dishes at breakfast or lunch. *4315 Mission Blvd., tel. 619/483–7666. Reservations accepted for dinner only. Dress: casual. AE, MC, V. Inexpensive.*

French **The Belgian Lion.** A somewhat fusty, ugly duckling of a restau★ rant, The Belgian Lion serves one of the best roast ducklings to be found in the city, along with marvelous creamy soups, excellent braised sweetbreads, poached salmon in a delicious sorrel sauce, sauerkraut braised in champagne with smoked meats and sausages, and a rich cassoulet. The service and wine list are worthy of the menu, and although the decor lacks that certain *je ne sais quoi*, the place has a great deal of charm. *2265 Bacon St., tel. 619/223–2700. Reservations suggested. Dress: casual. AE, DC, MC, V. Closed Sun. and Mon. Expensive.*

Seafood **McCormick and Schmick's.** Upon its opening in early 1988, this ★ excellent seafood house offered a serious challenge to the city's older fish eateries. The menu changes frequently and may include as many as 100 options, all uniformly well prepared and ranging from a lovely selection of fresh oysters to entire Dungeness crabs, a fine crab-and-salmon Newburg, grilled baby salmon, and just about everything else that swims, crawls, or ruminates under the waves. The service is good, the upstairs courtyard pleasant, and a few choice tables have ocean views. An especially good choice for a lazy, self-indulgent lunch. *4190 Mission Blvd., tel. 619/581–3938. Reservations suggested. Dress: casual. AE, DC, MC, V. Moderate.*

Salmon House. As the name implies, this handsome, waterfront restaurant specializes in salmon, grilled over alder wood in the style developed by the Indians of the northwest. Offerings run to other fish, prime ribs, and chicken, but the one real reason to visit this establishment is for the salmon, which *is* hard to top. *1970 Quivera Rd., tel. 619/223–2234. Reservations accepted. Dress: casual. AE, DC, MC, V. Moderate.*

Red Sails Inn. This is not technically at the beach, since it is on the San Diego Bay side of Point Loma. It's an old favorite with old salts, though, and a natural for anyone in search of good, simple seafood at a waterfront location. The restaurant is surrounded by yacht basins and thus enjoys a large following among nautical types, who especially treasure its hearty, all-American breakfasts and late-night snacks. *2614 Shelter Island Dr., tel. 619/223–3030. Reservations for large parties only. Dress: casual. AE, DC, MC, V. Inexpensive.*

Steak and Seafood **Saska's.** Walk through the doors and you're in the genuine heart of Old Mission Beach, whose lazy pulse still throbs here when the conversation in the bar turns to sports, especially San Diego's peculiar form of baseball called over-the-line. The food is simple but first rate; choices include shellfish cocktails, a fine crab chowder, the fresh fish offerings of the day (simply but beautifully grilled), and some of the best steaks in town. This is the only place that serves a full, quality menu until 3 AM nightly. *3768 Mission Blvd., tel. 619/488–7311. Reservations accepted. The waiters wear shorts, and you can, too. AE, DC, MC, V. No lunch weekdays. Moderate.*

Thai **Karinya.** Designed and operated by a Thai architect, Karinya is rather soothingly pretty while still every bit as casual as the most beachy beachgoer could desire (and in San Diego, that's pretty casual). Start with the spicy salad called *larb* and the sweet noodles called *mee krob*, and then move along to the tart, savory *tom yum gai* soup. The entree list gets hot and spicy with the curries (the beef *penang nuah*, and a fiery blend of shrimp and pineapple), and turns mild with myriad noodle dishes. Everything is quite, quite good, including the service. *4475 Mission Blvd., tel. 619/270–5050. Reservations accepted. Dress: Jeans will suffice. AE, MC, V. No lunch weekends. Closed Mon. Inexpensive.*

La Jolla

American **La Valencia Hotel.** Depending how you count them, there are from three to five dining rooms in La Jolla's famed and oh-so-fashionable "pink palace." Some locals just about live in the Whaling Bar dining room, which is why local shorthand designates the hotel "La V." Romantics will want to ascend the narrow tower to the Sky Room, however, which has the best (mostly French, and rather well done) food in the hotel, as well as a view of the Pacific that stretches into infinity. The downstairs rooms feature better lunches than dinners, but in any case, keep the seafood and poultry in mind. *1132 Prospect St.,* *tel. 619/454–0771. Reservations suggested. Dress: casual. AE, DC, MC, V. Moderate–Expensive.*

The Spot. As much a La Jolla tradition as the Hotel La Valencia, but at the exact opposite end of the scale, this place is popular with just about everybody for its easy, comfortable menu of burgers, ribs, sandwiches, and pizza; its ever-so-casual atmosphere; and its late-night dining. *1005 Prospect St., tel. 619/459–0809. Reservations accepted. Whatever you're wearing will be just dandy. AE, DC, MC, V. Inexpensive.*

California

★ **George's at the Cove.** A lovely, art-filled dining room, excellent service, a good view of La Jolla Cove and an imaginative, well-prepared menu make this one of the city's best restaurants. Pay special attention to the seafood, but the pasta, beef, and veal dishes and poultry specialties are also uniformly excellent. Desserts are outsized, grandiose, and irresistible. *1250 Prospect St., tel. 619/454–4244. Reservations suggested. Dress chicly because everyone else is sure to be. AE, DC, MC, V. Expensive.*

French

St. James Bar. A new offering from leading San Diego restaurateur Paul Dobson, the St. James Bar is a magnet for the area business folk at lunch and the glitterati at night. All are drawn by the creamy mussel bisque, the sweetbreads in truffle juice sauce, the delicate poached Norwegian salmon in saffron sauce, and other beautifully realized offerings. One of the city's top five eateries, it offers expert cuisine in a luxurious setting that includes marble floors, art from a top gallery, and an incongruous but handsome 100-year-old bar rescued from a Montana saloon. *4370 La Jolla Village Dr., tel. 619/453–6650. Reservations suggested. Dress: casual. AE, MC, V. No lunch Sat., closed Sun. Very Expensive.*

★ **Top O' the Cove.** More or less synonymous with romance, Top O' the Cove has been the scene of thousands of marriage proposals in its 35-year history. Yet another place that boasts an extravagant view of La Jolla Cove, it also boasts a competent kitchen that turns out beautifully garnished, luxury fare dressed with creamy and well-seasoned sauces. The menu hits all the bases—beef, veal, fowl, and seafood—but pay special attention to the nightly specials. The decor is lush, and the wine list, with more than 800 entries, the recipient of countless awards. *1216 Prospect St., tel. 619/454–7779. Reservations advised. Jacket and tie suggested. AE, MC, V. Very Expensive.*

L'Escargot. Yes, you've guessed it, this tiny hideaway in the Bird Rock district makes much of snails (escargot) and offers them in some 20 appetizer variations. To make something of a running joke of the situation, it also offers rich chocolate snails for dessert. In between these extremes lies some very solid, traditional French cooking, performed with flair by chef/proprietor Pierre Lustrat. Fresh fish, veal, beef, and duck dishes are equally rich and appealing. Skip the chocolate snails and instead order Lustrat's *tarte tatin* (upside-down apple tart) for dessert. He is so justly proud of it that his personalized license plates read "MA TATIN." *5662 La Jolla Blvd., tel. 619/459–6066. Reservations advised. Jacket suggested. AE, MC, V. Closed for lunch. Expensive.*

Indian

Star of India. As do so many other chic, big-city neighborhoods, La Jolla hosts a good selection of upscale ethnic eateries. The Star of India is a case in point: Grander and more expensive than the city's other Indian houses, it also offers a better selection of dishes and a more talented kitchen staff. In addition to all the typical curries and kebabs, the menu offers several tandoori meats (baked in a special, superheated oven), quite a number of vegetarian dishes, and a superb selection of freshly prepared Indian breads. *1025 Prospect St., tel. 619/459–3355. Reservations accepted. Dress: casual. DC, MC, V. Moderate.*

Italian   **Issimo.** La Jolla is blessed in its restaurants, and Issimo is third
★   in its trilogy of stars. Beautifully arranged plates are served in grand style in a small jewel box of a dining room. Start with a pasta or the incredible, homemade pâté de foie gras (yes, this is an Italian place, but the foie gras is fabulous), and then move along to a dandy osso buco, a wonderful plate of baby lamb chops, a fine veal sauté, or a steak in a delicate sauce. This restaurant also speaks seafood fluently, and the desserts rival those made by the finest European pastry chefs. *5634 La Jolla Blvd., tel. 619/454–7004. Reservations advised. Jacket suggested. MC, V. Closed Sun. Very Expensive.*

Avanti. For staid, old La Jolla, this starkly modern restaurant, with its mirrored ceiling and white and black and chrome interior design, comes as a refreshing surprise. Which explains why it is such a popular meeting place for trendy, successful natives looking for some sophisticated fun, with cuisine to match. An open-to-view kitchen lets you watch Chef John Cooke prepare such appetite-arousing dishes as tiny pasta rings mixed with ricotta and pistachios; scampi sauteed in olive oil, minced garlic, and white wine; beef fillet topped with a porcini mushroom sauce; and chicken breasts grilled with radicchio. Counting calories? There's a spa menu, too. *875 Prospect Ave., tel. 619/454–4288. Reservations advised. Dress: thoughtfully informal. AE, MC, V. Closed for lunch. Expensive.*

★   **Delicias.** Upon opening in 1990, this bright and cheerful trattoria was adopted by the natives of the tiny, pastoral village of Rancho Santa Fe (just east of La Jolla) as their local clubhouse. Wolfgang Puck acted as consultant in drawing up a Spago-like menu and training the chef, and the results include excellent pizza and calzone straight from a wood-burning oven, and, of course, a wide range of pastas and salads using fresh-daily ingredients from nearby vegetable farms. The service here benefits from being so far away from Los Angeles's moonlighting-actor pool. *6106 Paseo Delicias, Rancho Santa Fe, tel. 619/759–1739. Reservations suggested. Dress: casual. Full bar. AE, MC, V. Moderate.*

Manhattan. This little slice of the Big Apple became an overnight success when it brought a chic, cosmopolitan atmosphere and a rather good list of upscale Italian preparations to laid-back but hungry La Jolla. The deep-fried calamari make an outstanding starter, and the selection of pastas includes both familiar favorites as well as some unusual, relatively exotic choices. The kitchen also does a good job with fish and shellfish, but, oddly enough, its way with beef easily surpasses its talents in the veal department. Try the excellent ice cream specialties for dessert. Although Manhattan is located in the Empress Hotel, it is under separate management. *7766 Fay Ave., tel. 619/454–1182. Reservations accepted. Jacket suggested. AE, MC, V. Closed weekends for lunch. Moderate.*

Piatti. Another recent link in this very popular mini-chain of trattorias that now extends from one end of California to the other. Good pizza, calzone, pasta and an excellent selection of antipasti in a let's-have-fun setting. All in all, *molto simpatico.*

2182 Avenida de La Playa. 619/454–1589. Reservations advised. Dress: casual. MC, V. Moderate.

Mexican **El Crab Catcher.** Although this spot is just one of many along San Diego's most fashionable restaurant row, its spectacular view of La Jolla Cove and casual Hawaiian atmosphere (yes, Hawaiian) make it a favorite. Specialties include numerous crab dishes, other shell- and fin-fish, and simple beef and chicken dishes. Get here in time for the sunset. *1298 Prospect St., tel. 619/454–9587. Reservations suggested. Dress: casual. AE, MC, V. Moderate.*

Mixed Menu **Rancho Valencia.** A 15-minute drive east of La Jolla, in the idyl-
★ lic residential hamlet of Rancho Santa Fe, is John Gardiner's latest and most luxurious tennis resort. Open to the public for dining, it is an atmospheric and gastronomic treat that should not be missed. Chef Claude Segal's California/French menu includes such superb dishes as: a Napoleon layered with fresh foi gras, venison with wild currents, John Dory wrapped in crispy scallions with a lobster sauce, and rich desserts that require five sets of tennis to work off. (There's an equally appetizing spa-diet menu for the strong of will.) *5921 Valencia Circle, tel. 619/756–1123. Reservations required. Dress: sports clothes during day, jacket and tie at night. Full bar. AE, DC, MC, V. Moderate–Very Expensive.*

★ **Hard Rock Cafe.** It seems that every other city has a Hard Rock Cafe, and, of course, San Diego has one, too. The local college students and teens are rejoicing, and even their elders crack a smile when they stroll into this monument to ground chuck and Chuck Berry. Designed as a museum of rock 'n roll memorabilia, the place features Elton John's "Tutti Frutti" suit, guitars used by Def Leppard and Pink Floyd, and a pink Cadillac crashing through the ceiling. Most diners ogle all this while munching on hefty burgers and fat onion rings, but if you take a close look at the menu, you'll also find excellent grilled fish, a fine, lime-marinated chicken, and homemade apple pie that almost matches Mom's. *909 Prospect St., tel. 619/454–5101. AE, MC, V. No reservations. Dress: casual. Inexpensive.*

Seafood **Fisherman's Grill.** The oyster bar serves up an exceptional selection of raw bivalves and shellfish cocktails, and the kitchen follows suit by offering creamy chowders, clever sandwiches, mesquite-broiled fish, and good old-fashioned deep-fried shrimp coated with a zesty beer batter. *7825 Fay Ave., tel. 619/456–3733. Reservations accepted. Dress: casual. AE, MC, V. Closed lunch Sat. Closed Sun. Inexpensive.*

Coronado

For all its charms, Coronado always comes up short on the gastronomic side of the balance sheet. It is possible to eat reasonably well here, however, and the three establishments suggested offer romance and spectacular architecture in addition to acceptable cooking.

American– **Hotel Del Coronado.** Still gleaming from the wash-and-brush-
Continental up it received for its 1988 centennial celebration, Coronado's Victorian jewel sparkles with an evanescent, miragelike quality. The hotel offers three dining rooms, of which the informal Ocean Terrace, with its outdoor seating, is a natural for hearty sandwiches and salads at lunch. The formal, somewhat stuffy Prince of Wales Room serves a standard list of French classics

at dinner and does them competently, if without exceptional flair. An American–Continental menu prevails in the soaring, magnificent Crown Room, which has hosted state dinners for presidents and visiting dignitaries, and was the scene of a famous banquet given in honor of Charles Lindbergh after his historic flight across the Atlantic. The prime ribs and fresh fish are the best Crown Room bets, and the room is also very popular with the Sunday brunch crowd. *1500 Orange Ave., tel. 619/ 435–6611. Reservations advised for all rooms. The mood is casual, but jackets are suggested in the Prince of Wales. AE, DC, MC, V. Moderate–Expensive.*

French   **Marius.** This glamorously understated room in the ultrachic Le
★   Meridien hotel assumed leadership of San Diego County's restaurant scene the day it opened. Consulting chef Jany Gleize flies in regularly from his acclaimed La Bonne Etape in Provence to supervise the spectacular menu. Herbs, used abundantly but knowingly, perfume almost every dish. One of the true dining experiences of a lifetime is the roast fillet of lamb in a sauce redolent with the essence of fresh thyme. Other good choices include crab salad in sea urchin sauce, cold lamb terrine, sea bass in a sauce of crushed black olives, and a sly, wonderfully silly dessert of grilled pineapple in a sauce of orange juice, caramel, and black pepper. The service is faultless, and the place exudes an air of elegance. *2000 2nd St., tel. 619/ 435–3000. Reservations suggested. Dress: formal. AE, DC, MC, V. Dinner only, closed Mon. Very Expensive.*

Seafood   **Peohe's.** Built at the water's edge, this restaurant has a fabulous view of San Diego Bay and the gleaming new towers of downtown San Diego. A kind of Polynesian fantasyland, its tables are interspersed with gently flowing streams and placid ponds, all accented with lush tropical plants. The food could be secondary to all this, but the fresh fish of the day tends to be very well prepared; also look for such pseudo-Polynesian specials as the coconut-breaded fried shrimp. The Mexican-style lobster does not equal the version served south of the border, but is good in its way. Don't miss the banana-rum cake, which is as gooeyly delicious as it sounds. *1201 First St., tel. 619/437– 4474. Reservations suggested. Dress: casual. AE, DC, MC, V. Moderate.*

7 Lodging

by Sharon K. Gillenwater

A writer at San Diego *magazine, Sharon Gillenwater grew up in San Diego.*

When choosing lodgings in San Diego, the first thing to consider is location. The city has many neighborhoods, each one possessing unique characteristics. Consider the type of atmosphere you prefer. Do you want to be in the middle of a bustling metropolitan setting, or would you rather have a serene beach bungalow? Second, consider the hotel's proximity to attractions that you most want to see. And then, of course, there's the price.

San Diego offers a wide range of accommodations, from small, inexpensive, family-operated motels to large, luxury chains. New hotels are continually under construction, giving the city a surplus of rooms and lower room prices for those who shop around. The older hotels and motels in Hotel Circle frequently offer special rates and free tickets to local attractions. Many luxury hotels offer special weekend packages to fill rooms after the week's convention and business customers have departed. Check with your travel agent for the best buy. It's always a good idea to make reservations well in advance, especially during the busy summer season.

Accommodations Bureau of San Diego (tel. 619/226–8100) offers discounts on hotels and attractions.

If you are planning an extended stay or if you need lodgings for four or more people, you might consider an apartment rental. **Oakwood Apartments** (Oakwood Mission Bay West, 3866 Ingraham St., 92109, tel. 619/274–2780 or Oakwood Mission Bay East, 3883 Ingraham St., 92109, tel. 619/274–3240) offers comfortable, furnished apartments in the Mission Bay area with maid service and linens. **San Diego Vacation Rentals** (tel. 619/296–1000) offers coastal homes and condos at competitive weekly and monthly rates. It will send brochures and videotapes of rentals on request.

The most highly recommended hotels in each price category are indicated by a star ★.

Category	Cost*
Very Expensive	over $140
Expensive	$100–$140
Moderate	$60–$100
Inexpensive	under $60

for a double room

The following abbreviations for credit cards have been used: AE, American Express; DC, Diner's Club; MC, MasterCard; V, Visa.

Coronado

Although Coronado doesn't have many lodging facilities, it deserves a category of its own. The peninsula, which is connected to the mainland by the Silver Strand isthmus, can also be reached via the Coronado Bay Bridge or the ferry that leaves from San Diego's Embarcadero. Coronado is home to many wealthy retirees and naval personnel who work at the North Island Naval Air Station. Orange Avenue, with its quaint boutiques, leads directly to the town's famous landmark, The

Hotel Del Coronado. Coronado is a quiet, out-of-the-way place to stay, but if you plan to see many of San Diego's attractions, you'll probably spend a lot of time commuting across the bridge or riding the ferry.

Very Expensive **Hotel Del Coronado.** Built in 1888, the Del is a historic and social landmark made famous by the Marilyn Monroe film *Some Like It Hot*. The rooms and suites in the original Victorian-style building are charmingly quirky; some have baths larger than the sleeping areas, while others seem downright palatial. More standardized accommodations are available in the newer high rise. *1500 Orange Ave., 92118, tel. 619/435–6611 or 800/468–5335. 700 rooms. Facilities: pool, tennis courts, beach. AE, DC, MC, V.*

Le Meridien. Coronado's east shore has been transformed by this glamorous spot where guests can dock their yachts in the bay and wallow in the luxury of the hotel's spa. The rooms, which are actually suites with rattan chairs beside antiques, give the feeling of being in an exclusive beach resort. The Marius restaurant is superb, and Sunday brunch in the cafe has become a Coronado tradition. *2000 Second St., 92118, tel. 619/435–3000 or 800/543–4300. 300 rooms. Facilities: pool, spa, marina, restaurants. AE, DC, MC, V.*

Expensive **Glorietta Bay Inn.** Built around the mansion of the Spreckels family, who once owned most of downtown San Diego, this is now a spotlessly maintained hotel. Located adjacent to the Coronado harbor, the Del, and the Coronado village, there are many fine restaurants and quaint shops within walking distance. *1630 Glorietta Blvd., 92118, tel. 619/435–3101. 100 rooms. Facilities: tennis, golf, pool. AE, MC, V.*

Inexpensive **Coronado Motor Inn.** This motel is located away from the village toward the bay and the ferry stop. *266 Orange Ave., 92118, tel. 619/435–4121. 24 rooms. Facilities: pool. MC, V.*

Downtown

Downtown San Diego is presently in the midst of a decade-long redevelopment effort. The revitalization has attracted many new hotels. There is much to be seen within walking distance of downtown accommodations—Seaport Village, the Embarcadero, the historic Gaslamp Quarter, a variety of theaters and night spots, and the spectacular Horton Plaza shopping center. The zoo and Balboa Park are also nearby. For nonstop shopping, nightlife, and entertainment, the downtown area is an excellent location.

Very Expensive **Omni San Diego Hotel.** This high rise was completed in 1987 and is lavishly decorated with marble, brass, and glass. The rooms are luxurious and modern. The lobby lounge is packed every night with local financiers and weary shoppers from the adjacent Horton Plaza. *910 Broadway Circle, 92101, tel. 619/239–2200 or 800/THE–OMNI. 450 rooms. Facilities: tennis courts, sauna, spa, pool, complete health club, lounge, disco, 2 restaurants. AE, MC, V.*

San Diego Marriott Hotel and Marina. This luxurious high rise consists of two 25-story towers offering panoramic views of the bay and/or city. The North Tower rooms all have balconies but only the suites in the South Tower offer balconies. The Marriott has a prime location between Seaport Village and the conven-

San Diego Lodging

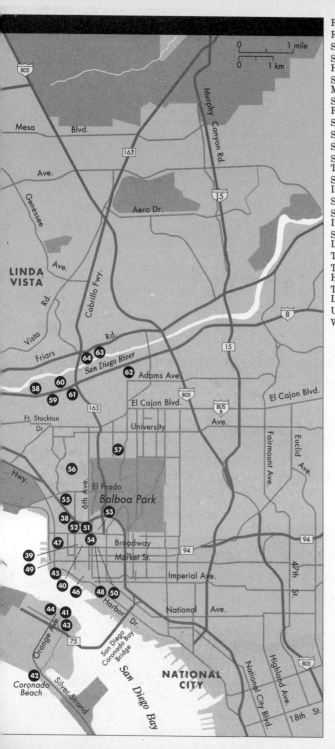

tion center. *333 W. Harbor Dr., 92101, tel. 619/234–1500 or 800/ 800/228–9290. 1,356 rooms. Facilities: 3 restaurants, 2 lounges with piano music, boutiques, full-service salon, jogging path, health spa, tennis courts, sauna, 2 outdoor pools, charter boat. AE, DC, MC, V.*

★ **U.S. Grant Hotel.** Originally built in 1910, this hotel, which faces the famed Horton Plaza, was renovated and reopened in 1985. The atmosphere is elegant and formal, with crystal chandeliers and marble floors. All rooms feature mahogany furnishings. Butlers and concierges serve the guests splendidly. There are two restaurants, the Garden Room and the Grant Grill, a longtime favorite of high-powered business types. The use of an associated health club is included. *326 Broadway, 92101, tel. 619/232–3121 or 800/237–5029, 800/334–6957 in CA. 280 rooms. AE, DC, MC, V.*

Westgate Hotel. This elegant high rise offers rooms uniquely furnished with genuine European antiques. Hand-cut Baccarat chandeliers adorn the lobby, which is modeled after the anteroom in the Palace of Versailles. The rooms feature Italian marble counters, oversize bathtubs, brass fixtures with 14-kt.-gold overlay, and breathtaking views of the harbor and the city (from the ninth floor up). Enjoy high tea and international coffee with piano accompaniment in the afternoon and the award-winning cuisine and white-glove service of Le Fontainebleau in the evening. The trolley can take you to Tijuana right from the hotel and complimentary transportation is available within the downtown area. *1055 Second Ave., 92101, tel. 619/238–1818 or 800/221–3802, 800/522–1564 in CA. 223 rooms. Facilities: restaurant, lounge. AE, DC, MC, V.*

Expensive **Britt House.** This grand Victorian inn offers charming rooms, each uniquely furnished with antiques. Each room has a sitting area in which fresh baked goodies are served for breakfast. Lovely gardens surround the building, and an elaborate high tea is served in the parlor every afternoon. Keeping in the Victorian tradition, there is a bathroom for every two rooms to share. Located within walking distance of Balboa Park and the zoo. Reservations are a must. *406 Maple St., 92101, tel. 619/ 234–2926. 10 rooms. AE, MC, V.*

Embassy Suites Downtown. It's a short walk to the convention center from one of downtown's most popular new hotels. All rooms are suites, and efficiency is the hotel's trademark. The decor is no more than pleasant, but everything is new and clean. Business travelers will find it easy to set up shop here, and families can make good use of the in-room refrigerators and separate sleeping areas. *601 Pacific Hwy., 92101, tel. 619/239– 2400 or 800/362–2779. 337 rooms. Facilities: pool, restaurant, bar. AE, DC, MC, V.*

★ **Horton Grand Hotel.** This is San Diego's oldest Victorian hotel, built in 1886 and restored in 1986 in the fashion of an elegant, European-style tourist hotel. The charming rooms are furnished with period antiques and feature ceiling fans, gas-burning fireplaces, and diaries, which provide guests with a sense of those who came before them and an opportunity to share with those who will come later. Each room is different from the next. The choicest rooms are those overlooking the garden courtyard that twinkles with miniature lights each evening. Afternoon high tea and evening jazz are offered. *311 Island Ave., 92101, tel. 619/544–1886. 110 rooms. Facilities: Chinatown museum, restaurant, lounge. AE, DC, MC, V.*

Moderate–
Expensive
Balboa Park Inn. Originally built in 1915, this charming European-style bed-and-breakfast inn was restored in 1982, with one- and two-bedroom suites with kitchenettes (for 2–4 people) housed in four two-story buildings that are connected by courtyards. Each suite has a different flavor—Italian, French, Spanish, or early Californian. Some suites have fireplaces, wet bars, and whirlpool tubs. Continental breakfast and the morning paper are delivered to every suite. Prices are reasonable considering all rooms are complete suites for 2–4 people. Balboa Park and the zoo are located directly across the street. *3402 Park Blvd., 92103, tel. 619/298–0823. 25 suites with baths. Facilities: outdoor bar, room service. AE, DC, MC, V.*

Moderate
Holiday Inn Harbor View. This is one of those round Holiday Inns you frequently encounter around the country. The rooms are standard Holiday Inn quality with views of the city and harbor. *1617 First Ave., 92101, tel. 619/239–6171. 205 rooms. Facilities: pool, restaurant, lounge. AE, DC, MC, V.*

Radisson Harbor View. This new high rise sits at the foot of the I–5 entrance ramp to downtown at Front Street. Near the courthouse and legal offices, the hotel is good for business travelers who don't mind the 10-block hike to the convention center—for those who do, there's a free shuttle. The pastel-decorated rooms are sparkling clean, with small harbor-view terraces. Business services and a health club are available. *1646 Front St., 92101, tel. 619/239–6800 or 800/333–3333. 333 rooms. Facilities: rooftop pool, health club. AE, MC, V.*

Saint James Hotel. Once a dingy flophouse, the St. James has been completely remodeled and renovated to its original turn-of-the-century elegance. The rooms are still small and cramped, and the Southwestern decor seems odd when the public spaces rely on heavy wood and crystal chandeliers. But the hotel staff is helpful, and the rates are more reasonable than most hotels downtown. *830 Sixth Avenue, 92101, tel. 619/234–0155. 99 rooms. MC, V.*

Inexpensive
Downtown Budget Motel. There's nothing fancy about this motel, but the location is less noisy than at other low-cost establishments. The rooms are nondescript but clean, and there are rooms for nonsmokers, and some with VCRs and refrigerators. *1835 Columbia St., 92101, tel. 619/544–0164 or 800/824–5317. 101 rooms. MC, V.*

Harbor Hill Guest House. This B&B offers quaint, comfortable rooms in a three-story home. Harbor view and kitchenettes are available. Continental breakfast included, families welcome. *2330 Albatross St., 92101, tel. 619/233–0638, 5 rooms. MC, V.*

Hotel Churchill. Originally built in 1915, this hotel underwent a major restoration and reopened in 1984. The interior resembles a medieval English castle, and each room is decorated in its own motif complete with a special name plaque on the door. Some rooms have their own bath while others share common baths. This hotel is located right on the trolley line and near all center city attractions. *827 C St., 92101, tel. 619/234–5186. 100 rooms. MC, V.*

★ **La Pensione.** At long last, a decent budget hotel downtown, with daily, weekly, and monthly rates. Some rooms have harbor views, all have kitchenettes. La Pensione is in a quiet neighborhood, and has a pretty central courtyard. *1546 Second Ave., 92101, tel. 619/236–9292. 20 rooms. Facilities: kitchenettes. MC, V.*

Rodeway Inn. Situated on one of the better streets downtown, it's clean, comfortable, and nicely decorated. *833 Ash St., 92101, tel. 619/239–2285. 45 rooms. Facilities: spa, sauna. AE, DC, MC, V.*

Harbor Island/Shelter Island

Harbor Island and Shelter Island are two man-made peninsulas located between downtown San Diego and the lovely community of Point Loma. Both islands are bordered by grassy parks, tree-lined paths, lavish hotels, and wonderful restaurants. Harbor Island is closest to the downtown area and less than five minutes from the airport. Shelter Island is on the Point Loma side. Both islands command breathtaking views of the bay and the downtown skyline. Although some lodgings we have listed are not located directly on the islands, they are in the vicinity.

Very Expensive **Sheraton Grand.** The Sheraton chain has taken over Harbor Island with the Sheraton Grand and the Sheraton Harbor Island East. The Grand is the more luxurious of the two, with lavish room furnishings, panoramic views, and butler service. The building has a sterile, impersonal feel to it, however, and the pool area seems like a low-budget afterthought. Still, the rooms are well arranged, with chairs and a large table for paperwork and a separate seating area for entertaining. *1590 Harbor Island Dr., 92101, tel. 619/291–6400 or 800/325–3535. 350 rooms. Facilities: pool, spa, 2 lounges, 1 restaurant. AE, DC, MC, V.*

★ **Sheraton Harbor Island East.** Although less luxurious than the neighboring Sheraton Grand, this hotel has more charm and romance. For a view, ask for a room above the eighth floor, preferably facing across the water to the lights of downtown. The restaurants and lounges here are popular for fine dining and dancing. *1380 Harbor Island Dr., 92101, tel. 619/291–2900 or 800/325–3535. 725 rooms. Facilities: tennis courts, sauna, spa, 2 pools, fitness facility. AE, DC, MC, V.*

Expensive **Bay Club Hotel & Marina.** Each room is comfortably furnished and has a view either of the bay or the marina. The room decor is subtle Polynesian, with bleached wood and natural colors. A buffet breakfast is included. *2131 Shelter Island Dr., 92106, tel. 619/224–8888. 105 rooms. Facilities: pool, spa, free underground parking. AE, DC, MC, V.*

★ **Humphrey's Half Moon Inn.** This sprawling South Seas—style resort has many open areas with palm trees, beautiful green grass, and tiki torches. The recently restored rooms have standard but pleasant modern decor; some have views of the pool area or the bay. The restaurant, Humphrey's, is famous with the locals for its good food and summer jazz concert series. *2303 Shelter Island Dr., 92106, tel. 619/224–3411 or 800/345–9995. 141 rooms. Facilities: putting green, pool, spa, bicycles. AE, DC, MC, V.*

Moderate **Best Western Posada Inn.** One of the nicer Best Western hotels, this is not on Harbor Island but on one of the neighboring thoroughfares adjacent to Point Loma. The location is good, and many rooms have a wonderful view of the harbor. The rooms are clean, comfortable, and nicely furnished. There are many fabulous seafood eateries within walking distance. *5005 N. Harbor Dr., 92106, tel. 619/224–3254 or 800/528–1234. 112 rooms. Facilities: pool, spa, restaurant, lounge. AE, MC, V.*
Kona Kai Beach and Tennis Resort. This hotel also serves as a

prestigious members-only club for locals, but all facilities are open to hotel guests. The rooms are simple and tasteful with Hawaiian decor. Rooms in the newer north wing are less expensive than the bayfront suites with lanais in the main building. *1551 Shelter Island Dr., 92106, tel. 619/222–1191. 89 rooms. Facilities: health club, tennis courts, racquetball courts, pool, spa, private beach, 2 restaurants, lounge. AE, DC, MC, V.*

Inexpensive   **Outrigger Motel.** Accommodations are less expensive here because the location is adjacent to the two resort peninsulas, not on them. It may be a bit noisier here, but the location is still picturesque. The sportfishing docks are across the street, and one can take a scenic walk along the bay to Harbor Island. Be sure to visit the famous Point Loma Seafoods Market and Restaurant across the street. *1370 Scott St., 92106, tel. 619/223–7105. 37 rooms with kitchens. Facilities: pool. AE, DC, MC, V.*

Richmar Inn. Again, lodgings are inexpensive here because the location is adjacent to the resort islands and on a busy thoroughfare. This is a large motel with comfortable rooms. *3330 Rosecrans St., 92106, tel. 619/224–8266. 98 rooms. Facilities: sauna, pool, restaurant. AE, DC, MC, V.*

TraveLodge Point Loma. The view is the same as at the higher-priced hotels, for a far lower price. Of course, there are fewer amenities and the neighborhood (near the Navy base) isn't as serene, but the rooms are adequate and clean. *5102 N. Harbor Dr., tel. 619/223–8171 or 800/255–3050. 45 rooms. Facilities: pool. AE, MC, V.*

Hotel Circle/Old Town

Hotel Circle, as the name implies, is headquarters to a number of hotels and motels, most of them moderately priced and catering to the individual traveler. A car is an absolute necessity here, since the "circle" consists of hotels on both sides of Interstate 8, the busiest stretch of freeway in San Diego. Although not particularly scenic or serene, Mission Valley is close to Balboa Park, the zoo, downtown, and the beaches. Atlas Hotels, which owns four hotels in this area, has a health club available to guests. Old Town, between downtown and Hotel Circle, is developing a crop of moderately priced chain hotels beside the freeway. As a general rule, try to reserve a room that doesn't face the freeway.

Expensive   **Doubletree Hotel.** One of the grandest hotels in the valley, this
★   high rise offers three floors reserved for nonsmokers. The decor is modern Southwestern. Children stay free and small pets are accepted. *901 Camino del Rio S., 92108, tel. 619/543–9000 or 800/528–0444. 350 rooms. Facilities: restaurant, lounge, spa, pool, fitness center. AE, DC, MC, V.*

Moderate–   **Heritage Park Bed & Breakfast Inn.** This inn is located a few
Expensive   minutes from Mission Valley in the Old Town area. The location
★   is picturesque and quiet. Nine guest rooms decorated with 19th-century antiques are housed in a romantic Queen Anne mansion from 1889. Five of the rooms have private baths; the others share facilities. The rooms are quaint and furnished with Victorian antiques. Breakfast and afternoon refreshments are included. *2470 Heritage Park Row, 92110, tel. 619/295–7088. 9 rooms, 5 with bath. MC, V.*

★   **San Diego Marriott Mission Valley.** This new high rise sits in the middle of the San Diego River valley, where the dry riverbed is being graded and transformed into a commercial zone with sleek office towers and sprawling shopping malls. The hotel has become the valley's glamour spot, and the rooms are far more spacious and contemporary than in nearby hotels. *8757 Rio San Diego Dr., 92108, tel. 619/692–3800 or 800/228–9290. 350 rooms. Facilities: pool, tennis court, health club. AE, DC, MC, V.*

Town and Country Hotel. Although the original part of this hotel was built in the 1950s, it has been refurbished many times and two high-rise sections were added in the 1970s. The rooms are decorated in a quaint Colonial fashion. With Hotel Circle's largest convention facilities, the hotel caters to convention and meeting groups, but it is resortlike enough to appeal to tourists also. *500 Hotel Circle N, 92108, tel. 619/291–7131. 1,000 rooms. Facilities: 6 restaurants, 5 lounges, 4 pools, golf, health club. AE, DC, MC, V.*

Moderate **Hacienda Hotel.** The white adobe hacienda-style buildings of this former shopping complex turned hotel spread up a steep hillside. Elevators are available, but you still have to do a bit of climbing. The reward is tranquillity above the bustle of Old Town. All rooms are suites with microwaves, refrigerators, and VCRs—all a family could need, plus tasteful Southwestern-style decor. *4041 Harney St., 92110, tel. 619/298–4707 or 800/888–1991. 150 suites. Facilities: pool, free indoor parking. AE, MC, V.*

Hanalei Hotel. If Interstate 8 were out of sight, you'd swear you were in a tropical paradise. This hotel has a definite island feel, with palm trees, waterfalls, koi ponds, and tiki torches. There is a two-story complex and a high rise. The two-story complex rooms are poolside and the high rise is built around a beautiful Hawaiian garden with ponds, palm trees, and plenty of spots to sit and take in the atmosphere. The rooms are clean and comfortable with Hawaiian decor. *2270 Hotel Circle S, 92108, tel. 619/297–1101. 425 rooms. Facilities: 2 restaurants, lounge, pool, spa. AE, MC, V.*

Kings Inn. This is a sprawling two-level motel complex. An Atlas property, it therefore affords access to a golf course and the nearby Atlas Health Club. *1333 Hotel Circle S, 92108, tel. 619/297–2231. 135 rooms. Facilities: restaurant, lounge, coffee shop. AE, DC, MC, V.*

Ramada Inn Old Town. New hotels and motels are appearing along I–5 at Old Town—a convenient location between downtown, Mission Valley, and the beaches. The most established of these new hotels is the hacienda-style Ramada, with fountains, courtyards, painted tiles, and Mexican decor in the rooms. The hotel is popular with medium-sized groups, and has a very good Sunday brunch. *2435 Jefferson St., 92110, tel. 619/260–8500 or 800/2–RAMADA. 151 rooms. Facilities: heated pool, Jacuzzi, restaurant. AE, MC, V.*

Red Lion Inn. The towering Red Lion is the landmark for Mission Valley's newest residential/commercial development along the San Diego River. The location is good for those doing business in the valley or travelers wanting easy access to the mountains and desert. The health club, indoor lap pool, and bountiful Sunday brunch are pluses, and the rooms are immaculately clean and new, though lacking character. The whole development, which includes the popular trendy restaurant Prego's and the beginnings of a riverfront park, isn't quite finished, but promises to be a focal point of the valley. *7450 Hazard Center*

Drive, 92108, tel. 619/297–5466. 300 rooms. Facilities: outdoor and indoor pools, hot tub, restaurant, meeting rooms, shops. AE, DC, MC, V.

Inexpensive **Circle 8 Motor Inn.** This large motel complex has a small refrigerator in every room. *543 Hotel Circle S, 92108, tel. 619/ 297–8800. 250 rooms. Facilities: pool, spa, deli. AE, DC, MC, V.*

Padre Trail Inn. This standard, family-style motel is located slightly southwest of Mission Valley. Historic Old Town, shopping, and dining are all within walking distance. *4200 Taylor St., 92110, tel. 619/297–3291. 100 rooms. Facilities: pool, restaurant, lounge. AE, DC, MC, V.*

La Jolla

La Jolla is one of the world's most beautiful, prestigious beach communities. Million-dollar homes line the beaches and cascade down the hillsides. Expensive boutiques, galleries, and restaurants make up the village—the heart of La Jolla. La Jolla is also a popular vacation spot and has many lodging possibilities even for those on a budget.

Very Expensive **Sea Lodge.** This hidden gem faces the ocean between La Jolla Beach and Tennis Club and La Jolla Shores, one of the best beaches in the county. Three-story buildings with red tile rooves form a low-lying compound on the beachfront, backed by the hills of La Jolla. The rooms have the sort of yellow, orange, and green decor popular in the 60s, and wooden balconies that look out on lush landscaping and the sea. Early reservations are a must here, and families will find plenty of room and distractions for both kids and parents. *8110 Camino del Oro, La Jolla, 92037, tel. 619/459–8271. 128 rooms, 19 with kitchenettes. Facilities: heated pool, hot tub, beach, 2 tennis courts, pitch-and-putt golf course, restaurant, lounge. AE, DC, MC, V.*

Sheraton Grande Torrey Pines. The view of the Pacific from atop the Torrey Pines cliffs can't be beat. This new low-rise, high-class hotel blends into the clifftop, looking rather insignificant until you step inside the luxurious lounge and look out at the sea and the 18th hole of the lush green Torrey Pines golf course. Amenities include 24-hour concierge service, limousine service, a health club, and a business center. The rooms are elegant but simple, done in pale pastels and off-white, and the restaurant is excellent. *10950 N. Torrey Pines Rd., 92037, tel. 619/ 558–1500 or 800/325–3535. Facilities: pool, health club, 3 tennis courts, adjacent to championship golf course, restaurant. AE, DC, MC, V.*

Expensive– **Hyatt Regency La Jolla.** The centerpiece of La Jolla's Golden
Very Expensive Triangle is the Aventine project, with the Hyatt as its cornerstone. The hotel was designed inside and out by Michael Graves, whose lithographs hang on the bedroom walls. The rooms are a combination of neo-classical and post-modern design, with lavish use of highly polished cherry wood, black lacquer, and marble. The adjacent restaurant court has four very trendy restaurants, and the health club includes an indoor basketball court. *377 La Jolla Village Dr., La Jolla 92122, tel. 619/ 552–1234 or 800/233–1234. 400 rooms and suites. Facilities: pool, 2 tennis courts, basketball court, hot tub, health club, 5 restaurants, lounges. AE, DC, MC, V.*

★ **La Valencia.** This European-style, pink-stucco hotel is a La Jolla landmark. A haven for the movie stars in the '30s and '40s, it has a courtyard for patio dining and an elegant lobby where guests congregate in the evenings to enjoy the spectacular view of the ocean while sipping cocktails. The clientele tends to be older, except in the Whaling Bar, which is a gathering spot for all ages. The restaurants have excellent food, and the hotel is ideally located for walking to the cove, shopping, and dining out. The prices are quite reasonable if you're willing to settle for a view of the village. For a view of the ocean, the prices almost double, but on a clear, sunny day, it might be worth every penny. *1132 Prospect St., La Jolla 92037, tel. 619/454–0771. 100 rooms. AE, MC, V.*

Expensive **The Bed & Breakfast Inn at La Jolla.** This charming inn offers elegant European-style accommodations and warm hospitality. Each room is individually decorated with Laura Ashley prints in the "elegant cottage" style. As the name says, breakfast is included. *7753 Draper Ave., La Jolla, 92037, tel. 619/ 456–2066. 16 rooms. MC, V.*

Colonial Inn. A tastefully restored Victorian-style building, this hotel offers turn-of-the-century elegance with features such as fan windows and a mahogany-paneled elevator. You can get a view of the village or of the ocean, but the ocean view will cost considerably more. Located in the center of La Jolla, the hotel is within walking distance of boutiques, restaurants, and the cove. *910 Prospect St., La Jolla, 92037, tel. 619/454–2181 or 800/832–5525. 75 rooms. Facilities: restaurant, lounge, pool. AE, DC, MC, V. .*

Embassy Suites Hotel. Although technically located in La Jolla, this hotel is a 10-minute drive away from the beach and the village. The area, known as the Golden Triangle, is a congested business and industrial region with condominiums and several shopping malls on the horizon. The hotel itself, completed in 1987, is a magnificent 12-story high rise with attractive, modern accommodations. Every room faces an indoor atrium courtyard, and the atmosphere is light and airy. Every room has a kitchen area with a wet bar, microwave, refrigerator, and coffee maker as well as a living room. A complimentary breakfast and evening cocktails are included. The hotel caters primarily to business travelers, but if you don't mind the congested location, it provides excellent lodgings for tourists as well. *4550 La Jolla Village Dr., San Diego, 92122, tel. 619/453–0400. 335 suites. Facilities: indoor pool, outdoor spa, weight room, restaurant, deli, lounge. AE, DC, MC, V.*

Summer House Inn. This is a pleasant, modern high rise located five minutes from the center of La Jolla and a few blocks from the beach. Freeway entrances are nearby, a plus in the congested La Jolla traffic. The room decor is modern with light oak furniture, some with brown colors, some with pastel blues and purples; those on the north side, away from Torrey Pines Road, are quieter. The view from the top floors is spectacular. On the very top, Elario's restaurant offers a splendid view, gourmet cuisine, and live jazz entertainment most nights. *7955 La Jolla Shores Dr., La Jolla, 92037, tel. 619/459–0261. 90 rooms. Facilities: pool. AE, MC, V. .*

Moderate– **La Jolla Cove Motel.** Offering studios and suites, some with
Expensive spacious oceanfront balconies, this motel overlooks the famous
★ La Jolla Cove beach. *1155 Coast Blvd., La Jolla, 92037, tel. 619/*

459–2621 or 800/248–COVE. 130 rooms. Facilities: solarium, sun deck, fresh-water pool, spa. AE, MC, V.

Prospect Park Inn. This charming European-style inn is newly redecorated. The rooms are quaint, and some have balconies with sweeping ocean views. Located in the village, it is within walking distance of shops and restaurants and one block from the beach. The higher the floor, the more you pay. *1110 Prospect St., La Jolla, 92037, tel. 619/454–0133, 800/345–8577, or 800/433–1609. 25 rooms. AE, MC, V.*

Moderate   **La Jolla Palms Inn.** This is a modest motel in a nice location within walking distance of shops and restaurants and beaches. The fairly large rooms are done in green, blue, and beige; ask for one by the pool. *6705 La Jolla Blvd., La Jolla, 92037, tel. 619/454–7101. 58 rooms. Facilities: pool, spa. AE, DC, MC, V.*

Torrey Pines Inn. Located on a bluff between La Jolla and Del Mar, this hotel commands a view of miles and miles of coastline. The hotel stands adjacent to the Torrey Pines Golf Course, site of the San Diego Open PGA golf tournament every January. Nearby is scenic Torrey Pines State Beach. Downtown La Jolla is a 10-minute drive away. The inn is a nice, reasonable, out-of-the-way place to stay. *11480 Torrey Pines Rd., La Jolla, 92037, tel. 619/453–4420. 75 rooms. AE, DC, MC, V.*

Inn by the Sea. The beach and the village of La Jolla are within five blocks, and the rates are considerably lower than at other La Jolla hotels. The five-story inn has more the feel of a motel than a resort, and the brown-on-beige rooms are far from imaginative, but it's a fine choice for those wishing to spend the big bucks dining and shopping rather than sleeping. *7830 Fay Ave., La Jolla 92037, tel. 619/459–4461 or 800/462–9732. 130 rooms. Facilities: pool, indoor hot tub. AE, MC, V.*

Mission Bay and Beaches

Most people who come to San Diego would like to stay close to the water. Mission and Pacific beaches have the highest concentration of small hotels and motels. Both these areas have a casual atmosphere and a busy coastal thoroughfare offering endless shopping, dining, and nightlife possibilities. Mission Bay Park, with its beaches, bike trails, boat-launching ramps, golf course, and grassy parks is also a hotel haven. You can't go wrong with any of these locations, as long as the frenzy of hundreds at play doesn't bother you.

Very Expensive   **Hyatt Islandia.** Located in one of San Diego's most beautiful seashore areas, Mission Bay Park, the Islandia has lanai-style units and a high rise. The landscaping is lush and tropical in flavor, and the room decor is tastefully modern with dramatic views of the bay area. This hotel is famous for its lavish Sunday buffet brunch. *1441 Quivira Rd., 92109, tel. 619/224–1234. 423 rooms. Facilities: pool, spa, 2 restaurants. AE, DC, MC, V.*

San Diego Hilton. This deluxe resort hotel is spread out in a picturesque park setting. There is a high rise offering rooms with lovely views of Mission Bay Park. The rest of the rooms are in little bungalows surrounded by trees and grassy areas. *1775 E. Mission Bay Dr., 92109, tel. 619/276–4010. 354 rooms. Facilities: jogging trail, tennis courts, coffee shop, restaurant, lounge, hotel yacht. AE, DC, MC, V.*

★ **San Diego Princess Resort.** This resort resembles a self-sufficient village with a wide range of amenities. Perhaps its greatest features are the marina and beaches. The grounds are so beautifully landscaped that this resort has been the setting for many movies. Accommodations consist of individual cottages. Kitchens and bay views are available. With something for everyone, this hotel is favored by families, particularly during the summer. *1404 W. Vacation Rd., 92109, tel. 619/274–4630. 450 cottages. Facilities: 3 restaurants, 8 tennis courts, 5 pools, bicycle and boat rentals. AE, DC, MC, V.*

Expensive **Catamaran Resort Hotel.** This is owned by the same family that owns the Bahia. Also located on the bay, this hotel is newly remodeled and luxurious. There are six 2-story buildings and one 14-story high rise. The view from the upper floors of the high rise is spectacular. The Pacific Ocean is a block away. *3999 Mission Blvd., 92109, tel. 619/488–1081. 315 rooms. Facilities: pool, spa, water-sport rentals, coffee shop, restaurant, bar. AE, DC, MC, V.*

Moderate– **Bahia Resort Hotel.** This huge complex is located on a 14-acre
Expensive peninsula in Mission Bay Park. The ocean is also within walk-
★ ing distance. The rooms are studios and suites with kitchens, tastefully furnished. The price is good, considering the location and amenities. *998 W. Mission Bay Dr., 92109, tel. 619/ 488–0551. 300 rooms. Facilities: tennis courts, water-sport rentals, spa, pool, evening bay cruises. AE, DC, MC, V.*

Dana Inn & Marina. This hotel, which has an adjoining marina, offers a bargain in the Mission Bay Park area. The accommodations are not as grand as in the other hotels in the area but they're perfectly fine if you're not going to stay cooped up in your room. *1710 W. Mission Bay Blvd., 92109, tel. 619/222– 6440. 196 rooms. Facilities: pool, spa. AE, DC, MC, V.*

Moderate **Pacific Shores Inn.** This is one of the nicer motels in the area and is only one-half block from the beach. The rooms are nicely decorated. Pets are accepted with a $50 refundable deposit. *4802 Mission Blvd., 92109, tel. 619/483–6300. 56 rooms. Facilities: pool. AE, MC, V.*

Surfer Motor Lodge. This hotel is located right on the beach and directly behind a new shopping center with many restaurants and boutiques. The rooms are plain, but the view from the upper floors of this high rise is very nice. *711 Pacific Beach Dr., 92109, tel. 619/483–7070. 52 rooms. Facilities: restaurant, cocktail lounge, swimming pool. AE, DC, MC, V.*

Inexpensive– **Ocean Manor Apartment Hotel.** Units rent by the day (with a
Moderate 3-day minimum), week, or month, and the owner says that
★ some people have been coming every year for 20 years! This hotel is located in Ocean Beach, a community south of Mission Beach that doesn't have many lodging facilities. This is a charming place with a lovely view, located right on Sunset Cliffs. The beach below has long since washed away, but there are beaches within walking distance. The rooms are studios or one- or two-bedroom suites with kitchens and living rooms. They are furnished plainly in 1950s style but are quaint and comfortable. There is no maid service but fresh towels are always provided. This is a quiet place and the owners want to keep it that way. Make reservations months in advance. *1370 Sunset Cliffs Blvd., 92107, tel. 619/222–7901 or 619/224–1379. 20 rooms. Facilities: pool. MC, V.*

Inexpensive **Mission Bay Motel.** Located one-half block from the beach, this motel offers centrally located, modest units. Great restaurants and nightlife are within walking distance, but you might find

the area to be a bit noisy. *4221 Mission Blvd., 92109, tel. 619/
483–6440. 50 rooms. Facilities: swimming pool. AE, MC, V.*

Santa Clara Motel. This is a small motel a block from the ocean
and right in the middle of restaurant, nightlife, and shopping
activity in Mission Beach. Location is the plus. Kitchens are
available, but there are no frills. Weekly rates are available.
*839 Santa Clara Pl., 92109, tel. 619/488–1193. 17 rooms. AE,
MC, V.*

Hostels

American Youth Hostels, Inc., San Diego Council (1031 India
St., 92103, tel. 619/239–2644 or 619/234–3330).

Imperial Beach International Hostel (170 Palm Ave., 92032, tel.
619/423–8039).

Point Loma Elliot International Hostel (3790 Udall St., 92107,
tel. 619/223–4778).

YMCA (500 W. Broadway, 92101, tel. 619/232–1133). Men and
women are welcome.

8 The Arts

*by Marael
Johnson*

Top national touring companies perform regularly at the Civic Theatre, Golden Hall, Symphony Hall, and East County Performing Arts Center. San Diego State University, the University of California at San Diego, private universities, and community colleges present a wide variety of performing arts programs, from performances by well-known artists to student recitals. The daily *San Diego Union, Evening Tribune*, and the San Diego edition of the *Los Angeles Times* list current attractions and complete movie schedules. The *Reader*, a free weekly that comes out each Thursday, devotes an entire section to upcoming cultural events, as well as current theater and film reviews. *San Diego* magazine publishes a monthly "What's Doing" column that lists arts events throughout the county and reviews of current films, plays, and concerts.

It is best to book tickets well in advance, preferably at the same time you make hotel reservations. There are various outlets for last-minute tickets, though you risk either paying top rates or getting less-than-choice seats—or both.

Half-price tickets to most theater, music, and dance events can be bought on the day of performance at the **TIMES ARTS TIX Ticket Center,** Horton Plaza, downtown (tel. 619/238–3810). Only cash is accepted. Advance full-price tickets may also be purchased through ARTS TIX.

Visa and MasterCard holders may buy tickets for many scheduled performances through **Teleseat** (tel. 619/283–7328), **Ticketmaster** (tel. 619/238–3810), and **Ticketron** (tel. 619/268–9686). Service charges vary according to event, and most tickets are nonrefundable.

Theater

The Bowery Theatre (1057 First Ave. in the Kingston Hotel, tel. 619/232–4088). A theater in search of a permanent home, the Bowery is acclaimed by critics and theater-goers for its premiers of high-quality works by both famous playwrights and soon-to-be-discovered artists.
Coronado Playhouse (1755 Strand Way, Coronado, tel. 619/435–4856). This cabaret-type theater, near the Hotel Del Coronado, stages regular dramatic and musical performances. Dinner packages are offered on Friday and Saturday.
Gaslamp Quarter Theatre (playhouse: 547 Fourth Ave., tel. 619/234–9583; showcase: 444 Fourth Ave., tel. 619/232–9608). The resident theater company performs comedies, dramas, mysteries, and musicals in the original 96-seat playhouse and in the new 250-seat showcase, both in the Gaslamp Quarter.
La Jolla Playhouse (Mandell Weiss Center for the Performing Arts, University of California at San Diego, tel. 619/534–3960). Exciting and innovative presentations, early summer to fall, under the artistic direction of Tony Award-winner Des McAnuff.
La Jolla Stage Company (750 Nautilus St., La Jolla, tel. 619/459–7773). Lavish productions of Broadway favorites and popular comedies, staged year-round in Parker Auditorium at La Jolla High School.
Lawrence Welk Village Theatre (8860 Lawrence Welk Dr., Escondido, tel. 619/749–3448). About a 45-minute drive from downtown, this famed dinner theater puts on polished Broadway-style productions with a professional cast.

Lyceum Theatre (Horton Plaza, tel. 619/235–8025). Home to the San Diego Repertory Theatre, San Diego's first resident acting company, which performs contemporary works year-round on the 550-seat Lyceum stage and in a 225-seat theater that can be rearranged to suit the stage set.

Marquis Public Theater (3717 India St., tel. 619/295–5654). Contemporary, experimental, and original plays are held on the main stage and in the smaller gallery.

Old Globe Theatre (Simon Edison Centre for the Performing Arts, Balboa Park, tel. 619/239–2255). The oldest professional theater in California performs classics, contemporary dramas, experimental works, and the famous summer Shakespeare Festival at the Old Globe and its sister theaters, the Cassius Carter Centre Stage and the Lowell Davies Festival Theatre.

Puppet Theatre (Palisades Building, Balboa Park, tel. 619/466–7128). Hand, rod, and marionette shows are held every weekend.

San Diego Gilbert and Sullivan Company (Casa del Prado Theatre, Balboa Park, tel. 619/231–5714). Four different productions of Gilbert and Sullivan and similar works are performed October–July.

San Diego Junior Theatre (Casa del Prado Theatre, Balboa Park, tel. 619/239–8355). Family favorites are performed by students, ages 8–18.

Sixth Avenue Playhouse (1620 Sixth Ave., tel. 619/235–8025). Different theatrical organizations stage an eclectic variety of entertainment in this 180-seat chapel.

Starlight Musicals (Starlight Bowl, Balboa Park, tel. 619/544–7827). A local summertime favorite is this series of popular musicals presented in an outdoor amphitheater from mid-June through early September.

The Theatre in Old Town (4040 Twiggs St., tel. 619/298–0082). Mostly musical theater and Broadway hits are staged by the International Company of United States International University, October–June. All the seats are good in this cozy, barnlike structure.

UCSD Theatre. (Warren Theatre and Mandell Weiss Theatre, University of California at San Diego campus, La Jolla, tel. 619/534–6467) The students of the University of California at San Diego's theater department take the stage in the theaters used by La Jolla Playhouse in the summer months, and present first-rate productions from September to May.

Concerts

Open-Air Theatre (San Diego State University, tel. 619/594–5200). Top-name rock, reggae, and popular artists pack in the crowds for summer concerts under the stars.

Organ Pavilion (Balboa Park, tel. 619/239–0512). Robert Plimpton performs on the giant 1914 pipe organ at 2 PM on Sunday afternoons, except in January, and on most Monday evenings in summer. All concerts are free.

Sherwood Auditorium (700 Prospect St., La Jolla, tel. 619/280–7013). Many classical and jazz events are held in the 550-seat auditorium within San Diego Museum of Contemporary Art. La Jolla Chamber Music Society presents nine concerts, August–May, of internationally acclaimed chamber ensembles, orchestras, and soloists. San Diego Chamber Orchestra, a 35-member ensemble, performs once a month, October–April.

Sports Arena (2500 Sports Arena Blvd., tel. 619/224–4176).

Big-name rock concerts play to more than 14,000 fans, using an end-stage configuration so that all seats face in one direction.

Symphony Hall (1245 Seventh Ave., tel. 619/699–4205). The San Diego Symphony is the only California symphony with its own concert hall. The performance season runs November–May, with a series of outdoor pop concerts held at Seaport Village during the summer.

Opera

Civic Theatre (202 C St., tel. 619/236–6510). The San Diego Opera draws international stars like Luciano Pavarotti, Joan Sutherland, and Kiri Te Kanawa. The season of four operas runs January–April in the 3,000-seat, state-of-the-art auditorium. English translations of works sung in their original languages are projected on a large screen above the stage.

Dance

3's Company (tel. 619/296–9523). Interpretative dance presentations, incorporating live music, are staged at major theaters and concert halls around San Diego County.

California Ballet (tel. 619/560–5676). Four high-quality contemporary and traditional works, from story ballets to Balanchine, are performed September–May. The *Nutcracker* is staged annually at the Civic Theatre; other ballets take place at Symphony Hall, East County Performing Arts Center, and Nautilus Bowl at Sea World.

San Diego Civic Youth Ballet (Casa del Prado Theatre, Balboa Park, tel. 619/233–3060). Classical story ballets are performed in spring and at Christmas by dancers aged 5–19.

Film

First-run international films are screened at the **Cove** (7730 Girard Ave., La Jolla, tel. 619/459–5404), **Guild** (3827 Fifth Ave., tel. 619/295–2000), and **Park** (3812 Park Blvd., tel. 619/294–9264).

Ken Cinema (4061 Adams Ave., tel. 619/283–5909). The roster of art/revival films changes almost every night, and many programs are double bills.

Sherwood Auditorium (700 Prospect St., La Jolla, tel. 619/280–7013). Foreign and classic film series and special film events are held regularly in the 550-seat auditorium within San Diego Museum of Contemporary Art.

9 Nightlife

by Dan Janeck

*A San Diego
resident, Dan
Janeck has years
of experience
writing on local
nightlife for a
variety of
publications,
including* San
Diego *magazine.*

The unbeatable variety of sun-and-surf recreational activities is considered the primary reason tourists love to visit San Diego, but most are unexpectedly delighted that the city gains new momentum after dark. The nightlife scene is one that's constantly growing and highly mercurial, given the chameleon-like character of clubs that aim to satisfy the crowd—one night it's Top 40 or contemporary; the next, reggae, pop-jazz, or strictly rock'n'roll. Live pop and fusion jazz have become especially popular—some say it's the ideal music for what is perceived as the typically laid-back lifestyle—and it can easily be found at a dozen or so venues throughout the county. Local rock clubs and nightclubs present music ranging from danceable contemporary–Top 40 to original rock and new-wave music by San Diego's finest up-and-coming groups. Discotheques and bars in Mission Valley and at the beaches tend to be the most crowded spots in the county on the weekends, but don't let that discourage you from visiting these quintessential San Diego hangouts. And should your tastes run to softer music, there are plenty of piano bars where frazzled nerves have a chance to wind down. Check the *Reader* for weekly band information or *San Diego* magazine's Restaurant & Nightlife Guide for the full range of nightlife possibilities.

California law prohibits the sale of alcoholic beverages after 2 AM. Bars and nightclubs usually stop serving at about 1:40 AM. You must be 21 to purchase and consume alcohol, and most places will insist on current identification. Be aware that California also has some of the most stringent drunk-driving laws, and roadblocks are not an uncommon sight.

The following credit card abbreviations are used: AE, American Express; DC, Diners Club; MC, MasterCard; V, Visa.

Bars and Nightclubs

Anthony's Harborside. The extra-spacious lounge looks out upon the beautiful harbor and features jazz and contemporary–Top-40 groups for dancing. *1355 N. Harbor Dr. downtown, tel. 619/232–6358. Open 11 AM–1:30 AM. Entertainment 8:30 PM–1:30 AM. AE, MC, V.*

Blarney Stone Pub and **Blarney Stone Too.** These two cozy Dublin-style pubs offer plenty of Irish brew and a wee bit of Irish folk music. *Original pub: 5617 Balboa Ave., Clairemont, tel. 619/279–2033. Pub Too: 7059 El Cajon Blvd., La Mesa, tel. 619/463–2263. Open 10 AM–1:30 AM. No credit cards.*

Cannibal Bar. A tropical-theme bar and nightclub in the Catamaran Resort Hotel, with nostalgic oldies and contemporary jazz. *3999 Mission Blvd., Pacific Beach, tel. 619/488–1081. Open 4 PM–1:30 AM. Entertainment 9 PM–1:30 AM. Closed Mon. AE, DC, MC, V.*

Diego's Loft. Downstairs is the raucous Diego's disco, while upstairs is the quieter, more sedate nightclub presenting live jazz groups and jam sessions. *860 Garnet Ave., tel. 619/272–1241. Open Thurs.–Sat. 8 PM–1 AM, Sun. 7 PM–midnight.*

The Hard Rock Cafe. A great place to dance and party amid an impressive collection of rock-and-roll memorabilia. *909 Prospect St., La Jolla, tel. 619/454–5101. Open daily 11 AM–1:30 AM. Live music Fri. and Sat. 8:30. AE, DC, MC, V.*

Islands Lounge. Tropical decor and lively contemporary music give this lounge in the Hanalei Hotel its unique character and attract a steady stream of regulars, 30–45. *2270 Hotel Circle N., Mission Valley, tel. 619/297–1101. Open 11 AM–1 AM. Entertainment 8 PM–midnight. AE, DC, MC, V.*

La Bodega Lounge. Located in the world-renowned Rancho Bernardo Inn, this comfortable and elegant spot with contemporary and big-band music is frequented by an older group. *17550 Bernardo Oaks Dr., Rancho Bernardo, tel. 619/277–2146. Open 10 AM–1:30 AM. Entertainment 8:30 PM–1:30 AM. AE, MC, V.*

Mercedes Lounge. The Bahia Resort Hotel's lounge has a superb view of the water and presents Top-40 rock and oldies for dancing. *998 W. Mission Bay Dr., tel. 619/488–0551. Open noon–2 AM. Entertainment 9 PM–2 AM. AE, DC, MC, V.*

Mick's P.B. In this spectacular club rich with Honduran mahogany, chicly dressed singles from 25 to 45 dance to live contemporary rock and Top 40 by bands predominantly from out of town. *4190 Mission Blvd., Pacific Beach, tel. 619/581–3938. Open 8 PM–1:30 AM. Entertainment 9 PM–1:30 AM. AE, DC, MC, V.*

Monk's. Down the street from the Mission San Diego de Alcalá, this down-to-basics spot attracts a steady clientele that listens and dances to Dixieland jazz, swing, rock, contemporary standards, and other varieties of music. *10475 San Diego Mission Rd., Mission Valley, tel. 619/563–0060. Open 11:30 AM–1:30 AM. Entertainment 9 PM–1:30 AM. MC, V.*

Old Del Mar Cafe. Offering rock to reggae, fusion jazz to oldies, and virtually every other popular style of music, this combination woodsy cafe–lounge is considered one of the best intimate venues in the North County. *2730 Via de la Valle, Del Mar, tel. 619/455–0920. Entertainment 9 PM–1:30 AM. MC, V.*

Old Pacific Beach Cafe. Certainly one of Pacific Beach's most popular after-dark spots, showcasing the broadest range of musical styles—fusion and pop jazz, R&B, rambunctious rock'n'roll, and reggae. *4287 Mission Blvd., tel. 619/270–7522. Entertainment 9:30 PM–1:30 AM. MC, V.*

Patrick's II. A downtown pub with definite Irish tendencies and a prime place for New Orleans–style jazz, blues, boogie, and rock. *428 F St., tel. 619/233–3077. Entertainment Tues.–Sat. 8:30 PM–1 AM, Sun. 5–10 PM. MC, V.*

Telly's Sports Bar. Named after actor Telly Savalas, this Sheraton bar has wide-screen TVs and all the acoutrements for sports fans, plus dance music with DJs. *1380 Harbor Island Dr., tel. 619/291–2900. Entertainment 9 PM–1 AM. Closed Sun.–Mon. AE, MC, V.*

Tio Leo's. A fun Mexican restaurant-cantina, often crowded with University of San Diego students, offers Top-40 dancing, fusion jazz, and popular reggae. *5302 Napa St., Bay Park, near Mission Bay, tel. 619/542–1462. Open 10 AM–1 AM. Entertainment 8 PM–1 AM. AE, MC, V.*

Vic's Bar & Restaurant. Located atop a first-rate steak house, the elegant bar and lounge host live contemporary bands for dancing on the weekends. *7825 Fay Ave., La Jolla, tel. 619/456–3789. Entertainment Fri.–Sat. 8:30 PM–12:30 AM. AE, MC, V.*

Jazz Clubs

B Street Cafe and Bar. Popular downtown watering hole for professionals, especially after 5, with above-average pop-jazz groups. *425 W. B St., tel. 619/236–1707. Entertainment 8 PM–1 AM. AE, MC, V.*

Cargo Bar. The San Diego Hilton Hotel's nautical-theme bar with a can't-beat view of the bay and a don't-miss lineup of jazz and contemporary bands. *1775 E. Mission Bay Dr., tel. 619/276–4010. Open 5 PM–1:30 AM. Entertainment 8:30 PM–1 AM. AE, DC, MC, V.*

Chuck's Steak House. A La Jolla institution, featuring jazz from a bevy of San Diego's better acoustic groups. *1250 Prospect St., La Jolla, tel. 619/454–5325. Entertainment Wed.–Thur. and Sun. 8 PM–midnight, Fri.–Sat. 9 PM–1 AM. AE, DC, MC, V.*

Croce's. The intimate jazz cave of restaurateur Ingrid Croce (singer-songwriter Jim Croce's widow) features superb acoustic-jazz musicians. *802 Fifth Ave., downtown in the Gaslamp Quarter, tel. 619/233–4355. Open 5 PM–1 AM. AE, MC, V.*

Elario's. A club on the top floor of the Summer House Inn, with a sumptuous ocean view and an incomparable lineup of internationally acclaimed jazz musicians every month. *7955 La Jolla Shores Dr., La Jolla, tel. 619/459–0541. Entertainment 8 PM–1 AM. AE, DC, MC, V.*

Fat City. Regulars sidle up to the extra-long bar in this nice Victorian-style lounge, where pop-jazz musicians take center stage Thur.–Sat. *2137 Pacific Hwy., near downtown, tel. 619/232–0686. Entertainment 8 PM–1 AM. AE, MC, V.*

Humphrey's. The premier promoter of the city's best jazz, folk, and light-rock summer concert series held out on the grass. The rest of the year the music moves indoors for some first-rate jazz Sat.–Sun. *2241 Shelter Island Dr., tel. 619/224–3577, taped concert information 619/523–1010. Entertainment 8 PM–midnight. AE, DC, MC, V.*

The Marine Room. Waves literally crash against the windows while jazz groups play. *2000 Spindrift Dr., La Jolla, tel. 619/459–7222. Entertainment nightly 7–11. AE, DC, MC, V.*

Pal Joey's. True to the roots of jazz, this comfortable neighborhood bar features Dixieland jazz Friday–Saturday. *5147 Waring Rd., Allied Gardens, near San Diego State University, tel. 619/286–7873. Entertainment 9 PM–1:30 AM. MC, V.*

Rock Clubs

Bacchanal. An all-concert venue that brings in a mixture of comedy, rock, nostalgia, jazz, R&B, and the like. *8022 Clairemont Mesa Blvd., Kearny Mesa, tel. 619/560–8022, taped concert information 619/560–8000. Entertainment 8:30–11:30 PM. MC, V.*

Belly Up Tavern. Located in converted Quonset huts, this eclectic live-concert venue hosts critically acclaimed artists who play everything from reggae, rock, new wave, Motown, and folk to—well, you name it. *143 S. Cedros Ave., Solana Beach, tel. 619/481–9022. Open 11 AM–1:30 AM. Entertainment 9:30 PM–1:30 AM. MC, V.*

Casbah. A small club showcasing rock, reggae, funk, and every other kind of band—except top-40—every night of the week. *2812 Kettner Blvd., near downtown, tel. 619/294–9033. Live bands at 9:30 nightly. No credit cards.*

Dance Machine. Plenty of room to dance to live rock groups. *1862 Palm Ave., Imperial Beach, tel. 619/429–1161. Open 4 PM–1:30 AM. Entertainment 9 PM–1:30 AM. Closed Sun.–Mon. MC, V.*

The Hype. One of San Diego's oldest bars keeps changing names but the scene stays much the same—loud top-40s from the DJs between the sets of top local bands. *3595 Sports Arena Blvd., tel. 619/223–5596. Open daily 6 PM–1:30 AM. MC, V.*

Iguanas. Though technically south of the border in Tijuana, Iguanas is considered a local club for those 18–21 years of age who cannot get into San Diego clubs. Iguanas hosts concerts by top-name bands and DJ dance music until 3 AM every night. A bus shuttles patrons back and forth from the border to the club. Tickets are available through Ticketron. *Pueblo Amigo Shopping Center, Tijuana, tel. 619/230–8585. Open 8 PM–2 AM, with concerts beginning at 10. MC, V.*

José Murphy's Nightclub and Pub. An enthusiastic though sometimes boisterous young crowd of beach-town regulars often packs this live-rock club-bar. *4302 Mission Blvd., Pacific Beach, tel. 619/270–3220. Open 11 AM–2 AM. AE, MC, V.*

Magnolia Mulvaney's. A mainstay for East County residents who come to listen to live rock'n'roll. *8861 N. Magnolia Ave., Santee, tel. 619/448–8550. Open 5:30 PM–1 AM. Entertainment Fri.–Sat. 9 PM–1 AM. AE, MC, V.*

Old Bonita Store & Bonita Beach Club. A South Bay hangout attracting singles 25–35 and featuring locally produced rock acts. *4014 Bonita Rd., Bonita, tel. 619/479–3537. Entertainment Tues.–Sat. 9:15 PM–1:15 AM. AE, MC, V.*

Park Place. Connected to a bowling alley, this rock club has a devoted East County following. *1280 Fletcher Pkwy., El Cajon, tel. 619/448–7473. Entertainment 9 PM–1:30 AM. MC, V.*

Rio's. Some of the most intriguing and innovative local rock, blues, and reggae bands like to perform here. *4258 W. Point Loma Blvd., Loma Portal, tel. 619/225–9559. Open 7 PM–1:30 AM. Entertainment 9 PM–1:30 AM. AE, MC, V.*

Spirit. An original-music club emphasizing the top local new-wave and experimental-rock groups. *1130 Buenos Ave., Bay Park, near Mission Bay, tel. 619/276–3993. Open 8 PM–1 AM. No credit cards.*

Winston's Beach Club. This bowling alley turned rock club features local bands, reggae groups, and occasional appearances by 60s rock bands. The crowd here can get a bit rowdy. *1921 Bacon St., Ocean Beach, tel. 619/222–6822. Live bands nightly 9 PM–2 AM. No credit cards.*

Country/Western Clubs

Abilene Country Saloon. An equal mix of tourists and local cowboys congregates at the Town & Country Hotel's urban version of the country dance club with live music. *500 Hotel Circle N, Mission Valley, tel. 619/291–7131. Open 4 PM–1:30 AM. Entertainment 9 PM–1:30 AM. Closed Sun. AE, DC, MC, V.*

The Country Bumpkin. The Dance Machine's country cousin is the best of South Bay's country clubs, featuring live bands. *1862 Palm Ave., Imperial Beach, tel. 619/429–1161. Open 4 PM–1:30 AM. Entertainment 9 PM–1:30 AM. Closed Sun.–Mon. MC, V.*

The Country Club. Live country bands nightly; jam sessions on Sunday. *1121 Third St., Chula Vista, tel. 619/426–2977. Live music nightly at 8 PM. No credit cards.*

Leo's Little Bit O' Country. The largest country/western dance floor in the county—bar none. *680 W. San Marcos Blvd., San*

Marcos, tel. 619/744–4120. Open 4 PM–1 AM. Entertainment 8:30 PM–1 AM. Closed Mon. MC, V.

Pomerado Club. The rustic dance hall, formerly a Pony Express station in the last century, now showcases the two-steppin' tunes of the house band, consisting of the owners. *12237 Pomerado Rd., Poway, tel. 619/748–1135. Entertainment Fri.–Sat. 9 PM–1:30 AM. No credit cards.*

Wrangler's Roost. A country/western haunt that appeals to both the long-time cowboy customer and the first-timer. *6608 Mission Gorge Rd., tel. 619/280–6263. Entertainment 9 PM–1:30 AM. MC, V.*

Comedy Clubs

Comedy Isle. Located in the Bahia Resort Hotel, this club offers the latest in local and national talent. *998 West Mission Bay Dr., tel. 619/488–6872. Shows Tues.–Thurs. 8:30, Fri.–Sat. 8:30, 10:30. AE, DC, MC, V.*

The Comedy Store. In the same tradition as the Comedy Store in West Hollywood, San Diego's version hosts some of the best national touring and local talent. *916 Pearl St., La Jolla, tel. 619/454–9176. Open Tues.–Thur. 8–10:30 PM, Fri.–Sat. 8 PM–1 AM. Closed Sun.–Mon. AE, MC, V.*

The Improv. A superb Art Deco–style club with a distinct East Coast feel, where some of the big names in comedy present their routines. *832 Garnet Ave., Pacific Beach, tel. 619/483–4520. Open 6:30 PM–midnight. Entertainment 8 PM–midnight. AE, MC, V.*

Discos

City Colors. Colorful and ritzy, attracting a classy crowd, City Colors is downtown's premier dance spot. *910 Broadway Circle, tel. 619/239–2200. Open 8 PM–2 AM for dancing. Closed Sun. AE, DC, MC, V.*

Club Diego's. A flashy discotheque and singles scene by the beach with excellent, nonstop dance music and friendly young (25–35) dancers. *860 Garnet Ave., Pacific Beach, tel. 619/272–1241. Open 8 PM–1:30 AM. AE, MC, V.*

Club Mick's. Vintage rock and roll in the midst of the beach scene. *4190 Mission Blvd., Mission Beach, tel. 619/581–3938. Open daily 5 PM–1:30 AM, Sat. 7 PM–1:30 AM. Closed Sunday. No credit cards.*

Confetti. A glitzy club, popular with young professionals, students, and anyone with an inclination to party. It metamorphoses into the alternative-music club **The Piranha Room** on Sunday only. *5373 Mission Center Rd., Mission Valley, tel. 619/291–8635. Open Mon.–Fri. 5 PM–2 AM, Sat. 7 PM–2 AM, Sun. 9 PM–2 AM. AE, MC, V.*

Crystal T's Live. A lounge, drawing the guests of the Town & Country Hotel along with local dancers 25–40. *500 Hotel Circle N, tel. 619/294–9010. Open 11:30 AM–1 AM. Entertainment Tues.–Sat. 9 PM–1:30 AM. AE, DC, MC, V.*

Emerald City. Alternative dance music and an uninhibited clientele keep this beach-town spot unpredictable—which is just fine with everyone. *945 Garnet Ave., Pacific Beach, tel. 619/483–9920. Open 8:30 PM–2 AM. Closed Sun.–Mon. No credit cards.*

Full Moon. North County's favorite nightspot is great for dancing to live and recorded music, with an ever-changing collection of acts, including occasional comedy and magic shows. *485 First St., Encinitas, tel. 619/436-7397. Open daily 2 PM-2 AM. Entertainment begins at 8. MC, V.*

Metro. Hip to the extreme and always hopping to the latest music mixes, this dance mecca has some of the most creatively dressed patrons in San Diego. *1051 University Ave., Hillcrest, tel. 619/295-2195. Open Wed.-Sun. 9 PM-2 AM. Closed Mon. and Tues. No credit cards.*

Time Machine. A club for dancing through the ages, from 1940s swing and big-band music on Sunday to the rock and contemporary standards of the 1980s during the rest of the week. *302 N. Midway Dr., Escondido, tel. 619/743-1772. Open 8 PM-1 AM. AE, MC, V.*

Torrey's. A beautifully appointed disco inside the La Jolla Marriott Hotel, where out-of-town guests and university students move to recorded Top-40 music. *4240 La Jolla Village Dr., La Jolla, tel. 619/587-1414. Open 8 PM-1 AM. AE, DC, MC, V.*

For Singles

El Torito. Notable happy hours and central location attract Yuppies and students to this Mission Valley Mexican restaurant. *445 Camino del Rio S, tel. 619/296-6154. Open 11 AM-2 AM. AE, DC, MC, V.*

Harbor House. In beautiful Seaport Village, the lounge of the popular seafood restaurant is packed equally with locals and tourists, dancing to Top-40 music. *831 W. Harbor Dr., tel. 619/232-1141. Open 4:30 PM-1:30 AM. Entertainment 9:30 PM-1:30 AM. AE, MC, V.*

The Red Onion. The beach scene doesn't get any hipper than this, with bikini-clad beach beauties perched on bar stools that overlook the dance floor. The noise level is several decibals beyond deafening. On the Mission Beach boardwalk at Belmont Park. *3125 Ocean Front Walk, tel. 619/488-9040. Open Sun.-Thurs. 10-10, Fri.-Sat. 10 AM-11 PM.*

T.G.I. Friday's. A prime after-work stop for young professionals and students, especially on Fridays; doesn't slow down until closing. *403 Camino del Rio S, Mission Valley, tel. 619/297-8443. Also at 8801 Villa La Jolla Dr., La Jolla, tel. 619/455-0880. Open 11:30 AM-1:30 AM. AE, DC, MC, V.*

The U.S. Grant Hotel. The classiest place in town to meet fellow travelers while relaxing with a scotch or martini at the mahogany bar. The best local jazz, R&B, and boogie-woogie bands alternate appearances during the week. Definitely for the over-30 business set. *326 Broadway, downtown, tel. 619/232-3121. Open daily 11 AM-1 AM. AE, DC, MC, V.*

Piano Bars/Mellow

Hotel Del Coronado. The fairy-tale hostelry that has hosted royalty and former presidents features beautiful piano music in its Crown Room and Palm Court, with dance-oriented standards in the Ocean Terrace Lounge. *1500 Orange Ave., Coronado, tel. 619/435-6611. Open 11 AM-1 AM. AE, DC, MC, V.*

Mille Fleurs. The comfortable piano bar of one of San Diego County's most celebrated restaurants features mood-setting standards. *6009 Paseo Delicias, Rancho Santa Fe, tel. 619/756-3085. Entertainment Wed.-Sat. 9 PM-1 AM. AE, MC, V.*

Top O' the Cove. Show tunes and standards from the '40s to the

'80s are the typical piano fare at this magnificent Continental restaurant in La Jolla. *1216 Prospect St., tel. 619/454–7779. Entertainment Wed.–Sun. 8 PM–midnight. AE, DC, MC, V.*

Westgate Hotel. One of the most elegant settings in San Diego offers piano music in the Plaza Bar. *1055 Second Ave., downtown, tel. 619/238–1818. Open 11 AM–1 AM. Entertainment 8:30 PM–midnight. AE, DC, MC, V.*

10 Excursions from San Diego

by Kevin Brass

San Diego County is larger than nearly a dozen U.S. states, with a population of over 2 million—the second largest county in California. It sprawls from the Pacific Ocean, through dense urban neighborhoods, to outlying suburban communities that seem to sprout overnight on canyons and cliffs. The Cleveland National Forest and Anza Borrego Desert mark the eastern boundaries. The busiest international border in the United States marks the county's southern line, where 53 million people a year legally cross between Baja and San Diego. To the north, the marines at Camp Pendleton practice land, sea, and air maneuvers in Southern California's largest coastal greenbelt, the demarcation zone between the congestion of Orange and Los Angeles counties and the mellower expansiveness of San Diego.

This chapter explores some of the day or longer trips you could schedule to areas outside the city of San Diego—to the North County, to inland and mountain communities, and to the desert.

The San Diego North Coast

To say the north coast area of San Diego County is different from the city of San Diego is a vast understatement. From the northern tip of La Jolla to Oceanside, a half-dozen small communities each developed separately from urban San Diego. In fact, they developed separately from each other, and each has its own flavorful history. Del Mar, for example, exists primarily because of the lure its wide beaches and Thoroughbred horse-racing facility extended to the rich and famous. Just a couple of miles away, agriculture, not paparazzi, played a major role in the development of Solana Beach and Encinitas. Up the coast, Carlsbad still reveals elements of its heritage, roots directly tied to the old Mexican rancheros and the entrepreneurial instinct of John Frazier, who told people the area's water could cure common ailments. In the late 19th century, not far from the current site of the posh La Costa Hotel and Spa, Frazier attempted to turn the area into a massive replica of a German mineral springs resort.

Today, the north coast is a booming population center. An explosion of development throughout the 1980s turned the area into a northern extension of San Diego. The freeways started to take on the typically cluttered characteristics of most Southern California freeways.

Beyond the freeways, though, the communities have maintained their charm. Some of the finest restaurants, beaches, and attractions in San Diego County can be found in the area, a true slice of So Cal heritage. From the plush estates and rolling hills of Rancho Santa Fe and the beachfront restaurants of Cardiff, to Mission San Luis Rey, a well-preserved remnant of California's first European settlers in Oceanside, the north coast is a distinctly different place.

Arriving and Departing

By Car I-5, the main freeway artery connecting San Diego to Los Angeles, follows the coastline. To the west, running parallel to it, is Old Highway 101, which never strays more than a quarter-mile from the ocean. Beginning north of La Jolla, where it is known as Torrey Pines Road, Old Highway 101 is a designated scenic route, providing access to the beauty of the coastline.

By Train Amtrak (tel. 619/239–9021 or 800/872–7245) operates trains daily between Los Angeles, Orange County, and San Diego. The last train leaves San Diego at approximately 9 PM each night; the last arrival is 11:30 PM. There are stops in Oceanside and Del Mar.

By Bus **The San Diego Transit District** (tel. 619/722–6283) covers the city of San Diego up to Del Mar, where the **North County Transit District** takes over, blanketing the area with efficient, ontime bus routes.

Greyhound-Trailways (tel. 619/239–9171) has regular routes connecting San Diego to points north, with stops in Del Mar, Solana Beach, Encinitas, and Oceanside.

By Taxi Several companies are based in the North County, including **Amigo Cab** (tel. 619/693–8681) and **Bill's Cab Co.** (tel. 619/755–6737).

By Plane **Palomar Airport** (tel. 619/758–6233), located in Carlsbad two miles east of I-5 on Palomar Airport Road, is a general aviation airport run by the County of San Diego and open to the public. Commuter airlines sometimes have flights from Palomar to Orange County and Los Angeles.

Guided Tours

Civic Helicopters (2192 Palomar Airport Rd., tel. 619/438–8424) offers whirlybird tours of the area from the air.

Exploring

Numbers in the margin correspond with points of interest on The San Diego North Coast map.

Any journey around the north coast area naturally begins at the beach, and this one begins at **Torrey Pines State Beach,** just south of Del Mar. At the south end of the wide beach, perched
❶ on top of the cliffs, is the **Torrey Pines State Reserve,** one of only two places (the other place is Santa Rosa Island off the coast of northern California) where the Torrey pine tree grows naturally. The park has a museum and an excellent set of hiking trails that snake through the 1,100-acre park, which is filled with exotic California shrubbery and features picturesque views from the cliffs. *Tel. 619/755–2063. Admission: $6 per car. Open daily 9 AM–sunset.*

❷ To the east of the state beach is **Los Penasquitos Lagoon,** one of the many natural estuaries that flow inland between Del Mar and Oceanside. Following Old Highway 101, the road leads into the small village of **Del Mar,** best known for its volatile political scene, celebrity visitors, and wide beaches. Years of spats between developers and residents have resulted in the new Del Mar Plaza, hidden by boulder walls and clever landscaping at

The San Diego North Coast

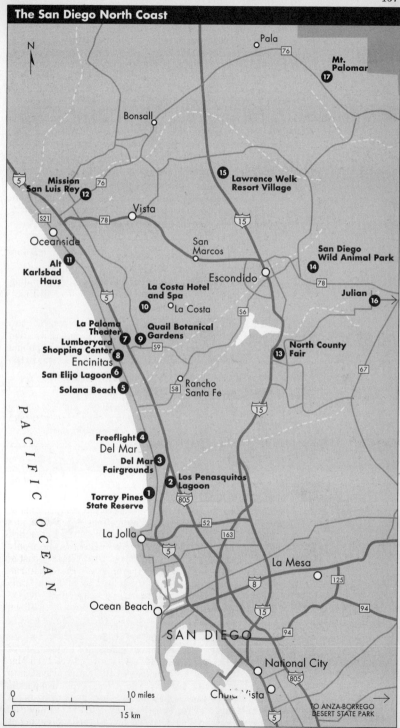

N

Pala

76

Mt. Palomar

17

Bonsall

5

Mission San Luis Rey

12

76

Lawrence Welk Resort Village

15

S21

Vista

78

15

Oceanside

San Marcos

Alt Karlsbad Haus

11

San Diego Wild Animal Park

5

Escondido

14

78

La Costa Hotel and Spa

10

La Costa

Julian

16

S6

La Paloma Theater

7 9

Quail Botanical Gardens

Lumberyard Shopping Center

8

S9

North County Fair

13

Encinitas

San Elijo Lagoon

6

Solana Beach

5

Rancho Santa Fe

S8

67

15

PACIFIC

Freeflight

4

Del Mar

Del Mar Fairgrounds

3

Los Penasquitos Lagoon

2

Torrey Pines State Reserve

1

805

OCEAN

La Jolla

52

163

5

La Mesa

125

Ocean Beach

8

SAN DIEGO

15

94

94

0 ____ 10 miles

0 ____ 15 km

National City

805

Chula Vista

5

TO ANZA-BORREGO DESERT STATE PARK

the corner of Old Highway 101 and 15th Street. The upper level
has a large deck and a view out to the ocean, and the restaurants and shops are excellent barometers of the latest in Southern California style. A left turn at 15th Street leads to
Seagrove Park, a small, extremely pleasant stretch of grass
overlooking the ocean. A right turn on Coast Boulevard provides access to Del Mar's beautiful beaches, particularly popular with Frisbee and volleyball players.

❸ Less than a half mile north, Coast Boulevard merges with Old
Highway 101. Across the road is the **Del Mar Fairgrounds,**
home to more than 100 different events a year, ranging from a
cat show to an auto race. *Via de la Valle Rd. exit west from I-5,
tel. 619/755–1161.*

The fairgrounds also host the annual summer meeting of the
Del Mar Thoroughbred Club (aka "Where the Turf Meets the
Surf"). The track brings the top horses and jockeys to Del Mar,
along with a cross section of the rich and famous, eager to bet
on the ponies. Crooner Bing Crosby and his Hollywood bud-
dies, Pat O'Brien, Gary Cooper, and Oliver Hardy, among
others, organized the track in the 1930s, primarily because
Crosby thought it would be fun to have a track near his Rancho
Santa Fe home. Del Mar soon developed into a regular stop for
the stars of stage and screen.

During the off-season, horse players can still gamble at the
fairgrounds, thanks to a satellite wagering facility. Races from
other California tracks are televised, and people can bet as if
the races were being run right there. Times vary, depending on
which tracks in the state are operating. *Tel. 619/755–1141. Racing season: July–Sept., daily except Tues. Post time 2 PM.*

❹ Near the fairgrounds, on Jimmy Durante Boulevard, there is a
small exotic bird-training facility, **Freeflight,** which is open to
the public. Visitors are allowed to handle the birds—a guaran-
teed kid pleaser. *2132 Jimmy Durante Blvd., tel. 619/481–
3148. Admission: $1. Open daily 9–5.*

Following Via de la Valle Road east from I-5 leads to the exclusive community of **Rancho Santa Fe,** one of the richest areas in
the country. Groves of huge, drooping eucalyptus trees, first
imported to the area by a railroad company looking to grow
trees for railroad ties, cover the hills and valleys, hiding the
posh estates. The little village of Rancho has some elegant and
quaint—and overpriced—shops and restaurants. But it is no
accident that there is little else to see or do in Rancho; the residents guard their privacy religiously. Even the challenging
Rancho Santa Fe Golf Course, the original site of the Bing
Crosby Pro-Am and considered one of the best courses in
Southern California, is still open only to members of the Rancho Santa Fe community.

❺ Back along the coast, along Old Highway 101 north of Del Mar,
is the quiet little beach community of **Solana Beach.** A highlight
of Solana Beach is **Fletcher Cove,** located at the west end of Lomas Santa Fe Drive, and called Pill Box by the locals because of
a bunkerlike lifeguard station on the cliffs above the beach.
Early Solana settlers used dynamite to blast the cove out of the
cliffs. It is an easy-access beach, with a large parking lot replete with a small basketball court, a favorite of local pickup
game players.

6 North of Solana Beach, separating Solana Beach from Cardiff, is the **San Elijo Lagoon,** home to many migrating birds. Trails wind around the entire area.

As you continue along Old Highway 101, past the cluster of hillside homes that make up Cardiff, past the campgrounds of the San Elijo State Beach, the palm trees of Sea Cliff Roadside Park (Swami's to the locals) and the golden domes of the Self Realization Fellowship mark the entrance to downtown **Encinitas.** The Self Realization Fellowship was built at the turn of the century and is a retreat and place of worship for the followers of an Indian religious sect.

7 Another landmark of old Encinitas (which was incorporated as a city in 1986, including the communities of Cardiff, Leucadia, and Olivenhain) is the **La Paloma Theater** on the north end of town on Old Highway 101 (at the corner of Encinitas Blvd., tel. 619/436–7469). The theater was built in the Roaring '20s as a stop for traveling vaudeville troupes. It has served as a concert hall, movie theater, and meeting place for the area ever since. Plays are still being rehearsed and performed here.

8 A newer landmark of Encinitas is the **Lumberyard Shopping Center,** a collection of small stores and restaurants that anchors the downtown shopping area. There is a huge selection of shopping centers inland at the intersection of Encinitas Boulevard and El Camino Real.

But Encinitas is known as the "Flower Capital of the World," not the "Shopping Center Capital of the World." Although the flower industry is not as prevalent as it once was, the city is still the home of Paul Ecke Poinsettias, the largest producer of the popular Christmas flower. A sampling of the area's dedication **9** to horticulture can be found at the **Quail Botanical Gardens,** home to thousands of different varieties of plants. *Encinitas Blvd. east from I-5 and turn left on Quail Gardens Dr., tel. 619/436–3036. Parking $1. Open daily 8–5.*

Old Highway 101 continues north through Leucadia, a small community best known for its small art galleries and stores. At the north end of Leucadia (which means "sheltered paradise" in Greek), La Costa Avenue meets Highway 101. Following La Costa Avenue east, past the Batiquitos Lagoon, leads to the fa- **10** mous **La Costa Hotel and Spa** (tel. 619/438–9111). It is noted for its excellent golf and tennis facilities and restaurants.

La Costa is technically part of the city of Carlsbad, which is centered farther north, west of the Tamarack Avenue and Elm Avenue exits of I-5. In Carlsbad, Old Highway 101 is called Carlsbad Boulevard. Large rancheros owned by wealthy Mexicans were the first settlements inland, while the coastal area was developed by an entrepreneur, John Frazier, who lured people to the area with talk of the healing powers of mineral water bubbling from a coastal well. The water was found to have the same properties as water from the German mineral wells of Karlsbad, hence the name of the new community. Remnants **11** from the era, including the original well, are found at the **Alt Karlsbad Haus,** a small museum and gift shop. *2802A Carlsbad Blvd., tel. 619/729–6912. Admission free. Open Mon.–Sat. 10–5, Sun. 1–4:30.*

North of Carlsbad is **Oceanside,** home of Camp Pendleton, the country's largest marine base, as well as a beautiful natural harbor teeming with activity. Oceanside Harbor is the north-coast center for fishing, sailing, and all ocean water sports. Oceanside Pier is a favorite hangout for fishermen. You can call for general harbor information (tel. 619/966–4570).

12 Oceanside is also home to **Mission San Luis Rey,** the largest and one of the best-preserved missions in the area. Built by Franciscan friars in 1798 to help educate and convert local Indians, San Luis Rey was the 18th and largest of the California missions. Today there is a picnic area, gift shop, and museum on the grounds. Self-guided tours are available through the grounds, where retreats are held. *Tel. 619/757–3651. Take Mission Ave. east from I-5. Open Mon.–Sat. 10–4, Sun. 1–4.*

Dining

Given the north-coast area's reputation as a suburban area, there is a surprisingly large selection of top-quality restaurants. In fact, San Diegans often take the drive north to enjoy the variety of cuisines offered in the North County. Prices are for one person and do not include drinks, taxes, or tip. The following credit card abbreviations are used: AE, American Express; DC, Diners Club; MC, MasterCard; V, Visa.

Expensive ($35–$50)

Del Mar **Remington's.** A luxurious and friendly atmosphere makes Remington's worth the high prices. The menu is exceptional and offers lobster, beef, lamb, and veal dishes. *2010 Jimmy Durante Blvd., tel. 619/755–5104. Reservations accepted. Jackets suggested. MC, V.*

La Costa **Pices.** Located near the La Costa Country Club, Pices represents the upper class of north-coast seafood restaurants. Traditional seafood, such as scallops and shrimp, is served in innovative and tasty dishes. *7640 El Camino Real, tel. 619/436–9362. Reservations accepted. Jackets required. AE, DC, MC, V.*

Rancho Santa Fe **Mille Fleurs.** This gem of a French auberge brightens a tiny village surrounded by country gentlemen estates. Just a few ★ miles from the county's famous vegetable farms, where the chef shops daily, this is a most romantic hideaway, with tempting cuisine to help the mood. *6009 Paseo Delicias, tel. 619/756–3085. Reservations advised. Jacket and tie advised. AE, DC, MC, V.*

Solana Beach **Frederick's.** This husband-and-wife-owned, friendly, relaxed bistro serves traditional French dishes with California-fresh overtones. Leave room for the freshly baked bread and one of the lush desserts. The menu changes weekly. *128 S. Acacia St., tel. 619/755–2432. Dress: casual. DC, MC, V. Closed for lunch. Closed Sun. and Mon.*

Moderate ($20–$35)

Cardiff **The Triton.** The beach and the sunset over the Pacific are the chief attractions of this outdoor dining spot. Although the seafood is just average, and when the surf is up the waiters tend to disappear, this place is fun, especially at lunch. *2530 S. Hwy. 101, tel. 619/436–8877. Dress: casual. AE, DC, MC, V.*

Del Mar **The Brigantine.** One of the stronger links in a chain of local fish restaurants, this one has a popular Oyster Bar. Unlucky gamblers from the nearby Del Mar Racetrack find the fair prices particularly attractive. *3263 Camino del Mar, tel. 619/481–1166. Dress: casual. AE, MC, V.*

Cilantros. For a taste of gourmet Mexican food—creative dishes full of subtle spices—Cilantros in Del Mar offers a wide variety of unusual creations, including shark *fajitas* and chicken with a mild chile sauce. The inexpensive tapas menu, with such delicacies as crab tostadas and three-cheese quesadillas, is a little easier on the wallet. *3702 Via de la Valle, tel. 619/259–8777. Reservations suggested. Dress: casual. AE, MC, V.*

Jake's. Another favorite of the racetrack crowd, Jake's is nestled on the shoreline, with the sort of view that turns one's thoughts to romance, not the Daily Double. There is a fresh fish special each day, as well as a different pizza offering. Those foolish enough to eat and run will appreciate the quick snack bar menu. *1660 Coast Blvd., tel. 619/755–2002. Reservations advised. Dress: casual. AE, MC, V. Closed for lunch Sat.*

Encinitas **Piret M.** This charming, sun-dappled French bistro looks as much like a sophisticated gourmet boutique (with delicacies for sale) as it does a countryside restaurant. The menu features hearty soups, quiches that will make a man of you, crisp fresh salads, a savory lamb ragout, large but elegant sandwiches, French omelets, and the sort of rich desserts that threaten the firmest of resolves. *897 First St., tel. 619/942–5152. Reservations advised. Dress: casual. AE, MC, V.*

Portofino's. This classy little restaurant attempts to re-create the atmosphere of the posh Riviera resort from which it gets its name. Homemade pasta and the seafood dishes are popular. *1108 First St., tel. 619/942–8442. Reservations accepted. Dress: casual. Full bar. AE, DC, MC, V.*

Santa Fe Grill. Despite its Mexican-sounding name, the Santa Fe Grill offers a straightforward selection of hamburgers, prime rib, and seafood dishes. *162 S. Rancho Santa Fe Rd., tel. 619/944–7455. Reservations accepted. Dress: casual. AE, MC, V.*

Inexpensive (under $20) **Los Olas.** Funky and inexpensive Los Olas, across the street from the beach in Cardiff, serves good food, especially the
Cardiff chimichangas, deep-fried flour tortillas stuffed with shredded, stewed beef, and the tasty fried burritos with heaps of guacamole and sour cream. The beachside atmosphere is better suited for lunch than dinner, though. *2655 S. Hwy. 101, tel. 619/942–1860. Dress: casual. MC, V.*

Solana Beach **Chung King Loh.** One of the better Chinese restaurants along the coast, Chung King Loh offers an excellent variety of Mandarin and Szechuan dishes. *552 Stevens Ave., tel. 619/481–0184. Dress: casual. AE, DC, MC, V. No lunch Sun.*

Fidel's. Rich in North County tradition, both Fidel's restaurants serve a wide variety of well-prepared dishes in a low-key, pleasant atmosphere. The original restaurant in Solana Beach, a two-story building with an outdoor patio area, is particularly nice. *607 Valley Ave., tel. 619/755–5292; 3003 Carlsbad Blvd., Carlsbad, tel. 619/729–0903. Dress: casual. AE, MC, V.*

Lodging

The prices below reflect the cost of a room for two people. Many hotels offer discount rates from October to May. The following credit card abbreviations are used: AE, American Express; DC, Diners Club; MC, MasterCard; V, Visa.

**Very Expensive
(over $120)**
Carlsbad

The Inn L'Auberge. By far the best hotel in Del Mar, the Inn sits across the street from the Del Mar Plaza and one block from the ocean. Modeled after the Tudor-style Hotel Del Mar, playground for Hollywood's elite in the early 1900s, the Inn is filled with dark wood antiques, fireplaces, and lavish floral arrangements—a high-style ambience, and a sense of refinement that clashes somewhat with the sun-drenched Southern California scene just outside its doors. The grounds are gorgeous, with stone paths winding throughout 5.2 acres, and leading to gazebos and pools; the spa specializes in European herbal wraps and treatments. *1540 Camino Del Mar, Del Mar, 92014, tel. 619/259–1515 or 800/553–1336. 120 rooms. Facilities: restaurant, 2 tennis courts, 2 pools, Jacuzzi, European-style spa. AE, MC, V.*

La Costa Hotel and Spa. This famous resort has recently gone through a $100 million renovation, and the style is now mildly Southwestern. Contemporary rooms are decorated in neutral tones, or rose and turquoise. You'll find all amenities, including supervised children's activities and a movie theater. *Costa del Mar Rd., 92009, tel. 619/438–9111 or 800/854–6564. 478 rooms. Facilities: 5 restaurants, pool, exercise room, golf, tennis, theater. AE, DC, MC, V.*

**Expensive
(over $75)**
Rancho Santa Fe

Rancho Valencia. This resort is so luxurious that several high-style magazines have chosen it for fashion backdrops, and have named it the most romantic hideaway in the United States. The suites are in red-tile-rooved casitas with fireplaces and private terraces. Tennis is the other draw here with 18 courts and a resident pro. *5921 Valencia Circle, tel. 619/756–1123 or 800/548–3664. 43 suites. Facilities: restaurant, 18 tennis courts, pool, 2 Jacuzzis, sauna. AE, MC, V.*

Carlsbad

Carlsbad Inn Beach and Tennis Resort. This hotel and time-share resort near the beach features modern amenities and rooms with an Old World feel. *3075 Carlsbad Blvd., 92008, tel. 619/434–7020. 200 rooms. Facilities: 2 restaurants, pool, health club, Jacuzzis, video room. AE, MC, V.*

Moderate ($55–$75)
Carlsbad

Best Western Beach View Lodge. Reservations are essential at this reasonably priced hotel at the beach. Some rooms have kitchenettes; others have fireplaces. Families tend to settle in for a week or more. *3180 Carlsbad Blvd., 92008, tel. 619/729–1151. 41 rooms. Facilities: Jacuzzi, sauna, swimming pool. AE, DC, MC, V.*

Del Mar

Stratford Inn. The inn offers a pleasant atmosphere just outside of town and three blocks from the ocean. Rooms are clean and well maintained; some have ocean views. Suites are available. Note: Not all rooms are air-conditioned, so be sure to ask before you reserve. *710 Camino del Mar, 92014, tel. 619/755–1501. 110 rooms. Facilities: 2 pools, Jacuzzi. AE, DC, MC, V.*

Encinitas

Moonlight Beach Hotel. This folksy laid-back motel is a favorite with those who enjoy the area's post-hippie aura and don't mind the traffic just outside their doors. All rooms have kitchens, and the beach is a few blocks away. *233 Second St., 92024, tel. 619/753–0623. 24 rooms. AE, MC, V.*

Radisson Inn Encinitas. Formerly called the Sanderling, this hotel on the east side of Old Highway 101 sits on a slight hill near the freeway. The rooms—some with an ocean view—are efficiently designed and unobtrusively decorated. *85 Encinitas Blvd., tel. 619/942–7455 or 800/333–3333. 92 rooms. Facilities: pool, whirlpool, putting green, restaurant. AE, DC, MC, V.*

Inexpensive (under $55)

Carlsbad

Carlsbad Lodge. The lodge is more than an easy walk from the beach, but there is a nice park nearby. The rooms are clean and pleasant. *3570 Pio Pico Dr., 92008, tel. 619/729–2383. 66 rooms. Facilities: Jacuzzi, sauna, swimming pool. AE, DC, MC, V.*

Encinitas

Budget Motels of America. This motel is adjacent to the freeway and within a block of the beach. Some rooms have VCRs and in-room movies—a good deal. *133 Encinitas Blvd., 92024, tel. 619/944–0260. 124 rooms. AE, DC, MC, V.*

Leucadia

Pacific Surf Motel. It will never be compared with The Ritz, but it is clean, comfortable, and near all the shops and restaurants of Encinitas. *1076 N. Hwy. 101, 92024, tel. 619/436–8763. 30 rooms. AE, MC, V.*

Oceanside

Oceanside TraveLodge. Near the beach and centrally located. *1401 N. Hill St., 92054, tel. 619/722–1244. 30 rooms. AE, DC, MC, V.*

Inland North County to Escondido and the Mountains

Even though the coast is only a few minutes away, the beach communities seem far removed from the mountain village of Julian or the quiet lakes of Escondido. Inland is the old California, where working farms and ranches are more common than the posh restaurants that mark the coastal landscape. The oak- and pine-covered mountains attracted prospectors seeking their fortune in gold long before tourists headed to the beaches. Home to wineries, old missions, freshwater lakes, and innumerable three-generation California families, the inland area of North County is the quiet, rural sister to the rest of San Diego County.

Escondido (aka the hidden valley) is a thriving, rapidly expanding residential and commercial city of more than 80,000 people and the center of a wide variety of attractions and destination points. To the south, the three-story, enclosed North County Fair shopping mall is something of a mecca for local shoppers, while animal lovers flock to the nearby Wild Animal Park, an extension of the San Diego Zoo, where animals roam free over the hills. To the north is an attraction of a completely different kind, Lawrence Welk Village, a museum and resort complex paying tribute to "Mr. Bubbles."

The mountains to the east of Escondido were once a remote outpost of the rugged West. Now they are a favorite spot for hikers, nature lovers, and apple-pie fanatics. Most of the apple lovers head to Julian, an old mining town that is now famous for its annual apple festival. Nearby Cuyamaca Rancho State Park is full of excellent trails and well-preserved picnic and camping areas. To the north, perched in a park atop Mt. Palomar, the Palomar Observatory is a haven for stargazers, and it has one of the most famous telescopes in the world.

The inland area may not be noted as a big tourist area, but a visit to San Diego wouldn't be complete without at least a drive through it.

Arriving and Departing

By Car Escondido is located at the intersection of Highway 78, which heads west from Oceanside, and I-15, the inland freeway connecting San Diego to Riverside, 30 minutes to the north of Escondido. Del Dios Highway winds from Rancho Santa Fe through the hills past Lake Hodges to Escondido. Highway 76, which connects with I-15 a few miles north of Escondido, veers east to Mt. Palomar. Highway 78 leads out of Escondido to Julian and Ramona. To reach the mountain areas from San Diego, take I-8 east to Highway 79 north.

By Bus The **North County Transit District** (tel. 619/743–6283) has routes crisscrossing the Escondido area.

By Taxi The **Yellow Cab Company** (tel. 619/745–7421) has a base in Escondido.

Important Addresses and Numbers

For general information on the inland area, contact the **Escondido Convention and Visitors Bureau** (tel. 619/745–4741). The **Julian Chamber of Commerce** (Box 413, Julian 92036, tel. 619/765–1857) can also supply useful information.

Exploring

Numbers in the margin correspond with points of interest on The San Diego North Coast map.

⑬ To shopping connoisseurs, **North County Fair** is a paradise, an 83-acre shopping complex with six major department stores and more than 175 specialty shops. *At the intersection of I-15 and Via Rancho Pkwy., tel. 619/489–2332.*

⑭ More than 2,500 animals roam the 1,800 acres of the **San Diego Wild Animal Park**, a zoo without cages. A 50-minute, five-mile monorail trip is the best way to see the animals, but the park is also a pleasant area to walk around. There are daily bird and trained-animal shows. *Tel. 619/234–6541. Take I-15 north to Via Rancho Pkwy. and follow the signs. Admission: $14.50 adults, $7.50 children under 16. Gates open daily 9–4; park open 9–6. Parking: $1.*

About a mile east of the Wild Animal Park, on San Pasqual Valley Road, is a monument and museum commemorating the site of the **Battle of San Pasqual.** On December 6, 1846, a troop of Americans, including famous frontier scout Kit Carson, was defeated by a group of Californios (Spanish-Mexican residents of California). This was the Californios' most notable success during the war (21 Americans were killed), but the Americans, with support from Commodore Stockton in San Diego, did gain control of the region. *15808 San Pasqual Valley Rd., Escondido, tel. 619/238–3380. Museum open 10–5. Admission free. Closed Tues. and Wed.*

Deer Park Vintage Cars and Wine (29013 Champagne Blvd., tel. 619/749–1666), also in Escondido, is a branch of the award-winning Napa Valley Deer Park Winery. Outside are a few select models from a collection of more than 50 vintage convertibles. There is also a delicatessen for impromptu picnics. Other popular local wineries: **Bernardo Winery** (tel. 619/

487–1866), **Menghini Winery** (tel. 619/765–2072), and **Ferrara Winery** (tel. 619/745–7632).

Following I-15 north past central Escondido leads to the **⑮ Lawrence Welk Resort Village.** Complete with a museum full of more Welk memorabilia than the average person may be able to tolerate, the complex also includes a golf course and dinner theater. *8860 Lawrence Welk Dr., tel. 619/749–3000. Admission free. Museum open Tues. and Thurs. 10–1, rest of the week 10–5.*

⑯ For more organic pleasures, the small mountain village of **Julian** provides an enchanting glimpse at life in the mountains. Gold was discovered in the area in 1869; quartz was unearthed a year later. More than $15,000,000 worth of gold was taken from local mines in the 1870s. Today, this charming mountain town retains many historic false-front buildings from the mining days. When gold and quartz became scarce, the locals turned to growing apples and pears, now the lifeblood of the little town. The pears are harvested in September and the apples, in October. The annual Julian Apple Days, first staged in 1909, begin October 1. *Take Hwy. 78 east from Escondido, tel. 619/765–1857.*

Tours of an authentic Julian gold mine are offered daily by the **Eagle Mining Company.** *Take C St. from the center of town, tel. 619/765–9921. Admission: $6 adults, $3 children under 16.*

Just a few minutes to the south of Julian are the 26,000 scenic acres of **Cuyamaca Rancho State Park** (tel. 619/765–0755). The park's hills feature several varieties of oak and pine trees, small streams, and meadows and provide a quiet escape for nature lovers. Primitive campsites are available. Camping is also permitted in the **Cleveland National Forest** (tel. 619/557–5050) to the south of I-8.

⑰ There are no apples or gold mines on **Mt. Palomar**—just one of the world's largest reflecting telescopes. Touring the observatory is a fascinating way to spend an afternoon. The park surrounding the observatory is full of lovely picnic areas and hiking trails. Also, don't forget to stop at Mother's Kitchen, the only restaurant on the mountain, which features some excellent vegetarian dishes. *Take Hwy. 76 east from I-15 and follow the signs, tel. 619/742–3462. Observatory open daily 9–4.*

For fans of the old California missions that pepper the Southern California landscape, **Mission San Antonio de Pala** still serves the Indians of the Pala Indian reservation. *Located on Hwy. 76 on the way to Mt. Palomar, tel. 619/742–3317. Museum and gift shop open Tues.–Sun. 10–3.*

Dining

The price categories below are based on the cost of a complete dinner for one, not including beverages, tax, or tip. The following credit card abbreviations are used: AE, American Express; DC, Diners Club; MC, MasterCard; V, Visa.

Expensive ($25–$40) Escondido **Lawrence Welk Resort Village Theater.** A prime-ribs buffet is a specialty of this dinner theater located in the Lawrence Welk museum and retirement community north of Escondido. *8860 Lawrence Welk Dr., tel. 619/749–3448. Reservations accepted. Jackets suggested. AE, MC, V.*

Rancho Bernardo
★
El Bizcocho. Chef Robert Blakeslee is well respected for the interesting veal, beef, and seafood dishes he creates and serves in the luxurious dining room of the Rancho Bernardo Inn. As an extra touch, low-calorie gourmet prix-fixe menus are available. The restaurant also serves an excellent Sunday brunch. *17550 Bernardo Oaks Rd., tel. 619/487–1611. Reservations accepted. Jackets required. AE, DC, MC, V.*

Moderate ($15–$25)
Fallbrook
Le Bistro. Located in the quiet, rural community of Fallbrook, this elegant restaurant specializes in shrimp and veal dishes. *119 N. Main St., tel. 619/723–3559. Reservations accepted. Dress: casual. AE, MC, V. Closed for lunch. Closed Mon.*

Julian
Pine Hills Lodge. The lodge is a dinner theater, mountain lodge, and restaurant all rolled into one. Sunday brunch is particularly popular at this 75-year-old establishment. *2960 La Posada Way, tel. 619/765–1100. Reservations accepted. Dress: casual. AE, DC, MC, V. Closed Mon.–Thurs.*

Lake San Marcos
Quails Inn. Part of the small Lake San Marcos Resort complex, this restaurant sits on Lake San Marcos. The menu is basic American fare, including prime ribs and lobster. *1035 La Bonita Dr., tel. 619/744–2445. Dress: casual. MC, V.*

Poway
Ristorante Galileo. This combination restaurant and tavern, perched on a hill in Poway, offers a wide variety of Italian and Continental dishes, including tasty homemade desserts. *12440 Poway Rd., tel. 619/748–2900. Reservations accepted. Dress: casual. AE, MC, V. No lunch weekends.*

Inexpensive (under $15)
Escondido
Hernandez' Hideaway. Isolated on a small road off Valley Parkway near Lake Hodges, this is a popular hangout for local Mexican-food lovers. *Rancho Lake Dr., tel. 619/746–1444. Dress: casual. Full bar. AE, DC, MC, V. Closed Mon.*

Rancho Bernardo
Acapulco. One of the better Mexican restaurant chains with outlets throughout the inland area. They are usually large, friendly restaurants with great margaritas. *16785 Bernardo Center Dr., tel. 619/487–6701; 1020 W. San Marcos Blvd., San Marcos, tel. 619/471–2150; 1541 E. Valley Pkwy., Escondido, tel. 619/741–9922. Dress: casual. AE, MC, V.*

Lodging

The following credit card abbreviations are used: AE, American Express; DC, Diners Club; MC, MasterCard; V, Visa.

Very Expensive (over $120)
Rancho Bernardo
Carmel Highland Golf and Tennis Resort. Country living is emphasized at this pale-pink compound of three-story town house-style buildings bordering a 6500-acre golf course. The packages for golf, tennis, or fitness regimes are quite reasonable. This is a good spot for a totally relaxing weekend. *14455 Penasquitos Dr., 92129, tel. 619/672–9100 or 800/622–9223. 176 rooms. Facilities: 3 restaurants, golf course, 6 tennis courts, 2 pools, health & fitness center. AE, DC, MC, V.*

Rancho Bernardo Inn. Pampering and a sense of tranquillity can be had here, while enjoying a game on the championship golf course or a sublime Sunday brunch at El Bizcocho, one of the county's best restaurants. The country-style rooms have large floral bouquets, plush easy chairs, and tiled baths. The health club offers three types of intense massages, and a children's camp is available in August. *17550 Bernardo Oaks Dr., 92129, tel. 619/487–1611 or 800/854–1065. 287 rooms. Facili-*

ties: 2 pools, tennis courts, golf course, restaurant, bar. AE, DC, MC, V.

Expensive **Lawrence Welk Village Inn.** About 15 minutes north of Es-
($90–$120) condido, this pleasant inn is far from everything except the the-
Escondido ater, museum, and golf course of the complex saluting Welk.
The rooms have a Southwestern flavor, with bleached woods
and mauve and turquoise furnishings. *8860 Lawrence Welk Dr.
92026, tel. 619/749–3000 or 800/932–WELK. 98 rooms. Facilities: Restaurant, shopping, pool, spa, 3 golf courses, tennis,
theater. AE, MC, V.*

Fallbrook **Pala Mesa Resort Hotel.** The main attraction at this isolated
property is an excellent golf course. The rooms have all been
recently redecorated in greys and burgundy and traditional
furniture. *2001 Old Hwy. 395, 92028, tel. 619/728–5881 or 800/
822–4600. 135 rooms. Facilities: tennis courts, spa, restaurant. AE, DC, MC, V.*

Moderate ($55–$75) **Julian Lodge.** A quiet bed-and-breakfast near the center of
Julian town, with a big fireplace in the lobby and antique furnishings.
The lodge offers the free use of bicycles to its guests. *Box 1930,
Fourth and C Sts., 92036, tel. 619/765–1420. 23 rooms. AE,
MC, V.*

Pine Hills Lodge. This secluded mountain lodge has an on-site
dinner theater (Fri.–Sat. year-round). The rooms are clean but
decorated in a very plain country style. The lodge rooms (moderate) have sinks and share baths. Some cabins have fireplaces.
*2960 La Posada, 92036, tel. 619/765–1100. 12 cabins, 5 lodge
rooms (shared bath). AE, DC, MC, V.*

The Desert

Every spring, the stark desert landscape east of the Cuyamaca
Mountains explodes with color. It's the annual blooming of the
wildflowers in the Anza-Borrego Desert State Park, less than a
two-hour drive from central San Diego. The beauty of this annual spectacle, as well as the natural quiet and blazing climate,
lures tourists and natives to the area.

The area features a desert and not much more, but it is one of
the favorite parks of those Californians who travel widely in
their state. People seeking bright lights and glitter should look
elsewhere. The excitement in this area stems from watching a
coyote scamper across a barren ridge or a brightly colored bird
resting on a nearby cactus, or from a waitress delivering another cocktail to a poolside chaise longue. For hundreds of years,
the only humans to linger in the area were Indians from the San
Dieguito, Kamia, and Cahuilla tribes, but the extreme temperature eventually forced the tribes to leave, too. It wasn't until
1774, when Mexican explorer Captain Juan Bautista de Anza
first blazed a trail through the area as a shortcut from Sonora to
San Francisco, that modern civilization had its first glimpse of
the oddly beautiful wasteland.

Today, more than 500,000 acres of desert are included in the
Anza-Borrego Desert State Park, making it the largest state
park in the United States. It is also one of the few parks in the
country where people can camp anywhere. No campsite is necessary; just follow the trails and pitch a tent anywhere in the
park.

Following the trails is an important point, since vehicles are prohibited from driving off the road in most areas of the park. However, there are 14,000 acres set aside in the eastern part of the desert near Ocotillo Wells for off-road enthusiasts. General George S. Patton conducted field training in the Ocotillo area to prepare for the World War II invasion of North Africa, and the area hasn't been the same since.

The little town of Borrego Springs acts as an oasis in this natural playground. Not exactly like Palm Springs—it lacks the wild crowds and preponderance of insanely wealthy residents—Borrego is basically a small retirement community, with the average age of residents about 50. For those who are uninterested in communing with the desert without a shower and pool nearby, Borrego provides several pleasant hotels and restaurants for travelers.

We recommend visiting this desert between October and May because of the extreme summer temperatures. Winter temperatures are comfortable, but nights (and sometimes days) are cold, so bring a warm jacket.

Arriving and Departing

By Car Take I-8 east to Highway 79 north. Turn east on Highway 78.

By Bus The **Northeast Rural Bus System** (NERBS) (tel. 619/765–0145) connects Julian, Borrego Springs, Oak Grove, Ocotillo Wells, Agua Caliente, Ramona, and many of the other small communities that dot the landscape with El Cajon, 15 miles east of downtown San Diego, and the East County line of the San Diego trolley, with stops at Grossmont shopping center and North County Fair.

By Plane Borrego Springs Airport (tel. 619/767–5548) has the nearest runway.

Important Addresses and Numbers

For general information about the Borrego and desert areas, contact the **Borrego Chamber of Commerce** (tel. 619/767–5555). For information on the state park, contact the Visitor Center, **Anza-Borrego Desert State Park** (Box 299, Borrego Springs 92004, tel. 619/767–5311). You can call the Visitor Center for information on when the wildflowers are blooming, or you can send a self-addressed postcard and they'll send it back when the flowers bloom. For campsite information, call **MISTIX** (tel. 800/444–7275).

Exploring

The **Anza-Borrego Desert State Park** is too vast even to consider exploring all its areas. Most people stay in the hills surrounding Borrego Springs. An excellent underground **Visitor Information Center** (tel. 619/767–5311) and museum are reachable by taking the Palm Canyon Drive spur west from the traffic circle in the center of town. The rangers are helpful and always willing to suggest areas to camp or hike. There is also a short slide show about the desert, shown throughout the day. A short, very easy trail from the Visitor Center to the campground will take you past many of the cacti illustrated in Visitor Center displays.

One of the most popular camping and hiking areas is **Palm Canyon,** just a few minutes west of the Visitor Information Center. A 1½-mile trail leads to a small oasis with a waterfall and palm trees. If you find palm trees lining city streets in San Diego and Los Angeles amusing, seeing this grove of native palms around a pool in a narrow desert valley may give you a new vision of the dignity of this tree. The Borrego Palm Canyon campground (on the desert floor a mile or so below the palm oasis) is one of only two developed campgrounds with flush toilets and showers in the park. (The other is Tamarisk Grove Campground at the intersection of Highway 78 and Yaqui Pass Road.)

Other points of interest include **Split Mountain** (take Split Mountain Rd. south from Hwy. 78 at Ocotillo Wells), a narrow gorge with 600-foot perpendicular walls. You can drive the mile from the end of the paved road to the gorge in a passenger car if you are careful (don't get stuck in the sand). Don't attempt the drive in bad weather, when the gorge can quickly fill with a torrent of water.

On the way to Split Mountain (while you are still on the paved road), you'll pass a grove of the park's unusual **elephant trees** (10 feet tall, with swollen branches and small leaves). There is a self-guided nature trail; pick up a brochure at the parking lot.

You can get a good view of the Borrego Badlands from **Font's Point,** off Borrego-Salton Seaway (S22). The badlands are a maze of steep ravines that are almost devoid of vegetation. Park rangers sometimes give guided tours of the region above the badlands.

You drive your own car in a caravan behind the ranger, stopping for closer looks and detailed information.

There is little to do in **Borrego Springs** itself except lie in the sun, lie in the shade, or take advantage of the hot days and recreate in the sun. The challenging 18-hole Rams Hill Country Club course is open to the public (tel. 619/767–5000), as is the Borrego Roadrunner Club (tel. 619/767–5652), but you'll have to know a member to play the private 18 holes of the De Anza Country Club located in the north end of the valley (tel. 619/767–5105).

For tennis fans, the Borrego Tennis Club (tel. 619/767–9725) has four lighted courts open to the public. One of the best and most appreciated deals in town is the Borrego Springs High School pool, located at the intersection of Saddle and Cahuilla roads, which is open to the public during the summer.

Most people prefer to explore the desert in a motorized vehicle. While it is illegal to ride two- or four-wheel vehicles off the trails in the state park, the **Ocotillo Wells State Vehicular Recreation Area** (tel. 619/767–5391), reached by following Highway 78 east from Borrego, is a popular haven for off-road enthusiasts. The sand dunes and rock formations are challenging as well as fun. Camping is permitted throughout the area, but water is not available. The only facilities are in the small town (or, perhaps, it should be called no more than a corner) of Ocotillo Wells.

To the east of Anza-Borrego is the Salton Sink, a basin that (although not as low as Death Valley) consists of more dry land below sea level than anywhere else in the hemisphere. The Salton Sea is the most recent of a series of lakes here, divided from the

Gulf of California by the delta of the Colorado River. The current lake was created in 1905–7 when the Colorado flooded north through canals meant to irrigate the Imperial Valley. The water is extremely salty, even saltier than the Pacific Ocean, and it is primarily a draw for fishermen seeking corvina, croaker, and tilapia. Some boaters and swimmers also use the lake. The state runs a pleasant park with sites for day camping, recreational vehicles, and primitive camping. *Take Hwy. 78 east to Hwy. 111 north, tel. 619/393–3052.*

Bird-watchers particularly will love the **Salton Sea National Wildlife Refuge.** A hiking trail and observation tower make it easy to spot the dozens of varieties of migratory birds stopping at Salton Sea. *At the south end of Salton Sea, off Hwy. 111, tel. 619/348–5278.*

For hunters, the **Wister Wildlife Area** (tel. 619/348–0577), off Highway 111 on the east side of Salton Sea, controls the hunting of water fowl in the area. There are campsites available.

Dining

Quality, not quantity, is the operable truism of dining in the Borrego area. Restaurants are scarce and hard to find, but the best are truly top quality. Prices are based on the cost of a complete meal for one, not including beverage, tax, or tip. The following credit card abbreviations are used: AE, American Express; DC, Diners Club; MC, MasterCard; V, Visa.

Moderate ($10–$20) **La Casa del Zorro.** An elegant Continental dining experience. The restaurant also serves Sunday brunch. *3845 Yaqui Pass Rd., tel. 619/767–5323. Reservations accepted. Dress: no shorts or jeans. AE, DC, MC, V.*

Rams Hill Country Club. An elegant, top-notch Continental restaurant in the middle of the desert. The club also serves Sunday brunch. *1881 Rams Hill Rd., tel. 619/767–5006. Reservations accepted. Dress: casual; jacket required on Sat. AE, MC, V. Closed for dinner Mon.–Wed., July–Oct. 1.*

Inexpensive (under $10) **Chefs for You.** A deli located in the largest shopping center in Borrego. *561 The Mall, tel. 619/767–3522.*

Lodging

If camping is not your thing, there are two very nice resorts near Borrego Springs that offer fine amenities without the overdevelopment of Palm Springs. Prices are based on the cost of a room for two. In the summer months, rates drop by as much as 50%. The following credit card abbreviations are used: AE, American Express; DC, Diners Club; MC, MasterCard; V, Visa.

Expensive (over $70) **Ram's Hill Country Club.** A relatively new hacienda-style country club in the middle of the desert. Patio units are on the golf course. *Box 664, Borrego Springs, 92004, tel. 619/767–5028. 20 units. Facilities: tennis courts, Jacuzzi. AE, MC, V.*

La Casa del Zorro. A small low-key resort complex in the heart of the desert, where you need only walk a few hundred yards to be alone out under the sky and you may well see roadrunners crossing the highway. The accommodations are in comfortable 1–3 bedroom ranch-style houses complete with living rooms and kitchens. *3845 Yaqui Pass Rd., 92004, tel. 619/767–5323 or 800/*

325–8274. 77 suites, 94 rooms, 19 casitas. Facilities: tennis courts, golf course, horseback riding, bicycles. AE, DC, MC, V.

Palm Canyon Resort. One of the largest facilities in the area, with a hotel, RV park, restaurant, and recreational facilities. *221 Palm Canyon Dr., 92004, tel. 619/767–5342 or 800/242–0044 in CA. 44 rooms. Facilities: 138 RV spaces, 2 pools, 2 Jacuzzis, restaurant, general store, laundromat.*

11 Ensenada and Tijuana

by Maribeth Mellin and Jane Onstott

San Diegan Jane Onstott is a travel writer and photographer and contributor to Fodor's Mexico *and* Fodor's South America *guides.*

Just 18 miles south of San Diego lies Mexico's Baja peninsula, a stretch of beaches, desert, and hills that has long been a refuge for Californians with an urge to swim, surf, fish, and relax in a country unlike their own. One usually enters Baja through Tijuana, Mexico's fourth-largest city. A teeming metropolis of more than one million residents, Tijuana can hardly be called a border town. It is a city, yet so unlike a U.S. city that the traveler feels instantly immersed in a foreign country. The language is Spanish, often called "Spanglish" for the local mix of Spanish and English spoken between residents and visitors. The currency is the peso, which fluctuates in value sporadically. The residents come from the south, from throughout Mexico and Central America. The visitors come from throughout the world. Tijuana's promoters like to call it "the most visited city in the world."

Tijuana's international border is the busiest, and often the most troublesome, international border in the United States. Tijuana attracts hundreds of new residents a week, drawn to bordertown wages that far exceed the income in their native towns. The border fence that stretches through the canyons and hills between Tijuana and California is filled with man-size holes; helicopters and jeeps patrol these barren landscapes, attempting to deter illegal immigration. Tijuana also attracts hordes of visitors, coming to work and play. Tourism in Tijuana and neighboring Rosarito Beach and Ensenada practically doubles each year and is easily the area's leading industry. In this sense, Tijuana is most assuredly a border town.

Until the toll highway to Ensenada was finished in 1967, travelers going south drove straight through downtown Tijuana, stopping along Avenida Revolución and the side streets for supplies and souvenirs. The free road, still used by those with plenty of time for wandering, curves over the hills through barren ranch land and eventually turns west to the coast at Rosarito Beach. The toll road now bypasses downtown (if you follow the signs carefully) and cuts down on the traffic through the hills, which have now become full-size towns called *colonias*.

During the seventies and eighties, Tijuana's population and tourism exploded. In 1970, Tijuana's population was under 300,000; today it is over a million. The city has spread into canyons and dry riverbeds and over hillsides and ocean cliffs. Many of its residents live in total poverty, in cardboard shacks far from electricity and running water. The city is crowded; services are constantly overwhelmed and the government is forever dealing with natural disasters such as floods. Still, Tijuana attracts more and more businesses setting up shop in *maquiladoras*, factories and plants that employ thousands of Tijuana's residents.

As a tourist spot, Tijuana is mostly visited on day trips or used as a layover for trips farther into Mexico. Southern Californians are accustomed to taking advantage of the lower airfares into Mexico from the Tijuana airport; if you are planning a trip farther into Mexico, you might want to compare the rates out of Tijuana. There are plenty of good-quality hotels in the city, and taxis to and from the airport are economical. Some of the hotels offer reduced-rate weekend packages, luring the travelers who normally just pass through town on their way to the coast. With tourism predicted to double again in the next few years, Tijuana is sure to continue to add more and more luxury hotels and attractions.

Not long ago, Rosarito Beach (or Playas de Rosarito) was a small seaside community with no tourist trade to speak of. It was, and still is, part of the municipality of Tijuana, an overlooked suburb of sorts on the way to Ensenada. Today, Rosarito has an identity of its own as an important resort area undergoing massive development. It is predicted that within the next few years, Rosarito will be a municipality with a local government overseeing a rapidly growing population of Mexicans and transplanted Americans.

The 1980s have brought an amazing building boom to Rosarito. The main street, alternately known as the Old Ensenada Highway and Boulevard Benito Juárez, is packed with restaurants, bars, and shops. The Quinta Del Mar resort, with its high-rise condos, lavish restaurants, and sprawling hotel buildings, has brought new life to the north end of town, where, in the past, there stood only a few taco stands and clusters of horses for rent. High-rise hotel towers, low-rise time-share resorts, and sprawling shopping malls are filling up every vacant lot. Rosarito Beach has hit the big time.

It is still, however, a relaxing place to visit. Southern Californians have practically made Rosarito a weekend suburb; surfers, swimmers, and sunbathers find a sense of adventure at the beach. The oceanfront seems much wilder and purer south of the border; for long stretches, both north and south of Rosarito, the coastline cliffs are free of houses and highways and the horizon seems miles away above the gray/blue/green waters. Whales pass not far from shore on their winter migration; dolphins and sea lions sun on rocky points in the cliffs. Whether you travel the toll road (Ensenada Cuota) or the free road (called Ensenada Libre or the Old Ensenada Highway), the view is startling, soothing, and sensational, particularly on a crystal-clear day.

Visitors find a combination of hedonism and health in Rosarito. One of the area's most popular attractions is its seafood; no visit is complete without a meal of lobster, shrimp, or abalone. Prohibition may have ended in the States, but the visiting Americans act as if they've been dry for months—margaritas and beer are the favored thirst-quenchers. People let down their hair and their inhibitions here (although the local constables keep things from getting out of hand). A typical Rosarito day might begin with a breakfast of eggs, refried beans, and tortillas followed by a horseback ride down the beach. Lying in the sun or strolling through the shops takes care of midday. Siestas are imperative, whether they're spent back on the beach, by the pool, or at a waterfront bar. More shopping, strolling, or sleeping, then it's time for dinner—a major event for most visitors. Rosarito's developers are working on building enough hotel rooms to meet the demand; its restaurant owners have acted more quickly. There has to be at least 50 restaurants in the Rosarito area. Most have similar menus—seafood, steak, and Mexican basics—but each has its own style of cooking, clientele, and ambience. There is no lack of food here.

Ensenada is a major port city 65 miles south of Tijuana on Bahia de Todos Santos. The view along Mexico Highway 1 from Tijuana to Ensenada is spectacular; the paved highway often cuts a path between low mountains and high oceanside cliffs; exits lead to rural roads and oceanfront campgrounds. The Coronado Islands can be clearly seen off the coast of Tijuana; below Rosarito Beach hang gliders lift off from towering sand dunes. Californians often weekend along this coastline. Their new condos and homes appear in resort communities with impressive white villas, but much of the coastline is still wild and undeveloped.

A small fishing community, San Miguel, sits on the highway just north of Ensenada; the smell of fish from the canneries lining the highway can be overpowering at times. The beach area between San Miguel and Ensenada has long been a haven of moderately priced oceanfront motels and trailer parks, but one luxury hotel has been completed, others are under construction, and still more are in the planning stages.

Like much of Baja, Ensenada has grown incredibly in the past five years, and its charms have been somewhat disguised by the construction. The harbor is one of Mexico's largest seaports and has a thriving fishing fleet and fish-processing industry.

Ensenada is a popular weekend destination; many of the travelers are repeat visitors who stick with their favorite hotels, shops, and restaurants. The beaches north and south of town are good for swimming, sunning, and surfing; there are no beaches in Ensenada proper. Many of the hotels have swimming pools; relaxation and tanning are popular pastimes. Ensenada turns into a real party town on holiday weekends, when the young, rowdy crowd spreads from Hussong's Cantina into the streets. Many of the hotels have strict rules about having guests and/or alcoholic beverages in the rooms; one look at the crowd and you can understand why. Be sure to ask for a room far from the hotel's center if you're planning on sleeping rather than partying.

Official Requirements

Passports and Tourist Cards
U.S. citizens entering Mexico by road are required to have proof of citizenship. The only acceptable proof of citizenship is either a valid passport or an original birth certificate plus a photo ID. Tourist cards are not needed unless you are traveling south of Ensenada or are planning to stay longer than 72 hours. Otherwise, tourist cards can be obtained from the information booth just inside the border.

Customs
U.S. residents may bring home duty free up to $400 worth of foreign goods, as long as they have been out of the country for at least 48 hours. Each member of the family is entitled to the same exemption, regardless of age, and exemptions may be pooled. Included in the allowances for travelers 21 or older are one liter of alcohol, 100 cigars (non-Cuban), and 200 cigarettes. Only one bottle of perfume trademarked in the United States may be imported. There is no duty on antiques or works of art more than 100 years old. Anything exceeding these limits will be taxed at the port of entry and may be taxed in the traveler's home state.

Since Mexico is considered a "developing" country, many arts and handicrafts may be brought back into the United States duty free. You will need to declare the items and state their value and use, but they won't count against your $400 limit.

Getting Around

Since you've come as far as the southwesternmost city in the United States, take advantage of the opportunity and go *un poquito mas alla* (just a bit farther) and experience Mexico. Baja California begins just 18 miles south of downtown San Diego. Tijuana, at the international border, can be reached from San Diego by bus, trolley, or car; from there, one has the option of continuing south by bus or car. Tijuana, Rosarito Beach, Ensenada, and points in between are viable day trips; the 67-mile trek from Tijuana to Ensenada takes about 2½ hours by car.

Passports are required of non-U.S. citizens for reentry at the San Ysidro or Otay Mesa border crossings.

By Bus For listings of bus lines connecting San Diego and Rosarito Beach and Ensenada, *see* Guided Tours, below.

Within Baja, **Autotransportes de Baja California** and **Tres Estrellas** link Tijuana with points beyond. The old Tijuana Bus Station is at Avenida Madero and Calle 2; tel. 668/6–9515. The new bus depot is located at the outskirts of town where Boulevard Lazaro Cardenas turns into the Airport Highway. Take a taxi or catch a bus on Calle 2 east of Avenue Constitución. If you wish to visit any other beach towns along the route, be sure to take a local, not an express, bus. In Ensenada, the bus station is at Avenida Riveroll between Calles 10 and 11, tel. 667/8–2322.

By Car Take U.S. I–5 or 805 to the border crossing in San Ysidro. If visiting Tijuana for the day, consider parking in one of the lots on the U.S. side and walking across the border. Be sure to purchase Mexican auto insurance, available at many stands before the last U.S. exit, before driving across the border. U.S. car-rental companies are beginning to allow drivers to take their cars into Mexico. You must purchase Mexican auto insurance when you rent the car and inform the company of your destination.

Mexico Highway 1, called Ensenada Cuota (toll road) runs from the border at Tijuana crossing to Rosarito and Ensenada along the coast; follow the Rosarito, Ensenada signs. The current toll between Tijuana and Ensenada is close to U.S. $10; the road is in good condition, but parts of it are often under construction, so drive with care. The free road, called the Old Ensenada Highway (Ensenada Libre) takes longer than the toll road and is a bit rough in spots, although perfectly serviceable. To visit beaches or small towns along the coast, get off the toll road and drive along the free road.

Beaches, restaurants, and other locations along the coast are often designated by the number of kilometers they are located from the beginning of the peninsular highway. A restaurant with an address of Km 55, therefore, would be 34 miles down the road; look for roadside markers to indicate these locations.

Rosarito Beach lies 18 miles south of Tijuana on the coast. To get there by car, simply take the toll road or the Ensenada Libre to the Rosarito Beach exit. You can tour Rosarito Beach proper on foot, which is a good idea on weekends, when Boulevard Juárez has bumper-to-bumper traffic. To reach Puerto

Nuevo and other points south, continue on Boulevard Juárez, also called Ensenada Libre, through town and south.

Ensenada is an easy city to navigate; most streets are marked. To reach the hotel and waterfront area, stay with alternate Highway 1 as it travels along the fishing pier and becomes Boulevard Costero, also known as Lázaro Cardenas.

By Boat The *Ensenada Express* (tel. 619/232–2109) provides round-trip transportation to Ensenada from San Diego (plus a Continental breakfast) for $59. It leaves the B Street Pier, downtown, at 9 AM daily (except Wednesday) and returns at 9 PM. **Norwegian Cruise Lines'** *Southwood* will transport you in style from Los Angeles to Ensenada. Three- and four-day excursions are available, beginning at around $400. Call 800/327–7030 for details or reservations. The **Admiral Cruise Lines'** *Azure Seas* has a similar schedule (tel. 800/327–2693).

By Trolley The bright red **San Diego Trolley** (tel. 619/231–8549) runs to the border and is the most convenient transportation for a day trip from San Diego to Tijuana. Trolleys depart from the station on Kettner Boulevard, across the street from the Santa Fe Depot in downtown San Diego, every 15 minutes during the day (every 30 minutes after 7:30 PM). The trip costs $1.50 and takes about 45 minutes. Once you reach the border, you must walk across a long freeway overpass to reach the pedestrian entrance into Mexico. There are taxis on the Mexican side of the border to take you to your destination.

By Taxi Taxis called *rutas* will drive you from downtown Tijuana, at Calle Madero and Calle 3, to Rosarito. The drivers usually won't leave until they have four passengers. The fare should be under $10 per person. In Ensenada, the central taxi stand *(sitio)* is located on López Mateos by the Bahia Hotel (tel. 667/8–3475). Be sure to negotiate the price before the taxi starts moving. Destinations within the city should cost $5 or less.

Scenic Drives

Though the toll road (Ensenada Cuota) is the quickest route from Tijuana to Ensenada, you bypass the charm of seeing Baja's coastal communities close up. To get a better look, leave the toll road at the Rosarito exit and travel the free road. Stop at the Rosarito Beach Hotel on the south end of town for a margarita and a lovely view of the ocean.

Traveling south, you pass huge yards of pottery figurines and a scattering of bars and restaurants. By far the most popular stop-off is at Puerto Nuevo, at Km 44. What was once a small fishing village with a few shacks serving as seafood restaurants is now a full-blown restaurant row, with over 25 restaurants all serving lobster and shrimp "Puerto Nuevo Style" with beans, rice, and homemade tortillas.

Notice the towering sand dunes a few kilometers south of Puerto Nuevo. Amateur and professional hang gliders perfect their skills here, and the sight of the colorful gliders against a clear blue sky is magnificent. The Plaza del Mar at Km 58, a hotel with an archaeological garden, is open to the public for no charge. Return to the toll road at Km 59, by La Fonda restaurant—another great place for lobster, shrimp, and margaritas. The free road south of the restaurant takes you inland; if you'd rather travel along the coast, get back on the toll road at La Mision.

Guided Tours

Baja California Tours runs eight different tours into Baja on air-conditioned motorcoaches, including daily departures to Ensenada from Mission Valley. All trips includes overnight accommodations. *6986 La Jolla Blvd. #204, La Jolla, CA 92037, tel. 619/454–7166. Fare: $99 per person per night to Ensenada.*

Five Star Tours provides transportation from the Amtrak station in downtown San Diego to the main drag in Tijuana. Buses leave both locations at intervals throughout the day, returning to San Diego as late as 9 PM on weekends. *1050 Kettner Blvd., San Diego, CA 92101, tel. 619/232–5049. Fare: $10 round-trip to Tijuana.*

Gray Line Tours arranges shopping and sightseeing tours on air-conditioned buses. A combination tour of Ensenada and San Felipe is available for $199 per adult ($50 for children 3–11) and includes transportation, hotel, and dinner, one night in both Ensenada and San Felipe. Make reservations two weeks in advance. *1670 Kettner Blvd., San Diego, CA 92101, tel. 619/231–9922.*

San Diego Mini-Tours offers guided tours to Tijuana and Ensenada. *837 S. 47th St., San Diego, CA 92113, tel. 619/234–9044. Fare: $22 half-day tour.*

In Mexico **Servicios Turisticos** (Av. Septiembre 213-B, tel. 668/6–1725; Viajes Carrousel, Blvd. Toboada and Orozco, tel. 668/4–0456; and Viajes Harold, Av. Revolución 608, tel. 668/8–1111) offers assistance with tours of Tijuana and beyond.

Touristicos de Baja California (Ave. Madero and Calle Mexico, tel. 668/8–3981) has charter buses and vans for trips into Baja, and is planning to offer tourist buses with air-conditioning and other such sought-after creature comforts on its excursions.

In Ensenada, half-day bus tours of Ensenada and the surrounding countryside are available from **Viajes Guaycura,** *López Mateos 1089, tel. 667/8–3718. Fare: $20.*

Tours of Baja's oldest winery, La Bodega de Santo Tomás, are conducted daily at 11 AM and 1 PM. *666 Av. Miramar, Ensenada, tel. 667/8–3333. Closed Sun. Admission: $1.*

Important Addresses and Numbers

To call Baja Norte from the United States, dial 70, the area code, and the number. The area code for Tijuana is 668; for Rosarito Beach, 661; and for Ensenada, 667.

Getting information or arranging reservations is infinitely easier for most people in the United States than in Mexico. Whenever possible, make inquiries and/or reservations before entering Mexico, through travel agents or other tourist information centers.

Tijuana/Baja Information (7860 Mission Center Court, no. 202, San Diego, CA 92108, tel. 619/299–8518, 800/225–2786 in the U.S., or 800/522–1516 in CA) handles reservations and provides valuable information about the area.

Mexico Travel West (Box 1646, Bonita, CA 92002, tel. 619/585–3033) will do the same.

Tijuana   There is a tourism office (tel. 668/3–1310) just after the border crossing that has maps, newspapers, and English-speaking clerks. Other tourist information booths are located at the foot of Calle 1, just after the pedestrian overpass across the border; at the airport; and at the intersection of Avenida Revolución and Calle 4. Listed below are some other important addresses and phone numbers.

Chamber of Commerce. The English-speaking staff is very helpful, and has maps and many brochures available. *Av. Revolución and Calle Comercio (Calle 1A becomes Calle Comercio as you head east toward the river), tel. 668/5–8472. Open daily 8–8.*
Main telephone office. Calle Pio Pico between Calles 10 and 11.
Main post office and telegraph office. Corner of Avenida Negrete and Calle 11, tel. 668/5–2682.
U.S. Consulate. Tapachula 96, Colonia Hipódromo, just behind the Tijuana Country Club, tel. 668/6–3886.

Rosarito   There is a tourist information office on Blvd. Juárez just south of La Quinta (tel. 661/2–0396 or 661/2–1005).

Ensenada   **Tourist Information** (State Tourism Office, Av. López Mateos 1305, tel. 667/6–2222).
Convention and Visitors Bureau (Av. López Mateos and Av. Espinoza, tel. 667/8–2411).
Police (Ortiz Rubio and Libertad, tel. 667/9–1751).
Hospital (Ave. Ruiz and Calle 11, tel. 667/8–2525).
Post Office (Av. Juárez 1347).
Red Cross (tel. 667/8–1212).

Emergencies   A new three-digit emergency dialing system is in effect throughout Baja Norte—for police, dial 134; Red Cross, 132; fire department, 136.

Air Evac International (tel. 619/425–4400) is an air ambulance that travels into Mexico to bring injured tourists back to the United States.

Exploring Tijuana

Numbers in the margin correspond with points of interest on the Tijuana map.

Avenida Revolución, Tijuana's main tourist street, once housed brothels and bars and attracted a raunchy, rowdy crowd. Today the avenue is lined with shops and restaurants, all catering to the tourists. Shopping here is an adventure; the shopkeepers call to shoppers from their doorways, offering low prices for an odd assortment of garish and grand souvenirs. Many shopping arcades open onto Avenida Revolución; inside the front doors are mazes of small stands with pottery and handicrafts and low prices.

❶ The **Frontón,** or **Jai Alai Palace** (at the far end of Avenida Revolución, at 7th, tel. 668/5–7833), is a magnificent building and an exciting place to watch fast-paced jai alai games. The restaurants and bars along Avenida Revolución offer excellent inexpensive meals and drinks, and the travelers love it. Many of Tijuana's tourists are regulars, with favorite shops and restaurants. San Diegans often travel south of the border just for din-

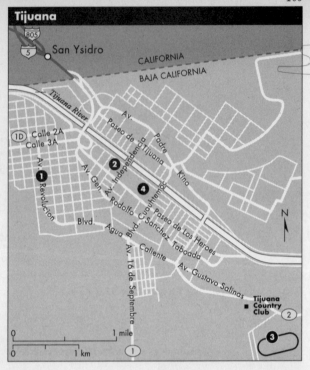

ner and become neighbors of a sort, making lifelong friends in Tijuana.

Time Out Among the many restaurants along Avenida Revolución, **Bol Corona** and **La Especial** are traditional favorites for authentic Mexican food, not fancied up for the tourists. The **Hotel Caesar** is the place to go for the real Caesar salad, which was created here. **Tia Juana Tilly's,** beside the Jai Alai Palace, is a good gathering spot for large parties with varying tastes in food.

2 The **Cultural Center,** in the Rio Tijuana area, was designed by the architect who created Mexico City's famous Museum of Anthropology. Its exhibits of Mexican history are the perfect introduction for all those thousands of visitors who first taste Mexico at the border. It is possible to wander past models of Mayan and Aztec temples, Indian pueblos, and missions, and get a true sense of the scope of Mexico's land, people, and history. Rotating exhibits focus on specific regions and cultures or highlight the works of present-day artists. The center has an Omnimax theater presenting films on Mexico. Guest artists appear at the Cultural Center regularly, attracting theatergoers from the United States as well as Tijuana. *Paseo de los Héroes y Mina, Zona del Rio, tel. 668/4–1111. Open daily 9 AM–8:30.*

Time Out The restaurant within the Cultural Center serves fairly good Mexican food throughout the week. It's a good place to relax and absorb all you've seen.

❸ Agua Caliente Racetrack (tel. 668/6–2002) was recently renovated, but it still speaks of the glamorous years when Hollywood stars gambled and played at the now-closed Agua Caliente Resort. Horses and greyhounds race regularly, and new satellite dishes make it possible to bet on and watch races from Southern California.

The **Rio Tijuana** area is quickly becoming the city's glamorous zone. A new pedestrian walkway connects the border and the Rio. Follow the signs for Pueblo Amigo. The area is not far from the border, just past the dry riverbed of the Tijuana River along Paseo de los Héroes. This boulevard is one of the main thoroughfares in the city, with large statues of historic figures, including one of Abraham Lincoln, in the center of the *glorietas* (traffic circles). The Cultural Center is in the midst of the Rio area, as are empty lots that are frequently used for fairs and **❹** fiestas. The **Plaza Rio Tijuana,** built a few years back, was Tijuana's first major shopping center. It is an enormous affair, with good restaurants, major department stores, and hundreds of shops. The plaza has become a central square of sorts, where holiday fiestas are sometimes held. Smaller shopping centers are opening all along Paseo de los Héroes; Plaza Fiesta and Plaza de Zapatos are two of the finest.

The **Playas Tijuana** area, at the oceanfront, is slated next for development. For now, the area is a mix of modest neighborhoods, with a few restaurants and hotels. The beaches are long and pleasant and visited mostly by locals.

Exploring Rosarito Beach

Numbers in the margin correspond with points of interest on the Northwestern Baja map.

Rosarito Beach is the main stop-off on the way from Tijuana to Ensenada; its early development presaged its current dominance of the area. The beach is one of the longest in Northern Baja, an uninterrupted stretch of sand from the power plant at the northernmost end of town to below the Rosarito Beach Hotel, about five miles south. This stretch is perfect for horseback riding, jogging, and strolling, from sunrise to sunset, or under a full moon.

Boulevard Benito Juárez is Rosarito's main drag, a super sideshow of sorts, with hotels, restaurants, stores, taco stands, horse fields, open-air markets, and plenty of people to watch. The best shops are clustered around the Rosarito Beach Hotel and Quinta del Mar Hotel. The best bargains are at the open-air flea market that operates on weekends just north of Quinta del Mar Hotel.

❶ The **Rosarito Beach Hotel** (on Blvd. Juárez at the south end of town, tel. 661/2–1106) has been this area's main draw since the Prohibition era in the United States, when Hollywood's glamorous crowd traveled en masse to the palatial hotel and clean, empty beaches. The hotel has since added high-rise towers and a parcours trail, but its history is evident in the enormous dining room, betting hall, and swimming pool areas. The lobby's walls are covered with intricate, colorful murals depicting Mexico's history; in one hallway there's an elaborate reproduction of the Mayan calendar on goatskins affixed with an egg

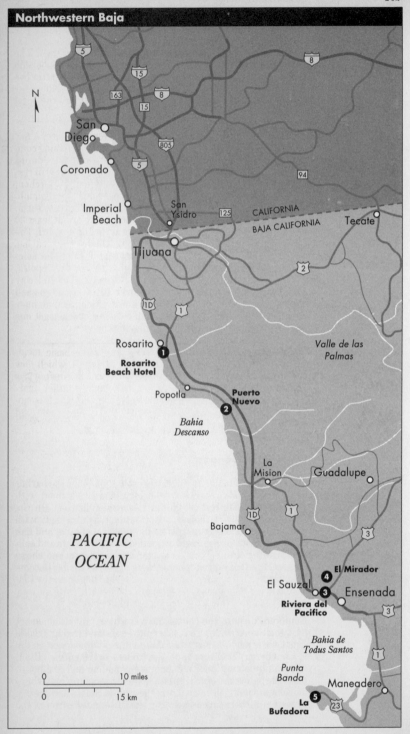

N

San Diego

Coronado

Imperial Beach

San Ysidro

CALIFORNIA

BAJA CALIFORNIA

Tecate

Tijuana

Rosarito

Rosarito Beach Hotel

Popotla

Puerto Nuevo

Bahia Descanso

Valle de las Palmas

La Mision

Guadalupe

Bajamar

PACIFIC OCEAN

El Mirador

El Sauzal

Riviera del Pacifico

Ensenada

Bahia de Todus Santos

Punta Banda

Maneadero

La Bufadora

0   10 miles

0   15 km

tempera. The beach here is the cleanest in Rosarito, and horses can be rented for sunset rides beside the surf.

Time Out The hotel's dining room serves a lavish Sunday brunch. The best place for watching the surf is from the lounge and poolside tables, where beers and margaritas taste ever so good after the long drive down. Those traveling on to Puerto Nuevo or Ensenada often stop here for a drink just to explore the hotel and get a good view of the sea.

❷ **Puerto Nuevo** is the most popular side trip from Rosarito. A few years ago, the only way to know you'd reached this fishing community was by the huge painting of a 7-Up bottle on the side of a building. You'd drive down the rutted dirt road to a row of restaurants—some just a big room in front of a family's kitchen. There you were served the classic Newport meal—grilled lobster, refried beans, rice, homemade tortillas, butter, salsa, and lime. The meal became a legend; now there are at least 30 restaurants on quaint brick-paved lanes at the top of a cliff. The place is packed on weekends, all day long, though the meal has few variations. And now there are Newport T-shirts for sale. Those seeking a less frenetic spot, stop at La Fonda, Popotla, Calafia, or Bajamar, all on the road to Ensenada. The Halfway House is popular with hang gliders, who fly off the high sand dunes nearby, over the scores of dune buggies. And at busy times, it seems nearly every clifftop clearing has at least one car parked there, its passengers enjoying the view.

Time Out Puerto Nuevo's restaurants all serve the same basic meal. Their differences are in their ambience. Ortega's, which now operates lobster restaurants in Rosarito as well as Newport, is popular with rowdy crowds who freely imbibe killer margaritas. Among the quieter places is Ponderosa, which is run by a friendly family who live behind the dining room and kitchen.

Exploring Ensenada

The city of Ensenada, the third largest in Baja, hugs the harbor of Bahia de Todos Santos with a long boardwalk lined with sportfishing charters, restaurants, and warehouses. On the northernmost point sits an indoor/outdoor fish market, with stand after stand selling fresh fish, seafood cocktails, and fish tacos. The market is packed on weekends with buyers and sellers; browsers can pick up some standard souvenirs and cheap eats and take some great photographs. The market has become a bit harder to find now that construction has begun on the Plaza Marina. Just look for an enormous construction site on your left as you enter town; the market is right behind it.

Boulevard Costera runs along the waterfront from the market past the Sportfishing Pier; after the shops and shacks trickle out there is a long stretch of palms and rocky coast next to the ❸ Plaza Civica. The beautiful old **Riviera del Pacifico** (Blvd. Lázaro Cardenas), once a glamorous gambling hall and hotel, faces the palms and ocean, recalling the Ensenada of old, where movie stars and politicians from the United States and Mexico drove by in their limousines. Be sure to wander through the building, now used primarily for government offices, to get a feel of the good old glamour days.

Avenida López Mateos is Ensenada's tourist zone, situated one block east of the waterfront. High-rise hotels, souvenir shops, restaurants, and bars line the avenue from its beginning at the foot of the Chapultapec Hills for eight blocks to the dry channel of the Arroyo de Ensenada. South of the riverbed is a row of inexpensive motels, across the street from the Tourist Office (Av. López Mateos 1305). The tourist zone spreads farther and farther each year toward Avenida Juárez, Ensenada's true downtown where the locals shop for furniture, clothing, and necessities.

❹ El Mirador is where you go for a true sense of the expanse of Ensenada. To get there drive up Calle 2 into the Chapultapec Hills toward the radio tower. From there, one can see the entire Bahia de Todos Santos, from the canneries of San Miguel south to Punta Banda and La Bufadora. The city of Ensenada spreads out for miles under the hills; by checking the scene against a map, you can pretty well figure out how to get anywhere. Behind El Mirador, the hills rise even higher; here are the palatial homes of the town's wealthier citizens.

The hillsides and valleys outside Ensenada are known for their grapes and olives; many of the wineries have tours that can be arranged through hotels in Ensenada. The **Santo Tomás Winery** is located in town and has tours daily except Sunday. The **Cetto** and **Calafia** wineries are located in the Guadalupe Valley, on Highway 3 toward Tecate. The valley is about a 30-minute drive from Ensenada on a good, paved highway that runs up into the hills past cattle ranches and orchards. In San Antonio de Las Minas, about 15 minutes from Ensenada, there is the excellent gourmet Restaurante Mustafa; other than that, there's nothing to do along the road except marvel at the boulders, cliffs, and scenery. Valle Guadalupe has a few small markets and a Pemex station; Olivares Mexicanos, called the world's largest olive plantation, with 120,000 trees, lies just outside the town. The Cetto and Calafia vineyards run for miles along the road toward Tecate. The drive is a pleasant half-day adventure, and the view coming back over the hills to the coast is spectacular.

❺ La Bufadora is an impressive blowhole in the coastal cliffs at Punta Banda. Take Highway 1 about 15 minutes south of Ensenada to Maneadero, then drive 12 miles west on Highway 23. This is a slow and somewhat risky trip, but the scenery at the coast is worth the effort. The geyser has been known to shoot as high as 75 feet; tourists gather on a concrete platform at the edge of the cliffs and take their chances with the water's spray. Small seafood restaurants, taco stands, and souvenir shacks line the road's end.

Though you don't need a tourist card if you are staying in Ensenada for less than 72 hours, those traveling south of Ensenada will have to fill out tourist cards (using birth certificate, passport, or voter's registration card for identification) and go through the checkpoint at Maneadero, a small farming community.

Time Out   For a special evening, dine at **La Cueva de los Tigres,** just south of town on the beach (km 112 at Playa Hermosa, tel. 667/6–

4650). The restaurant is famous for its abalone and calamari, and the view of the beach is spectacular.

Shopping

There has never been a lack of souvenirs to bring back from a trip to Northern Baja, and whether you're interested in traditional handicrafts from around Mexico, tequila (with or without the worm) and Kahlua, or T-shirts and gigantic straw hats, you'll find plenty on which to spend your pesos (or dollars, since they are universally accepted in the tourist towns). Among the most popular items are woolen rugs, serapes, and shawls; silver jewelry; stained-glass lamps; tin mirrors, candelabra, and trinkets; pottery dishes and planters; piñatas; paper flowers; leather goods; wooden and wicker furniture; and much more.

Tijuana Shopping in Tijuana is changing, although many of the old rules still apply. The traditional shopping area is Avenida Revolución, from calles 1 through 8. Bartering is not as common there as it once was, although it still never hurts to try (in a polite way of course) offering a price lower than the one marked. Casual interest and a nonchalant attitude are key factors for successful bartering.

The Drug Store, Maxim's, Dorian's, and Sara's have good selections of clothing and imported perfumes. Tolan, across the street from the Jai Alai Palace on Avenida Revolución, has a nice selection of high-quality crafts. Sanborn's, at Avenida Revolución and Calle 9, has fine crafts from throughout Mexico, a great bakery, and gourmet chocolates. Espinosa, on Avenida Revolución and at the Cultural Center, has fine silver, brass, and gold jewelry. Liquor stores dot the avenue; remember that you may bring only one liter of alcohol back into the United States.

Pueblo Amigo, on Paseo de los Héroes just beyond the border, is a fanciful, pseudo-colonial marketplace with boutiques in brightly colored adobe buildings.

Plaza Rio Tijuana, on Paseo de los Héroes in the Rio area near the Cultural Center, is a major shopping center with department stores, specialty shops, and restaurants. **Plaza Fiesta,** another new center, is located across from Plaza Rio Tijuana at Paseo de los Héroes, and next door the **Plaza de Zapatos** is an entire center dedicated to nothing but shoe stores.

Rosarito Beach At the shopping arcade near Quinta del Mar Hotel, Tienda Gonzalez carries nice wool serapes and rugs. Oradia Imports specializes in French perfumes, and Taxco Curios has a large selection of silver jewelry. The last shop in the row, Interios Los Rios, has exquisite custom furniture, unusual pottery from Michoacán, and a delightful selection of ceramic "Tree of Life" candelabra. Between the 7-11 liquor store and the Calimax, you can get all the beach supplies you need. Santa Fe Bazar & Curios, across Boulevard Juarez from the hotel, has exquisite handcarved desks, chairs, and picture frames.

Farther south on Boulevard Juárez, midway between Quinta del Mar and the Rosarito Beach Hotel, is **Mexicana Viejo y Nuevo,** a shop with museum-quality hand crafts and carved wood furniture.

Across the street, Maricarmen Fashions carries a line of women's clothing made with Guatemalan fabrics.

Just outside town on the Old Ensenada Highway heading south, are three large pottery yards with rows of clay pots and other ceramic goods. Another stretch of pottery yards has appeared just before Puerto Nuevo. Puerto Nuevo has a few good curio shops as well, with silkscreened T-shirts, shell art, and hanging papier-mâché birds and animals.

Ensenada Most of the tourist shops are located along Avenue López Mateos by the hotels and restaurants. Dozens of curio shops and arcades line the street, all selling basically the same selection of pottery, woven blankets and serapes, embroidered dresses, and onyx chess sets. Four blocks inland from López Mateos is Avenue Juárez, the center of downtown for the locals. Large department stores, farmacias, and shoe stores line the avenue.

La Rana (López Mateos 715) has a wide selection of beach attire and surfing supplies. Originales Baja (623 López Mateos) sells large brass and copper birds, wood carvings, and glassware. Artes de Quijote (503 López Mateos) has an impressive selection of good-quality carved wooden doors, huge terra-cotta pots, wooden puzzles and games, tablecloths and napkins from Oaxaca, and large brass fish and birds. Joyeria Princess, a few doors down, has a good selection of gold and silver jewelry at reasonable, set prices. In the Mitla Bazaar, Elles and Fila have designer men's and women's clothing.

Mike's Leather (621 López Mateos) has a nice selection of leather clothing and dyed huaraches. Fantasias del Mar (821 López Mateos) has exotic shells, coral jewelry, and paintings. The government craft store, Fonart (1303 López Mateos), next door to the tourism office, is filled with high-quality crafts from all over Mexico. Especially nice are the black pottery from Oaxaca and wooden dolls and animals from Michoacán. La Mina de Solomon, next to the El Rey Sol restaurant on López Mateos, carries handcrafted gold jewelry. Artes Bitterlin, in the same building, is a gallery carrying antiques, sculptures, paintings, and Sergio Bustamante copper and brass animals.

On Avenue Ruiz, Hussong's Edificio, next door to the infamous Hussong's Cantina, has a collection of shops selling silkscreened T-shirts, surfboards, and Ensenada bumper stickers and souvenirs. Avila Imports, across the street from Hussong's, sells French perfumes, Hummel statues, and crystal. Along Boulevard Costera at Avenue Castillo a new artisan's market has opened, geared toward the droves of cruise ship passengers who arrive continually. Most shops carry typical souvenirs, but the Unique Art Center is a real find. The owners collect unusual pottery pieces made by the Casa Grande and Taranhumara Indians, and their display is extraordinary. The owners supply galleries throughout the Southwest, where these pieces cost double what they do here. The Astra Shopping Center, at Calle Delante and Highway 1, has major department stores and small handicraft shops.

Los Globos, a large swap meet on Calle 9, is open on weekends.

Beaches

"Baja" is synonymous with "beaches." The peninsula has over 1,000 miles of coastline on the west coast alone. There are many pretty beaches and excellent views of the coast within a day's drive of San Diego. Once past Tijuana, it isn't hard to find a solitary stretch of beach, if that suits your swimming, surfing, or diving fancy. Lifeguards are rare if they exist at all, so swim with caution. Good beachfront hotels are situated on some of the prettiest beaches, so if you're looking for a nice beach with amenities such as food, drink, and rest rooms nearby, you'll want to check out the beachfront hotels.

The Playas Tijuana, or Tijuana beach area, is located south of town off the toll road, Ensenada Cuota. The area has been under development for years, but as of yet, there are no major hotels and few restaurants in the area. The beaches are frequented primarily by locals; in the winter, the area is fairly deserted.

Rosarito has beautiful beaches, with long sandy stretches for walking, running, or horseback riding, and good waves for swimming and body surfing. Horses are available for rent on the beach and along the main street; early morning rides on the beach are popular. During peak seasons, roaming vendors sell crafts and drinks. There are no lifeguards.

The waterfront in Ensenada proper is taken up by fishing boats; the best swimming beaches are south of town. Estero Beach is long and clean, with mild waves. Surfers populate the beaches off Highway 1 north and south of Ensenada, particularly at San Miguel, California, Tres Marias, and La Joya beaches; scuba divers prefer Punta Banda, by La Bufadora. The tourist office in Ensenada has a map that shows safe diving and surfing beaches.

Participant Sports

Tijuana *Golf*	The Tijuana Country Club has an 18-hole course, open to the public. Rental clubs, carts, and caddies are available. *Av. Agua Caliente, just east of downtown. Call 619/299–8518 for information and reservations.*
Rosarito Beach *Fishing*	There is a small fishing pier at Km 33 on the Old Ensenada Highway, and surfcasting is allowed on the beach. There is no place in Rosarito to get fishing licenses, but tourism officials say they are not necessary if you fish from shore.
Golf	Golf may be played at the Bajamar, an excellent 18-hole course 20 miles south of Rosarito at a vacation resort.
Horseback Riding	Somewhat scrawny horses can be rented from the north end of Boulevard Juárez and on the beach. Rates average around $5 per half hour.
Surfing	The waves are said to be particularly good at Popotla, Km 33; Calafia, Km 35.5; and Costa Baja, Km 36 on the Old Ensenada Highway.
Tennis	Tennis may be played at the Bajamar, mentioned above under "Golf."
Ensenada *Hunting*	The hunting season for quail and other gamebirds runs from September through December. Hunting trips can be arranged

through **Uruapan Lodge** (Gastelum 40 downtown, tel. 667/8–2190). The lodge package includes transportation from the border, room, meals, hunting equipment, and licenses for $100 per day.

Sportfishing Fishing boats leave the Ensenada Sportfishing Pier regularly. The best fishing takes place from April through November, but bottom fishing is also good in the winter. Charter vessels and party boats are available from several outfitters who also offer whale-watching trips in the winter. Most hotels can arrange fishing trips. Licenses are available at the tourist office or from charter companies. The following are some companies that organize fishing trips and rent equipment:

Ensenada Clipper Fleet (tel. 667/8–2185) at the Sportfishing Pier has charter and group boats.
Gordo's Sportfishing (tel. 667/8–3515) is one of the oldest sportfishing companies on the pier, with charter and group boats and a smokehouse.
Pacific Anglers Fleet (tel. 667/4–0865) at the Sportfishing Pier arranges charters.
El Royal Pacifico (26651 Naccome Dr., Mission Viejo, CA 92691, tel. 714/859–4933) offers advance-sale tickets and reservations on sportfishing boats in Ensenada from their U.S. office in Mission Viejo.

Tennis Tennis may be played at the Baja Tennis Club at San Benito 123; a few hotels have their own courts.

Spectator Sports

Tijuana Bullfighting season is May through September, and the con-
Bullfights tests usually take place on Sunday afternoons and holidays. The first seven matches are held at the El Torreo Tijuana, on Agua Caliente just outside downtown, and at the Plaza Monumental; the next seven at the Plaza Monumental arena in Playas Tijuana. Admission ranges from $4 to $20. For ticket information, call 668/4–2126 or 668/7–8519. The luxurious Fiesta Americana Hotel (tel. 619/298–4105, or 800/223–2332 in CA) offers a package including transportation from San Diego, Orange County, or Los Angeles to the hotel, live music, free tequila, and pre- and post-bullfight parties, as well as the bullfight itself.

Charreadas A Mexican mixture of amateur rodeo and fiesta, these lively events take place at one of several rings around town on Sunday mornings. Tel. 668/4–2126 for information.

Jai Alai This fast-paced betting game is played in the Frontón, or Jai Alai Palace, an impressive old building worth seeing even if you don't attend the games, which are held nightly except Thursdays, but don't usually begin until 9 or 10 PM. *Av. Revolución and Calle 8, tel. 668/5–7833. Admission: $2.*

Racing The recently refurbished Caliente Racetrack is popular with both locals and tourists. Horses race on weekend afternoons beginning at noon; greyhounds race nightly throughout the year, first race at 7:45 PM. The Jockey Club and restaurant are quite lavish. Satellite betting is available at the track and at Pueblo Amigo.

Rosarito Beach Of interest to spectators as well as participants, a variety of
Bicycling Baja bike races draw cyclists from around the world. The

Tecate–Ensenada race, held in April or May, was the original Baja bike race; the newer Tri-City race, beginning in Tijuana and ending in Ensenada, is usually held the last Sunday in March. The Rosarito–Ensenada race is currently in vogue; as many as 15,000 cyclists have participated in the race. Large street fiestas naturally occur after these events, with many refreshment and food stands and often a band or two.

Charreadas   The rodeo/fiestas are held on summer Sundays at the Lienzo Tapatio Charro Ring south of town and the new Ejido Mazatlan Charro Ring on the east side of the toll road.

Polo   The game will soon be played at the new field under construction in the middle of town; the Polo Club will be private but the meets may be open to the public.

Ensenada   Charreadas are occasionally scheduled at the ring at Avenvida
Charreadas   Alvarado and Calle 2; tel. 667/4–0242.

Racing   There is no racetrack in Ensenada, but those hooked on horse racing can go to López Mateos, behind the Riviera-Pacifico building (tel. 667/6–2133) to place their bets and watch televised races of Tijuana's Agua Caliente Racetrack and Los Angeles's Santa Anita and Hollywood tracks.

Dining

Category	Cost*
Expensive	$11–$15
Moderate	$7–$10
Inexpensive	under $6

*per person, not including tax, tip, or beverage. Prices are given in dollars because of the instability of the Mexican peso.

The following credit card abbreviations are used: AE, American Express; DC, Diners Club; MC, MasterCard; V, Visa.

Tijuana   Tijuana has restaurants to serve every taste, from the taco stands on the street to gourmet French and regional Mexican cuisine. And, with a constantly growing city—the population is now over two million—even the Chamber of Commerce has trouble keeping track of the latest restaurants. Seafood is abundant; beef and pork are common, both grilled and marinated as *carne asada* and *carnitas*. Pheasant, quail, rabbit, and duck are popular in the more expensive places. Dress is informal, though T-shirts and shorts are frowned upon in the evening. Reservations are not required or even accepted at most restaurants.

Expensive   **Alcazar del Rio.** Nouvelle cuisine amid mirrors has hit Tijuana with this upscale, see-and-be-seen restaurant. Patrons are the city's success stories—the casually elegant, sophisticated elite. Everything considered to be exotic in Tijuana is here— smoked salmon with capers, Australian lamb, Serrano ham with sweet cantaloupe, cherries jubilee. The halibut with pine nuts is sublimely simple, and the wine list is excellent. *Paseo de los Héroes, tel. 668/4–2672. Reservations suggested. Jacket and tie suggested. AE, MC, V.*
Cilantro's. Wonderful regional Mexican dishes in a beautiful two-story restaurant. Dishes are described on the English

menu—try Chiles Nogada, filled with meat and fruit and topped with pomegranate seeds, or the chicken in almond sauce. *Paseo Tijuana #213, tel. 668/2–8340. MC, V.*

Pedrin's. This is one of Tijuana's best seafood restaurants, overlooking the Jai Alai Palace from the second-story garden room. Meals include deep-fried fish appetizers, fish chowder, salad, entree, and a sweet after-dinner drink of Kahlua and cream. The rajas shrimp, covered with melted cheese and green chilis, is great, as is the grilled lobster. *Av. Revolución 1115, tel. 668/5–4052. AE, MC, V.*

Moderate **El Abajeño.** Tops for homemade *carne asada*, tamales, and enchiladas, the dining room at El Abajeño is colorfully decorated with murals and folk art, and the waiters are friendly and accommodating. Live mariachi music alternates with a piano bar. *Blvd. Agua Caliente 101, tel. 668/5–6980. MC, V.*

La Leña. The sparkling clean white dining room faces an open kitchen, where chefs grill beef specialties such as *Gaonera*, a fillet of beef stuffed with cheese and guacamole, while women prepare fresh tortillas. *Blvd. Agua Caliente 4560, tel. 668/6–2920. MC, V.*

Margarita's Village. Twelve flavors of margaritas, baked kid, and other Mexican dishes are served by singing waiters in the large indoor dining room and outdoor second-story patio overlooking the shoppers on Avenida Revolución. The inexpensive weekend buffet bolsters shoppers' spirits for further bargaining. *Av. Revolución at Calle 3, tel. 668/5–7362. AE, DC, MC, V.*

Tia Juana Tilly's. Popular with tourists and locals looking for a busy, bustling place to party and dine on generous portions of specialties from throughout Mexico, this is one of the few places where you can get *cochinita pibil*, a Yucatecan specialty made of roasted pork, red onions, and bitter oranges. *Av. Revolución at Calle 7, tel. 668/5–6024. Part of the same chain and catercorner to the original is Tilly's Fifth Ave., a popular watering hole. AE, DC, MC, V.*

Inexpensive **Bol Corona.** Arches and porticoes have made this spot a Revolución landmark since 1934. The bar is a lively place with wide-screen televisions blasting seasonal sporting events. The restaurant serves traditional Mexican food, including over a dozen types of burritos, enchiladas, and *chilaquiles* made with corn tortillas simmered in chicken broth. *Av. Revolución 520, tel. 668/5–7940. No credit cards.*

Carnitas Uruapan. The main attraction at this large, noisy restaurant is carnitas, marinated pork sold by the kilo and served with homemade tortillas, salsa, cilantro, guacamole, and onions. Patrons mingle at long wooden tables in rustic surroundings, toasting each other with chilled cervezas. *Blvd. Diaz Ordaz 550, tel. 668/5–6181. No credit cards.*

Chiki Jai. A tiny Basque place, redolent of the blue cheese served on each table, Chiki Jai is popular for squid served in its own ink and Basque-style chicken. *Av. Revolución 1042, tel. 668/5–4955. No credit cards.*

La Especial. Located at the foot of the stairs leading to an underground shopping arcade, this restaurant is a traditional favorite for down-home Mexican cooking at low prices. *Av. Revolución 770, tel. 668/5–6654. No credit cards.*

Mr. Fish. Cosmopolitan Tijuana is not where you normally find the *palapa* (beach shack) seafood houses so popular at the coastal resorts. But three blocks from the Fiesta Americana is a 12-table palapa strung with fishing nets, and the ubiquitous mounted marlin on the wall. The corn chips and salsa are fresh, the fish soup is filled with chunks of bass and tomatoes, and the shrimp *al mojo de ajo* comes smothered in garlic, butter, and cilantro. If you like frogs' legs, you've got four styles to choose from. This is definitely the place to go for fish. *Bd. Agua Caliente 6000, tel. 66/86–3603. No reservations. Dress: casual. MC, V.*

Rosarito Beach New restaurants open here constantly, and though the competition is heavy, nearly all the places have the same items on their menus—lobster, shrimp, fresh fish, and steak—at nearly the same prices. The restaurants compete heavily with their drink prices; many offer free margaritas or a bottle of wine with dinner.

Expensive **Dragon del Mar.** This elegant Chinese restaurant is decorated
★ with furniture and paintings imported from China. A miniature waterfall greets guests in the marble foyer and a pianist plays relaxing music. Partitioned with movable carved wooden panels, the expansive dining room is still an intimate dining experience. The food is exquisitely prepared, appealing to the eye as well as the palate. *Blvd. Juárez 20, tel. 661/2–0604. AE, MC, V.*

La Masia. The beach's most elegant restaurant, near the high-rise Quinta del Mar Hotel, is heavy on flaming torches and Polynesian decor. The cuisine is Continental. *Quinta del Mar Hotel, Blvd. Juárez 25500, tel. 661/2–1300. AE, MC, V.*

La Mision. This lovely, quiet restaurant, with white adobe walls and carved wood statues nestled in molded niches under the high-beamed ceilings, serves gourmet seafood and steaks in an international style. There is also patio dining in the enclosed courtyard. *Blvd. Juárez 182, tel. 661/2–0202. MC, V.*

Los Pelicanos. One of the few restaurants on the beach, with huge windows, a great sunset view, and a casual upstairs overlooking the beach, and the hotel next door with balconies. The menu includes the ever-present lobster, served with vegetables and baked potato rather than rice and beans. *At the end of Calle Ebano, tel. 661/2–1757. MC, V.*

Moderate **Las Cazuelas del Mar.** This family restaurant across from Quinta del Mar serves fresh seafood, traditional Mexican dishes, and hand-made tortillas. The food is average, but the prices are lower than usual. Upstairs is an authentic Mexican nightclub. *Blvd. Juárez 77, no phone. No credit cards. Closed Tuesdays.*

La Fachada. A quiet place by Rosarito standards, La Fachada is preferred by more subdued diners. The food is good, and the atmosphere is authentic Mexican. At night a guitarist and pianist perform soothing ballads. *Blvd. Juárez 2884, tel. 661/2–1785. Open 8 AM–10 PM. MC, V.*

La Flor de Michoacán. Pork roasted over an open pit Michoacan style, called *carnitas*, is the house specialty. Chunks of the marinated meat are served with homemade tortillas, guacamole, and salsa for make-your-own tortillas. The surroundings are simple but clean, and the tacos, *tortas* (similar to hero sandwiches), and tostadas are great. Takeout available. *Blvd. Juárez 146, no phone.*

El Nido. A woodsy, leather-booth-type restaurant, this is one of the oldest in Rosarito and still popular with Rosarito regulars unimpressed with the new, fancier establishments. Steaks are grilled over mesquite wood at the open grill just off the dining room. *Blvd. Juárez 67, tel. 661/2–1430. MC, V.*

★ **Las Olas.** Upstairs, this restaurant and bar are worth finding. Specialties are served with a second-story view of the main street. Live music for dancing on weekends. *Blvd. Juárez 298, no phone. No credit cards. Closed Tuesdays.*

Ortega's. A member of the Ortega chain of lobster houses, and with a more varied menu, this restaurant serves lobster Puerto Nuevo style with beans, rice, and tortillas. The lavish Sunday brunch is very popular. *Blvd. Juárez 200, tel. 661/2–0022. MC, V.*

★ **René's.** Specialties include *chorizo* (Mexican sausage), quail, frogs' legs, and lobster. There is an ocean view from dining room and a lively bar with mariachi music. *Blvd. Juárez, tel. 661/2–1020. MC, V.*

Inexpensive **Azteca.** The enormous dining room at the Rosarito Beach Hotel has a view of the pool and beach area. Visitors come to the hotel regularly just for the lavish Sunday brunch, where margaritas are the drink of choice. Both Mexican and American dishes are offered, and the portions make up for the erratic quality of the food. *Rosarito Beach Hotel, Blvd. Juárez, tel. 661/2–1106. Reservations accepted. MC, V.*

Carnitas el Cachanilla. As the name implies, the specialty here is carnitas. The *menudo* (tripe soup) is also great. *Km 20 Old Ensenada Hwy., tel. 661/2–0250. No credit cards.*

Juice 'n Juice. Rosarito's healthfood restaurant is a no-frills lunch counter with lots of salads, juices, yogurt, and granola. But you can also order burgers and fries. *Blvd. Juárez 11, tel. 661/2–0338. No credit cards.*

South of Rosarito Beach
Expensive **Calafia.** Private haute cuisine dining is available by reservation only at this elegant cliff-top restaurant that serves up a terrific ocean view with its food. You can dine indoors or sit outside at tables that perch on terraces down the side of the cliff. Dance floors inside and at the bottom of the cliff are ideal for open-air dancing. *Km 35.5 Old Ensenada Hwy., tel. 661/2–1581. MC, V.*

La Fonda. This traditionally popular rest stop on the way to or from Ensenada has a nice outdoor patio overlooking the beach, and it serves killer margaritas with oily corn chips and hot salsa. The restaurant serves fresh lobster, grilled steaks, and traditional Mexican dishes. The bar gets crowded and boisterous at night, especially on weekends when a live band plays pop music and the patrons dance wildly on the tiny dance floor. *Km 59 Old Ensenada Hwy., no phone. MC, V.*

Moderate **Francisco's Steak & Seafood.** More familiarly known as "Calafia," this moderately priced Mexican restaurant sits atop the cliffs above Cava Calafia. The dining room, large bar, and dance floor face out to the ocean, but on sunny days the nicest place to sit is at the picnic tables scattered outside along the edges of the cliffs. Catering is available for group events. *Km 35.5 at Calafia, tel. 661/2–1581. MC, V.*

Puerto Nuevo, or Newport. Puerto Nuevo is a village of about 25 restaurants, at Km 44, off the Old Ensenada Highway, all serving what has become known as lobster Newport-style. Some of the restaurants are just large dining rooms in front of the owners' homes; others are full-fledged fancy places with table linens and views of the ocean. The traditional Puerto Nuevo meal is grilled lobster served with homemade tortillas, refried beans, rice, salsa, lime, and dishes of melted butter. Some places also serve shrimp, tacos, and burritos, but lobster is the main draw. Among the smaller spots, **Ponderosa** and **Maria's** are especially nice. **Ortega's,** with at least three restaurants operating in the village, has the corner on the rowdy crowd. *Take the La Fonda exit from the toll road and drive south to reach Puerto Nuevo. You can tell you're there when you see hundreds of cars and taxis parked in a large dirt lot. No phone. No credit cards.*

Ensenada   Since Ensenada is a sportfishing town, fish is the prime dining choice. The lobster, shrimp, and abalone are great, and a variety of fresh fish is prepared in French, Italian, and Mexican sauces. On the street, at the Fish Market and in inexpensive restaurants, seafood cocktails, ceviche, and fish tacos are the main delight. During the winter hunting season, quail and pheasant are popular.

Expensive   **El Rey Sol.** This is a 40-year-old family-owned French restaurant in a charming building with stained-glass windows, wrought-iron chandeliers, heavy oak tables and chairs, and linen tablecloths. Specialties are French and Mexican presentations of fresh fish, poultry, and vegetables grown at the family's farm in the Santo Tomás Valley. Appetizers come with the meal. Excellent pastries are baked on the premises. *Av. López Mateos 1000, tel. 667/8–1733. AE, MC, V.*

La Cueva de los Tigres. The dining room, which is especially nice at sunset, looks out on the water. The enduring specialty, abalone in crab sauce, has won international awards. The restaurant is so popular that patrons regularly drive down from California for dinner. *About 2 mi south of town at Km 112 at Playa Hermosa, tel. 667/6–4650. AE, MC, V.*

Valentino. The setting is romantic, in a dimly lit room with candles and blue tablecloths, across the street from the waterfront. The menu features seafood and steaks. There is a Sunday champagne brunch. *Blvd. Costero 915, tel. 667/4–0022. AE, MC, V.*

Moderate   **Carnitas Uruapan.** A branch of the famous Tijuana hangout, this restaurant primarily serves *carnitas:* chunks of marinated, roasted pork served with fresh tortillas, salsa, onion, tomatoes, and cilantro. Patrons share long wooden tables in this informal setting. *Av. Sangines 36, tel. 667/6–1044. No credit cards.*

Casamar. Large groups, families, and couples seem equally comfortable in the main dining room, which bustles with activity and is popular for its wide variety of excellent seafood. Lobster and shrimp are prepared several ways but seem the freshest when served *con mojo y ajo*—simply grilled with garlic and butter. The upstairs bar has live jazz on weekend nights. *Blvd. Lázaro Cardenas 987, tel. 667/4–0417. MC, V.*

Casamar no. 2. Seafood, Mexican specialties, and breakfast are served indoors and out at this casual offshoot on the waterfront. *Av. Macheros 499, just off Blvd. Lázaro Cardenas, tel. 667/8–2540.*

Smitty González. One of the premier fun spots, Smitty's has great food, Puerto Nuevo lobster, potent daiquiris, and a fireman's pole that guests can use to get from the second-story bar to the dining room. *Av. Ryerson and López Mateos, tel. 667/4–0636. MC, V.*

Inexpensive **Calmariscos.** Some of Ensenada's best seafood is served in this modest restaurant, with formica-top tables and plastic chairs. No frills, but the food is great, plentiful, and cheap. It's best known for its tender turtle steaks. *Calle 3 no. 474, near Av. Ruíz, tel. 667/8–2940. Open 24 hours. V.*

Señor Taco. This is a clean, inviting storefront taco stand with benches and stools along the walls and good, inexpensive tacos, burritos, and enchiladas. *Av. Ruíz 171, no phone. No credit cards.*

Via Veneto. Ensenada's favorite pizza place is in a dark dining room with latticework walls, stained-glass lamps, and posters of Italy. The thin-crust pizza is served with some unusual toppings, such as shrimp, crab, and pineapple. *Blvd. Costero no. 853, tel. 667/8–2516.*

Lodging

The hotel business is booming in Baja. All levels of accommodations are available, from luxury suites in Tijuana to trailer parks south of Rosarito Beach. Northern Baja is a popular weekend getaway most of the year, and the hotels fill up on holidays and weekends, when reservations are a must. The Tijuana Convention and Tourism Bureau has an office in San Diego that can reserve hotel rooms; call or write **International Marketing and Promotions** (7860 Mission Center Court, No. 202, San Diego, CA 92108, tel. 619/298–4105, 800/225–2786 in the U.S., 800/522–1516 in CA.). They represent several tourism offices in Baja, make hotel reservations at a large number of properties, and are a great source of information. **Pan American Hotels International** (P.O. Box 2776, Chula Vista, CA 92012, tel. 619/422–6918 or 800/678–7244) reserves rooms at a large number of properties throughout Baja. **Baja Lodging** (4659 Park Blvd., San Diego, CA 92116, tel. 619/491–0682) reserves rooms in hotels and small, more remote properties throughout Baja. **Mexico West Travel Club** (Box 1646, Bonita, CA 92002, tel. 619/585–3033) will give advice and make reservations for you. Most hotels listed have parking available.

Category	Cost*
Very Expensive	over $100
Expensive	$50–$100
Moderate	$25–$50

for a double room. Prices are given in dollars because of the instability of the Mexican peso.

The following credit card abbreviations are used: AE, American Express; DC, Diners Club; MC, MasterCard; V, Visa.

Tijuana Hotels in Tijuana are clustered downtown, along Avenida Revolución, near the Country Club on Boulevard Agua Caliente, and in the Rio Tijuana area on Paseo de los Héroes.

Very Expensive **Fiesta Americana.** These gleaming towers seem somewhat incongruous amid the cluttered streets leading away from Avenida Revolución to the Agua Caliente Racetrack and the Tijuana Country Club. With its expansive marble lobby, glistening crystal chandeliers, and expensive boutiques, the Fiesta Americana has brought a new sense of luxury to Tijuana's hotel scene. The rooms near the top of the towers command a wonderful view of Tijuana's urban sprawl; their marble baths and modern paintings give the feel that Tijuana has come of age as a major tourist destination. The nightclub, with live rock music and huge video screens, has become a popular weekend gathering spot for those seeking glamour and glitz, and the lobby restaurant is a good spot for a relaxing lunch. During the bullfighting season, the hotel offers special packages, including reduced room rates and post-fight parties with the matadors. *Blvd. Agua Caliente 4550, tel. 668/1–7000 or 800/343–7821. 422 rooms. Facilities: restaurants, health club, tennis courts, golf course, pool, sauna, whirlpool, banquet and convention facilities, travel agency. AE, DC, MC, V.*

Expensive **Lucerna.** Those seeking colonial charm and restful surroundings head for the Lucerna, one of Tijuana's oldest hotels. The swimming pool is surrounded by hibiscus bushes and giant, ancient trees that pleasantly shade the lounging area. The rooms are decorated with a Mexican flair, with heavy wood furnishings and an emphasis on comfort rather than glitz. The Lucerna has a particularly good travel agency, complete with English-speaking travel agents. *Paseo de los Héroes 10902, tel. 668/6–1000. 178 rooms, 9 suites. Facilities: coffee shop, restaurant, lounge, pool. AE, DC, MC, V.*

Moderate **La Mesa Inn.** This Best Western hotel is well situated near the Agua Caliente Racetrack, and the new shopping center, Plaza Patrica, is just a few steps away. The rooms are plainly furnished, more like a motel than a hotel, but the inn is a good low-cost selection far enough from the center of town to offer some peace and quiet. There is no charge for children under 12. *Blvd. Diaz Ordaz 50, tel. 668/1–6522 or 800/528–1234. 122 rooms. Facilities: coffee shop, lounge, nightclub, pool, cable TV. AE, DC, MC, V.*

Rosarito Beach Though Rosarito is going through a building boom with a lot of new hotels and motels under construction, there is still a shortage of accommodations. Accordingly, the rates have climbed considerably.

Expensive **Plaza del Mar.** The mock archaeological ruins along the roadside point the way to this oceanfront resort community, where snowbirds hibernate during winter months. The resort is spread out from the main road to the cliffs over the sea, with long rows of motel-like rooms interspersed with courtyards filled with blooming plants. The rooms are plain and simple, with an orange and yellow color scheme. The pool sits atop the cliffs; steep stairways down the cliffs lead to the rocky beach. The restaurant and bar are also on the cliffs; the outdoor tables are a good place for early breakfasts and sunset drinks. *Km 58 on the Old Ensenada Hwy. (take the La Misión exit from the toll road and go north 1 mi), tel. 668/5–9152 or 800/528–1234. Reservations: Box 4520, San Ysidro, CA 92073. 100 rooms. Facilities: restaurant, bar, heated pool, sauna, game room, volleyball, shuffleboard, tennis courts, rooms. AE, MC, V.*

Quinta del Mar. Once you've seen this high-rise hotel and condominium complex on the north end of town, you realize just how much Rosarito Beach has grown up. The towers rise above the dirt streets and taco stands, and the rooms, in whites and pastels with giant bathrooms and an endless supply of hot water, offer a luxurious reprieve from the noisy crowds of shoppers, beachgoers, and locals outside. Amusements within the complex include tennis, basketball, volleyball, and a well-equipped children's playground. The resort has its own beach access, and the sand is raked daily to remove the seaweed and debris. Sunsets are particularly dramatic from the rooftop patio, while the shops along the streetfront side of the hotel offer some of the best Mexican crafts to be found in Rosarito. The resort also operates the Quinta Chica Motel, which is more moderately priced but lacks beach access. *Blvd. Juárez 25500, tel. 661/2–1145. Reservations: Box 4243, San Ysidro, CA 92073, tel. 800/228–7003. 143 rooms. Facilities: 3 restaurants and bars, pool, whirlpool, steam baths, beauty shop. AE, MC, V.*

★ **Rosarito Beach Hotel.** During Prohibition, Hollywood stars discovered the opportunities for continuing their carousing in Mexico, and they made Rosarito their south-of-the-border resort. They invested heavily in the Rosarito Beach Hotel, a sprawling hotel and gambling hall that has retained its charm and elegance through a series of owners and renovations. The seaside hotel has red tile roofs and a white adobe archway leading to the main entrance. The cavernous ballroom was once a gambling hall. These days, rock bands blast away on weekend nights. The hotel's nicest features are its large swimming pool and the glassed-in deck and lounge area overlooking a long beach. The original rooms in the main hotel are quaint but a bit rundown; those on the beachside have nice views. The rooms in the outer wings are basic, with mismatched bed linens and erratic plumbing. The most comfortable accommodations are in the newer high-rise buildings, though you lose charm in exchange for newness. The restaurant serves a lavish Sunday brunch, and the terrace bar overlooking the beach is a good place for margaritas. *Blvd. Juárez at the south end of town, tel. 661/2–1106. Reservations: Box 145, San Ysidro, CA 92073. 70 rooms, 80 suites. Facilities: restaurant, pool, health club, racquetball, tennis, track. AE, MC, V.*

Moderate **La Fonda.** This oceanfront hotel has for years been the haven of those seeking an evening or weekend of pleasure by the sea. The restaurant and bar are popular with locals and tourists, and the dance floor gets rowdy on weekends. The small outdoor patio sits atop the cliffs over La Fonda's beach and fills up quickly near sunset. The hotel rooms are sparsely furnished but clean; many have ocean views. La Fonda attracts young couples and singles looking for surf, sun, and an unlimited supply of cold beer. *Km 59 Old Ensenada Hwy., no phone. Reservations: Box 268, San Ysidro, CA 92073. 18 rooms and several kitchenette apartments. Facilities: restaurant, bar, and disco. AE, MC, V.*

Ensenada The most popular hotels are concentrated in a five-block area along Avenida López Mateos, the center of tourist activity. Rates during the week are sometimes cheaper than those on weekends.

Expensive **Las Rosas.** This pink palace just north of town is by far the most glamorous hotel in the area, with an atrium lobby and a green-glass ceiling that glows at night. All rooms face the pool, which seems to flow over the edge of the cliffs into the sea. Some rooms have a fireplace and hot tub. *Mexico Hwy. 1 north of town, tel. 667/4–4310 or 800/225–2786. 32 rooms and suites. Facilities: pool, hot tub, restaurant, lounge, shops. MC, V.*

San Nicolas. Quieter than some hotels in town, San Nicolas is about 10 blocks from central Ensenada and set beside residential neighborhoods. A huge wall covered with murals depicting Mexico's history surrounds the hotel, which was once the area's main resort. The hotel has recently been renovated, and the immense new suites with private hot tubs are the most elegant rooms in town. The walk to town is long and not very scenic, but the sense of being removed from the hustle and bustle makes up for the distance, and taxis are readily available. *Av. López Mateos at Av. Guadalupe, tel. 667/9–1901. Reservations in U.S., tel. 800/522–1516. 150 rooms and suites. Facilities: restaurant, lounge, disco, 2 pools, whirlpool, beauty salon, gift shop, cable television. AE, MC, V.*

Moderate **Misión Santa Isabel.** The only colonial-style hotel near the water, the Misión has recently undergone a complete renovation, including a new disco and banquet facilities. Despite the new facade, the rooms remain dark and dreary, with heavy wood furnishings and dull gold drapes. Still, if you're looking for a more authentic sense of Mexico rather than the familiarity of a high-rise chain hotel, this is your best bet in town. The desk clerks are particularly helpful. *Av. López Mateos at Av. Castillo, Box 76, Ensenada, tel. 677/8–3616. 52 rooms, 6 junior suites. Facilities: restaurant, bar, pool. AE, MC, V.*

TraveLodge. There are no surprises here, just your basic American chain-hotel rooms with white walls, mass-produced paintings, and color TVs. Some rooms have VCRs, which are popular in Ensenada because TV reception is only fair. All rooms have service bars, but prices can run quite high. The coffee shop serves some basic American dishes—burgers, bacon and eggs, chicken on white toast, along with Mexican dishes. *Av. Blancarte 130, tel. 667/8–1601. Reservations: Box 1467, Ensenada, tel. 800/255–3050. 50 rooms. Facilities: heated pool, whirlpool, cantina, restaurant, recreation room. AE, MC, V.*

Nightlife

Tijuana Tijuana has toned down its "Sin City" image, and much of the night action takes place at the Jai Alai Palace and the racetrack. Several hotels, especially the Lucerna and Fiesta Americana, have entertainment. For those who want to experience the seamier side of old Tijuana, several places along Revolución, including Sans Souci, Bambi, and Les Girls, have strip shows around the clock.

The best Revolución bars for disco dancing are **Club A** (Av. Revolución and Calle 4a, tel. 668/5–2081) and **Regine** (Av. Revolución 1000, tel. 668/2–2761). The **Odyssey** (Av. Revolución between Calles 2a and 3a, tel. 668/7–2477), a watering hole and disco, has a fifth-story terrace overlooking the action on Revolución.

Several new discos and clubs have made the Zona Rio a happening night spot. **Iguanas** (Pueblo Amigo, tel. 668/2–4967) is a beyond-hip setting for live music by the latest groups favored by the younger set. For total immersion in the flashy, high-tech disco scene try **OH! Laser Club** (Paseo de los Héroes 56, tel. 688/4–0267), **Heaven & Hell** (Paseo de los Héroes 10501, tel. 668/4–8484), and **Baby Rock** (1482 Diego Rivera, tel. 668/4–9438).

Rosarito Beach The many restaurants in Rosarito Beach try to keep their customers entertained at night with live music, piano bars, or folklorico dance shows. The **Quinta del Mar hotel** has live music Wednesday–Sunday, recorded disco music other nights, and a large dance floor. Watch the ocean from the piano at the **Beachcomber Bar** at the Rosarito Beach Hotel.

Check out **Francisco's** (Calafia, Km 35.5 Old Ensenada Hwy., tel. 661/2–1581) and **Popotla** (Km 33 Old Ensenada Hwy., tel. 661/2–1504) for live music and dancing Friday to Sunday. **Rene's** (Blvd. Juárez south of town, tel. 661/2–1061) gets rowdy on weekend nights with a live dance band.

Ensenada Ensenada is a party town for college students, surfers, and young tourists, and the bars, particularly along López Mateos and Ruíz, get rowdy at night. Most of the expensive hotels have bars and discos that are less frenetic. **Hussong's** (Av. Ruíz) is perhaps Ensenada's most prominent landmark; no trip is complete without entering this dark, dingy, noisy, enormous saloon where vendors hawk rugs, roses, and Polaroid photos. **Papas and Beer,** across the street, is newer, cleaner, and trendier, but the crowd is just as rowdy, yelling down from the second-story balcony to the strollers below. **Bandito's,** in the same block, is a boisterous disco. Billiard parlors line Calle 2 between Ruíz and Gastelum; this is definitely men-only territory.

Tortilla Flats, on the harbor with a view of the fishing boats, has dining and dancing of a more mellow sort; **Carlos and Charlie's** (Blvd. Costero) is more family oriented but rowdy. **Club Bananas,** nearby, is a neon-video-disco bar popular with the college crowd, as is **Tequila Connection** (Alvarado 12 just off Costera). **La Taberna Española** (Blvd. Costero 1982) is a great place to gather for a night-long feast of tapas and sangria, along with Flamenco shows. **Smitty y Gonzales** (Av. Reyerson), a new restaurant and disco, attracts devoted disco dancers. **Joy's Disco** (López Mateos and Balboa) is popular with the locals, as is **Xanadu Disco** (Ejercito Nacional).

Casamar restaurant's small lounge features live jazz on Friday and Saturday nights. The **El Cid Hotel** has a disco where folklorico dances are held every Saturday at 7 PM.

Index

Personal Itinerary

Departure *Date*

Time

Transportation

Arrival *Date* *Time*
Departure *Date* *Time*
Transportation

Accommodations

Arrival *Date* *Time*
Departure *Date* *Time*
Transportation

Accommodations

Arrival *Date* *Time*
Departure *Date* *Time*
Transportation

Accommodations

Addresses

Name	*Name*
Address	*Address*
Telephone	*Telephone*
Name	*Name*
Address	*Address*
Telephone	*Telephone*
Name	*Name*
Address	*Address*
Telephone	*Telephone*
Name	*Name*
Address	*Address*
Telephone	*Telephone*
Name	*Name*
Address	*Address*
Telephone	*Telephone*
Name	*Name*
Address	*Address*
Telephone	*Telephone*
Name	*Name*
Address	*Address*
Telephone	*Telephone*
Name	*Name*
Address	*Address*
Telephone	*Telephone*

Fodor's Travel Guides

U.S. Guides

Alaska
Arizona
Boston
California
Cape Cod, Martha's
 Vineyard, Nantucket
The Carolinas & the
 Georgia Coast
The Chesapeake
 Region
Chicago
Colorado
Disney World & the
 Orlando Area
Florida
Hawaii

Las Vegas, Reno,
 Tahoe
Los Angeles
Maine,Vermont,
 New Hampshire
Maui
Miami & the
 Keys
National Parks
 of the West
New England
New Mexico
New Orleans
New York City
New York City
 (Pocket Guide)

Pacific North Coast
Philadelphia & the
 Pennsylvania
 Dutch Country
Puerto Rico
 (Pocket Guide)
The Rockies
San Diego
San Francisco
San Francisco
 (Pocket Guide)
The South
Santa Fe, Taos,
 Albuquerque
Seattle &
 Vancouver

Texas
USA
The U. S. & British
 Virgin Islands
The Upper Great
 Lakes Region
Vacations in
 New York State
Vacations on the
 Jersey Shore
Virginia & Maryland
Waikiki
Washington, D.C.
Washington, D.C.
 (Pocket Guide)

Foreign Guides

Acapulco
Amsterdam
Australia
Austria
The Bahamas
The Bahamas
 (Pocket Guide)
Baja & Mexico's Pacific
 Coast Resorts
Barbados
Barcelona, Madrid,
 Seville
Belgium &
 Luxembourg
Berlin
Bermuda
Brazil
Budapest
Budget Europe
Canada
Canada's Atlantic
 Provinces

Cancun, Cozumel,
 Yucatan Peninsula
Caribbean
Central America
China
Czechoslovakia
Eastern Europe
Egypt
Europe
Europe's Great Cities
France
Germany
Great Britain
Greece
The Himalayan
 Countries
Holland
Hong Kong
India
Ireland
Israel
Italy

Italy 's Great Cities
Jamaica
Japan
Kenya, Tanzania,
 Seychelles
Korea
London
London
 (Pocket Guide)
London Companion
Mexico
Mexico City
Montreal &
 Quebec City
Morocco
New Zealand
Norway
Nova Scotia,
 New Brunswick,
 Prince Edward
 Island
Paris

Paris (Pocket Guide)
Portugal
Rome
Scandinavia
Scandinavian Cities
Scotland
Singapore
South America
South Pacific
Southeast Asia
Soviet Union
Spain
Sweden
Switzerland
Sydney
Thailand
Tokyo
Toronto
Turkey
Vienna & the Danube
 Valley
Yugoslavia

Wall Street Journal Guides to Business Travel

Europe

International Cities

Pacific Rim

USA & Canada

Special-Interest Guides

Bed & Breakfast and
 Country Inn Guides:
 Mid-Atlantic Region
New England
The South
The West

Cruises and Ports
 of Call
Healthy Escapes
Fodor's Flashmaps
 New York

Fodor's Flashmaps
 Washington, D.C.
Shopping in Europe
Skiing in the USA &
 Canada

Smart Shopper's
 Guide to London
Sunday in New York
Touring Europe
Touring USA